THE EXISTING CHRIST

An Existential Christology

being in God of and from God…
we…
with God in us forming us
…manifest God

Contents

I

II

III

Introduction

Scripture contains the history of the temporal Christ and of the early Christian movement. What could be more important to a Christian than scripture? The reality and accessibility of the existing presently accessible Christ is more important. The former merely tells of the latter... as best it can, given that the telling is of events and people lost in a history that now eludes us. For many reasons and on many levels, preferring to use the word representations of reality as experienced by others, over personal immediate and direct experience, is to prefer imaginary abstractions to life itself. That is especially true when we are considering our personal spiritual existence. Immediate and direct experience is what matters. Abstract spoken or written words concerning the present or the past can help, but it is through immediate and direct personal experience that God touches us personally.

Consider that you and a companion are walking in a hilly wood on a sunny fall day, with leaves all about in resplendent colours. Your companion writes down notes of what you both seem to be experiencing. That evening you use *your companion's note*s as a guide for deeper understanding and knowing about *your personal experience* of your personal walk. Unawares, you let go your personal experiences because your companion's notes seem clearer, more compelling and 'easier' to grasp cognitively.

In time your grandchildren find your companion's notes and your comments on those notes concerning your experiences. They try to use those notes to sensibly and intelligibly encounter and engage the experience you personally and uniquely had walking in the woods on that fall day. Your grandchildren are seeking an experience like yours for themselves. They come to believe that your companion's notes and your comments on your companion's notes are the means of finding that experience. They replace actual experience of walking in the woods with the experience of reading and studying the notes and the comments. What poor reflections and vague shadows your grandchild would use in pursuit of experiencing what you experienced on that fall day in the woods. All the while the immediate and direct accessible experience of a walk in the woods with resplendent leaves, is actually presently available to your grandchildren; they have only to take such a walk themselves.

What is true about the experience of walking in the woods is also true when it comes to 'walking in the Kingdom of God' among the spiritual things of God indwelling our person. By relying entirely on abstract spoken or written words of such personal experience, people who can actually and personally encounter and engage God, can lose their way, while God is all about within his or her person. Within our person we experience God indwelling in human terms. We can experience it, then sensibly and intelligibly grasp that experiencing. God indwelling is forming our spiritual person, in human terms (that is in terms of the reality of Christ). In union with God we experience the essence and essential properties of God as these are within our person.

In the most simple of terms, the reality people know today and will come to know in future is not and will not be what it has been for most people in past millennia. The few shreds of 'reality' that have survived the last few centuries are being disintegrated by the advances of science and philosophy any credible replacement.

In our existence and existing, what is real and what is not? This question is the backdrop of personal existential significance, meaning and purpose. The answer is with God or Existence ("I AM".)

What ultimately matters is not that God created or caused us; rather that God indwelling through Christ is ***creating or causing*** us. In the time we have and with what we are given in that time, it is for us to personally exist with ultimate existential significance, meaning and purpose in what we are and what we do. We are created to share in God of, from and through God. We are being created sharing God's "I AMness".

While we can intuit and reason that God is present in all things, God is not present to us in all things. We interact with God in ways that are subject to our nature and make-up. There exist aspects of reality which are inaccessible to us. We do no access such things and we do not interact with them. What are of concern for us are those things that are accessible to us. Our union with God is limited by our nature and make-up. God's presence and manifestation to us is limited to our own nature and make-up. In essence, that is the essence and the properties of the essence of God, God is present and manifests to us spiritually. It is our spiritual nature that enables our union with God. God's presence and manifestations are in our experience of carnal actions, regardless of the wonder and power of carnal actions. Carnal actions have no ultimate existential value in regards to existential significance, meaning or purpose. For this reason, Christ's carnal actions, including miracles, do not cause our union with God, nor our salvation or holiness. Spiritual birth is a natural part of human nature, which is made up of flesh and blood and of Spirit in us as well as in Christ. Resurrecting a carnal life after a carnal death does not make a person spiritual; that person was carnal and remains carnal. Only spiritual birth and life makes a person spiritual. God is only present to us and is manifest to because we are personally born and live spiritually. God then is indirectly present and manifest to us because others who are spiritual born and living are present to us. God's presence and manifestation to us is either spiritually direct or spiritually indirect through our person or the person of others. The notions that God is present to us in what clearly carnal actions emerge and are sustained by our carnal nature in pursuit of its carnality.

Two theatres of being are before us: one experiences the world of objects external to our person (biblically, the world after the flesh); the other experiences as the world of the things of God internal to our person (biblically, the world after the spirit). The latter is identified by Paul as the world according to Christ after the spirit. The world according to Christ after the spirit is the arena of *existential Christology*.

Action in this arena is driven by a radical existential Christian paradigm. The root of radical existential Christianity is not extremism itself. Extremism can serve many masters. The root of radical existential Christianity is not us or what we do. We do not make or create our Christian existence. It does not come as a result of a decision we personally make. The existence we presume to shape is not the existence that actually shapes us. The root of radical existential Christianity is in being or existing in the extreme, without anyone or anything standing between or interfering in the individual personal relation of union between the person's spirit and the spirit of Christ.

Existential Christians are *radical* Christians in that their faith is in their sensible and immediate and direct experience of God indwelling in human terms. They do not use or accept any mediators and media between themselves and their experience of God indwelling. The radical Christian is existentialistic[1] in essence and in existence.

The ultimate existential significance, meaning and purpose of God, manifests in persons' immediately and directly being formed spiritually by God indwelling in intelligible human terms. The Word of God indwelling them makes the essence of God and the things of God intelligible in human terms by way of the character or make of Christ after the spirit forming them spiritually according to that character or make up. God is revealed to individuals face to face. Metaphorically, the potter's actions unify the potter and the clay. The potter's essence properties become manifest in the union, by means of which the clay takes on the essence and properties of the potter in clear distinct and specific terms. The ultimate existential significance, meaning and purpose of the forming and formed clay come into being and exist. As a result, the potter's work shares the properties of the potter. The union of the potter and the potter's work is more intimate, immediate and direct that a face to face encounter would be.

Existential Christology as approached in this book provides a practical framework for Christianity in the 21st century that securely withstands scrutiny of critical reflection and thought. More importantly Existential Christology establishes the ground on which Christian practice frees people from bondage and captivity.

When we read scripture, we put our bodies between God and our personal self. (We also have the bodies of those who wrote the scripture between their authentic experiences and their abstracted writings. We are twice removed.) To resolve this shortfall, people have adopted superstitious practices to suggest that this temporal and inadequate process is 'inspired' or magically transformed

---

[1] In his introduction to his booklet, *Existence and the Existant*[1],, titled *Varieties of "Existentialisms"*, Jacques Maritan, reclaimed the fullness of existentialism and its intellectual history, from the negating limits set to it by some philosophers of the late 19th and of the 20th century.

in the processing by God. The temporal media or mediators supplant God in personal existential engagement. For the moment temporal aspirations and delights, as well as temporal fears and anxieties are satisfied in terms of the flesh. Such people seem to not realize or they seem to forget that God is alive within them to be presently existentially encountered and engaged directly and immediately --- not through any media or mediator.

When we are spiritually forming in God of and from God indwelling according to Christ after the spirit, nothing separates us from God. Our communion in the union itself is intelligible to us through the specifics and distinctions that are Christ after the spirit.

As this century and the millennium opens before Christians and people in general, spiritual life is confronted by diverse currents of change flowing in oceans of confusion, over which irrational winds blow wantonly without purpose. Nothing stands upon which to establish spiritual being, except spiritual reality itself waiting to be realized in our existing. Other constructs will fail and fall, as they have always failed and fallen.

Questions concerning meaning and existence arise. Does God exist? Is God's love real? Is mercy real? Is kindness real? Are justice and righteousness real? What is the foundation of and substance of spiritual life? What does God's existence mean to me personally? What is religion for? Why do we use religion? What do we accomplish in the use of religion? Some religions serve bodily desires and wellbeing. Some aim to alleviate pain or secure rewards and pleasure. Some undertake to explain life in corporeal or carnal terms. Rightly or wrongly, for better or worse,

Christian religion has been used and can be used for all of those purposes.

It is the nature of existence to exist. It is our nature to exist in nature. How do we exist in existence or what is our nature in existing? In existence, we are differentiated spiritually because *we can live in existence* according to God as specified in human terms; that is, *according to the distinctions and specifics that are Christ.* We become differentiated according to the specific properties and essence of Christ after the spirit. The very nature or essence of God, which is the ultimate existential significance, meaning and purpose of God or Existence ("I AM."), is manifest in the reality of Christ. That reality as the Word of God specifies and makes distinct the things of God that are ultimately existentially significant, meaningful and purposeful. Love, mercy, kindness, justice and righteousness are all in the nature of Christ and are all held in common by persons who have been formed to be Christ-like.

The coming century promises that the grounding and framing of Christian living will move and shift. The challenges will cause faith to stumble, if not fall. In the reality of the infinite and eternal existing Christ there is a Covenant --- a Christ Covenant --- that will ground and frame or form spiritual living.

The first part of this book is about the reality Christ and how that presently existing reality forms our spiritual person. Drawing on some 17th Century Radical Protestant writings, as well as Quaker, Wesleyan and Reformist legacies of Light and Experimental Religion, this book delves into the pursuit and securing of salvation and holiness.

The second part of this book draws on the book of John and its Gospel message regarding the existing Christ, as well as the authenticated letters of Paul and the work of Spinoza. It reflects on some salient themes from the Gospel of John, presenting thought provoking and 'creative' reflections on some of those texts.

The existing Christ is the infinite and eternal reality that shapes Christian understanding, knowledge and theology. Christian religion is our existential proclamation of salvation and holiness manifest or expressed in our living. On such existential proclamation Christian theology stands.

Our reality that is formed according to the intelligible distinctions and specifics Christ is our existing with the ultimate existential significance, meaning and purpose of Christ. Our reality in God of and from God forming our spiritual person according to Christ after the spirit is not merely our reality existing as a meaningless and insignificant thing among other meaningless and insignificant things. The things of God are real. In Christ, the things of God take on human nature. While we cannot relate to God directly we can relate to Christ directly because the nature of Christ and our nature, when we have been formed by Christ after the spirit, are the same nature, with the same common properties.

To know Existence itself or to know God is to be love, mercy, kindness, justice and righteousness. It is to have knowledge of existentially ultimate significance, meaning and purpose. For us to personally experience and know our spiritual person in Existence or in God as loving, merciful, kind, just and righteous; is to know my personal ultimate existential significance, meaning and purpose.

In regards to spiritual life, Christian religion is the actual union, connection and relation of people to God, so that people have and live their existence: being in God of and from God. The existence of God is one issue. What God's existence signifies, means or purposes is a different issue. More importantly what God's existence means to me personally, is also a different issue. The existence and meaning of God is nothing to me personally, because God is beyond my personal limitations in every way. What is not beyond me is the existence of God in human terms, and the meaning of the existence of God *in human terms.* I can relate to God in human terms and God in human terms is of ultimate existential significance, meaning and purpose to me as a spiritual person. God in human terms is the reality of Christ. While I may generally intuit and sense God ineffably within me, I actually grasp specific significance, meaning and purpose being in God of and from God in human terms, while being in God and having God be in me. That is, in my existentially being of the reality of Christ, is my personal ultimate existential significance, meaning and purpose.

In the twentieth century philosophy came to the conclusion that each person's reality is his individual reality. This is seen in the work of Heidegger and Wittgenstein and some of the 20th century existentialists.

Reality of personal union with God, while not objective, is not subjective. A person does not make up reality itself. We participate in it and *experience* it. In itself reality is all in all, but that also includes specifics and distinctions. The distinctions can be trialed, measured, tested and demonstrated[2]. Is the same vein, Christ as reality and our personal salvation and holiness in that reality, has distinctions that can be trialed, measured, tested and demonstrated. Trialing, measuring, testing, and demonstrating is not limited to objects external to our person. Nor is trialing, measuring, testing demonstrating limited to particular 'objects' internal to our person. Experience of union with God is neither objective nor subjective, yet it is experiential. It is distinct, sensible and intelligible.

Experience of union with God indwelling forming our spiritual being according to Christ after the spirit is experience of God's essence and the essential properties of God, in Christ-specific or human terms.

We do not create reality, and we do not create salvation and holiness, though all these are personal and individual. Salvation and holiness is not a 'club' that wants admission criteria or that we can join by signing a contract. There is no action or work that is valid evidence of membership to other observers. There is no tangible carnal evidence that we can sense through our bodies and its members to be had concerning another person's spiritual birth or living. There are no images to see, words to hear,

[2] It goes without saying that the religion of science is not the science of religion.

no feelings to be felt to demonstrate the spirituality of another person. Salvation is between a person and God, as is personal holiness. No one can confirm another person's real state of salvation or holiness, one way or any other.

Pious living, which is a passive following according to cues (images, words, rules, events, experiences, etc.) external to our person, is merely a blessed echo of the reality that is Christ. The Christ-reality is present in human terms, is present in distinct Christ-specific intelligibility. To an extent piety catches reflections of spiritual reality but as through a glass darkly, as Paul put it. This echoing or reflecting is not built on the solid rock of existence itself. Piety allows for pious living, which is salutary and good as far as it goes. It allows us to participate in the things of God indirectly.

Christ is the reality of God intelligibly and sensibly present to us within our existing person in human terms. The reality which is the infinite and eternal Christ proceeds from 'the mouth of God'. The 'specifics in human terms' are 'mouthed' (or Worded) by God. This reality proceeds from the Word of God into a creation we are able to relate to because we exist with God indwelling our person. We ourselves do not set the terms of Christ as reality; the terms are set by God through the Word of God. Individually, we do not invent or create the reality of which we are a creative part. Nor collectively do churches magically create or embody the entirety of that Christ reality in itself. We manifest the reality of Christ or express it through our existing personally and collectively manifesting the spirit of Christ in human terms through our personal existing or being. Having said that, it remains for us to discover and discern the reality of Christ in us and in existence; and, for us to not be hindered in that existential manifestation.

When we speak of God or Christ's indwelling, that is Inner Light or the Word of God in us; we do not mean that God is *inside us alongside us*. Spiritually God is not separate from us. We are not bodies or minds, with God inside our bodies or minds yet outside our person created to only experience and know God or Christ as objects external to us. The situation would be depraved and depressing because we would be separated from the Spirit of God. When we say, we are in God of and from God, according to Christ after the spirit in Christ of and from Christ, we mean spiritually our entire person's essence in actually presently existing and being is in God according to Christ after the spirit and is of God and is from God according to Christ after the spirit.

The reality of God present in us and to us in human terms reconciles our personal existing or atones our personal existing to God by way of union through Christ. When we put on Christ[3], we are formed into Christ-likeness and become in Christ of and from Christ. That is, we are being in God, being of God and are becoming from God through the reality of the infinite and eternal spirit of Christ. We are given ultimate existential significance, meaning and purpose in the creating or birthing of our spiritual person or in our being spiritually formed or

---

[3] In the practice of piety, we put on Christ in the flesh; we do as Christ would do. In union with God indwelling according to Christ after the spirit, we put on Christ after the spirit because we are formed to be as Christ would be.

generated through the reality of Christ into the infinite and eternal Kingdom of God.

I exist as a carnal person, born of water as put in John 3:5. There is a transient, finite carnal body and carnal mind connected to that carnal person. The person is formed out of finite, temporal events that are random and absurd in relation to ultimate existential significance, meaning or purpose. Though there may be a trail of cause and effect, the trail ends in the absurdity and randomness of activity in the void and nothing of darkness which has no being or existence. As a carnal person, I am confined in bondage to the carnal world after the flesh. Just as I know I exist as a carnal person, I also know I exist as a spiritual person, born of spirit as put in John 3:5. There is experience in and evidence of both. With the advent or birth in the spirit, of and from the spirit, the carnal body and canal mind persist as carnal objects. The carnal person does not persist. The carnal person dies, while the carnal body and mind continue to live in the carnal world. The spiritual person is born from the infinite eternal things of God: the essence and properties of God in human terms. The spiritual person formed in, of and from the infinite and eternal things of God, tabernacles or is housed in the carnal body and carnal mind, until the carnal death of that body and mind. The reality or existence of the spiritual person is housed in the world after the flesh, but is simultaneously actually existing in essence in union with God, which existence is not a finite existence of and from the flesh but is an eternal existing without limits, therefore infinite. We experience these spiritual things. Actually experiencing spiritual things, we sense them and intelligibly know them distinctly and specifically in our person illuminated by God indwelling according to the human distinctions and specifics that make up the Christ reality.

It is useful to consider how we experience Christ and which is the *certain and true experience and knowledge of the spirit of Christ in us* and working in us, leading us to spiritual being and spiritual wellbeing. Such considerations of our personal Christ-specific experiences contribute to the formation and implementation of Christ-specific plans or rules of living, with which we and others can experience and use to obey God in us, through Christ in us.

****

The first part of this book concerns the reality of the existing Christ. The existing Christ is God in human terms. The first section concerns our access to the reality of Christ, through which spiritual life is generated and through which forming we are *personally* formed and live spiritually. The present reality of the existing eternal Christ, which was and always will be, is discussed in relation to our personal temporal existence. God's ever-present message: the Word as Gospel, proclaiming human purpose, meaning and significance is presented as the actualizing of the reality of Christ in us individually and collectively.

The second part discusses the existing Christ as expressed in John's Gospel. From a different time and place, the Gospel of John speaks about the eternal Christ existing and ministering temporally. Here is a record of the Gospel proclaimed by Christ according to John. In the process of expressing what occurred at the time, the writer also expresses Christ as Christ was in the writer during the actual writing of the content of the book of John. As it is read and considered by the reader, the book of John speaks about the eternal Christ existing within us as readers; and, in our actual experiences of our reaching into the book for Light. What John expresses and we impress upon ourselves, generates a presentation of the Word of God to us personally. The testament of the Book of John is considered with a view to finding presently relevant expressions of Light in that text.

The third part of this book presents a step-by-step approach to sensibly and intelligibly experience Christ as reality internally and externally, utilizing experiential and experimental methods of discovery and learning. The approach empowers people's seeking, finding and accessing spiritual formation in actually and existentially encountering God. Such encountering and engaging sensitizes personal existence to the spiritual things of God and changes life in practice and in essence.

The Existing Christ and Existence

God exists as God. God also exists infinitely and eternally in human terms[4]. Christ is God in human terms. As such, we have an actual and accessible existential explication of God in human terms through the eternal spirit, mind and heart of Christ. In essence and in existence Christ is *personal*, God is not. As individual spiritual person, we share or have the personal essence or personal spirit and personal properties of Christ in common with Christ. This commonality is the fundamental character of Christ imaging God in human terms, which character we experience, sense and know by way of union with God indwelling according to Christ after the spirit. The spirit, heart and mind of Christ are not 'objects' that we can bodily sense or know through our carnal mind's intelligence.

Some imagine that they a social relationship with Christ. They view the reality of Christ as something external to them that they can sense and relate to as they other external objects, for example other people. Our relationship to God is not a social relationship between two people or objects. It does not involve any kind of social contract or covenant. Our relationship to God is existential: it is in the existing of our union with God. We are in God and God is in us. We are united as one. That is our

[4] Christ is the eternally present reality of the infinite and eternal God in human terms.

existential experience. But, given the limits our human person, our experience of God is in human terms, that is: we experience the spirit of Christ who is God in human terms. This is our reality. In addition to intelligibly knowing Christ, we can also imagine. Christ as an abstract model, exemplar or character. Those who believe they have a social relationship with Christ are treating the imagined Christ as a presently existing person who is an object external to them.

Our second birth is in the spirit of Christ and is of and from that spirit, which is God in human terms. Things exist as spiritual reality which we experience by union with God through our spiritual birth and living according to Christ after the spirit. From our spiritual experience we actually immediately and directly sense and know the essence or spirit and properties of Christ indwelling. Our relation is in Existence and Existing, not a contracted social relationship between two 'people' objects.

The essence of God is the spirit of Christ. The essence of the idea of God is the idea of the spirit of Christ. Both these are the same idea, which we experience sense and know to providing Light that reveals spiritual Life given in Existence by the Word.

In his Tractatus Theologico-Politicus, Spinoza suggests that *unlike all other persons* Christ[5] knows God

[5] When Spinoza uses the word Christ, he refers not merely to the flesh and blood aspects of the historical temporal Christ but refers at the same time to the spirit of Christ aspects of the historical, temporal Christ. Unlike the former, the spirit of Christ aspects existed before the historical, flesh and blood existence of Christ; and, they continue to exist after the death of the historical, temporal flesh and blood Christ.

immediately and directly, mind to mind. For our part, as Christ knows God, so we know Christ: mind to mind and immediately and directly. In existing or being in, of and from Christ, we spiritually are and we spiritually exist in Christ-specific terms, presently existing of and from the Word of God. We are and we know our selves and know God within us in the existential act of being Christian through union with God indwelling forming us according to Christ after the spirit.

We are not made to be God. As it is put in scripture, we are made in the image of God. Better said, *we are made in the image or character of God*[6] *to be the image of God to each other*. The purpose is not to mimic God, but to represent God to other people. In our makeup, there is an active trace or active presence of the essence of God. We are made with the spark of God within our person. We can actually express or manifest God in our existing, not simply because we are created by God, but because the essence of God is present in our being or existing. We are designed to ultimately manifest God's spiritual properties, which are in the spirit of Christ and in the mind of Christ. Being in, of and from God, our minds share in the common notions of the mind of Christ.

Unlike other people who exist temporally and historically in time and space, Christ could not be formed (by a second birth) according to Christ after the spirit. At the time Christ was the spirit of Christ in human terms. Spinoza uses the phrase 'Christ Jesus' only once in letter 73 (EP73) to Oldenburg in response to Oldenburg's queries about the flesh and blood aspects of Christ. Spinoza's view would have been that as merely Christ after the flesh, the flesh and blood aspects of Christ did not and does not generate spiritual life or being.

[6] The essence and properties of God manifest in human terms by Christ after the spirit.

The writers of Scripture thread their accounts together with numerous reoccurring and inter-related images, metaphors and themes. These are venues for the writers' messages. One such theme is that people are created in God's image. The message is that the very essence of God is also the essence of a person born from above in God of and from God indwelling according to Christ after the spirit. This makes the person a child of God in spiritual union with God. Existentially, in our existing we exist with an essence that is God's essence in human terms within us, and our existential significance, meaning and purpose is in our essence, which is God's essence in us.

Consider the chemical elements[7] as we experience them. Iron exists as a chemical element. All instances of Iron that exist have the same chemical make-up. A particular instance of Iron has the same chemical make-up of all instances of Iron. All the instances of Iron that exist in time and place, do not account for the *creating* of Iron, *what creates or causes* Iron, *how the distinctions or specifications* that make the Iron *exist or come to be*, or *what the make-up of the cause or creator* of Iron *might be*, etc.

A living person, like Iron, exists in time and place. Unlike Iron, a person has an idea of its own 'person' along with other ideas of things in the world. The person has a mind derived from the world according to the flesh. Such a person after the flesh has an essence of his or her person after the flesh. Such an essence does not have *ultimate existential* significance, meaning or purpose.

---

[7] There may be some connection between Spinoza's understanding of Chemistry and his views on Substance and its modes. Boyle's experiments on Nitre were critiqued by Spinoza in Spinoza's Correspondence to Henry Oldenburg.

For a real actually living person to have ultimate existential significance, meaning and purpose they must manifest the essence of God or Existence itself in their personal individual existing. Their person would have to be formed essentially and existentially in God of and from God; they would have to be born from above according to Christ after the spirit in human terms. We can demonstrate chemical truths and truths about people after the flesh with reasoning and experiment in regards to things after the flesh. We can and should demonstrate spiritual truths with reasoning and experiment in regards to the spiritual things of God indwelling forming us according to Christ after the spirit.

When our being or existing is in God of and from God (that is made in the image or character of God), our immediate and direct experience of the spiritual things of God is *like* our indirect experience through our bodies, of Iron. *It is our personal immediate and direct actual experience.* God's essence *spirits* our existing and being, so that we in fact have and intelligibly sense God's essence and we intelligibly manifest and sense the fruits of the Spirit from within. When being born from above, we are existing in God of and from God and we are being the most our personal existence can be. Because of this existential union, we manifest the ultimate essence of Existence itself: we are not mere existential widgets alienated and separate from the whole of Existence itself. As God or Existence is, and as we are immediately caused spiritually by the idea of God indwelling within; so we are in our person, in our mind, in our hearts and in our spirit.

In our temporal existence: we are 'of' the carnal, *and* we are 'of' the spiritual. In ultimately fulfilling our creation, we become and are 'of' God. We become and are of God through the activating presence of the Word of God, not remotely in scripture but actually presently active within us as the spirit and mind of Christ. In the course of existing, we "put on" the spirit, mind and heart of Christ as the core of our mind and the centre of our heart.

In existence itself, there is a reality that is Christ. This is the indwelling reality through which a person finds salvation and holiness. It is the reality through which we relate to God, through which we undertake God's work and are enabled to be Godly. Within existence is our own existence. We encounter Christ in that existence of ours that involves God indwelling our person. Notably, while we primarily encounter Christ most immediately within ourselves, we also have reports from others of that Christ reality in their personal existence.

We actually and presently encounter God in human terms, here and now. We present Christ in our existing and being, not merely in mediated audible words or temporal images. When we manifest or express God through Christ in us, we present or 'prophesye' the spirit, mind and heart of Christ to ourselves and to one another. The better way to hear, see and understand is to be actually manifesting and presenting our experience of Christ to ourselves and to one another in congregation or in community. The better way to live is to live to express or manifest God through Christ in our living or being. This is the better way to find, know and follow Christ to become of God and to do the things of God, is to do the work of God within us as well as 'without' or external to us..

When Christ is manifest in our being of God, then God in human terms is among us and is with us: personally and collectively. Christ was incarnate in human terms in the historical Christ. When now we put on the mind and spirit of Christ, Christ incarnates through the Word of God in us.

Our experience of triangles is analogous. What do we know about triangles? Triangles are all about us. We see them and interact with them. While we may initially think that what we know is known only to us, over time we ascertain that others also know about triangles. We find common understanding and experiences. We develop concepts, theories and understanding. At some point, it comes clear that triangles are subjective creations, but triangles have existence apart from us, which existence we experience. We come to understand that triangles are real apart from our experience. The reality of triangles does not depend on us individually or collectively. Triangles are actualized in temporal experience through us. We express triangles in what we do. Triangles are but a small part of infinite and eternal existence and being. What we experience and learn about triangles, we teach to others.

We have texts that describe triangles. We have authoritative geometricians who can speak to the issue of triangles. Neither the texts nor the authorities are our personal experiential source of the reality of triangles. Our firsthand knowledge of triangles comes from our first experience of triangles regardless of the knowledge we have of triangles from texts or from authorities. Indeed, for us personally triangles are neither real nor true, regardless of any teaching or texts, until we experience the reality of triangles and the reality of their truths in our own personal existence.

In regards to our ultimate personal purpose, meaning and significance: we are not of triangles and we do not become triangles. Triangles have no life or life giving essence. In regards to our ultimate personal purpose, meaning and significance, we are of God and we can become of God. God is life and God through Christ is spiritually life-giving. The reality of triangles is a little thing, with little consequence in regards to overall infinite and eternal being. The reality of God in human terms is, for us, everything that is purposeful, meaningful and of ultimate existential significance.

Because I exist, I know that I exist temporally. Because I exist, I also know that Christ exists temporally in my inner-self individually (and, in us collectively), here and now. I have present immediate and direct experience that Christ exists today in temporal reality in and through myself. All evidence from others indicates that others have similar firsthand experience of the present temporal reality of Christ in and through them. As far as I understand eternal existence, my experience of Christ, including the spirit of Truth, reveals the temporal existence of Christ in and through me. It also reveals the eternal existence of Christ in my experience, apart from my experience of my self.

I do not know and I cannot know that Christ existed temporally 2,000 years ago. If I believe that Christ existed 2,000 years ago, that is something I subjectively choose to believe by faith and not because of solid historically acceptable evidence.

Substantive faith is authentic belief rooted in the actual make of temporal and eternal existence. This is what our existence is and it is what God is in our experience. As such, faith is what we know and believe because we exist. It is in what we are and what we do. In temporal existence, we are flesh and we are spirit. Our personal being or existence moves from flesh to spirit: from being of flesh to being of Spirit. The body or flesh itself does not transform. The Spirit does not transform. It is actual personal existence that lets go being of and from flesh, to embrace being of and from the Spirit. The formation of our temporal existence from being of carnal things to being of choosing, preferring or 'selecting for' spiritual things, through our real, active participation in the present and eternal reality of Christ[8], is our salvation. Salvation is driven by choices[9] and decisions and it emerges out of those choices and decisions. The choices and decisions are to follow[10] the eternal and infinite realty that is Christ. In following Christ, we lift

---

[8] That is in our 'following' Christ.

[9] We function and we should function as presently freely choosing. Determinate or free choice debates presume too much. We do what we do ... and that works. To arrest and abort our functioning because we do not fully understand existence or God, is foolishness sustained when we attend to the dark rather than the Light. We may never fully understand God, but we are not required to understand what is beyond understanding. Whether we are determined or free, we act as we are free. How free choice relates to abstract theology or philosophy of determinism or free choice, does not concern us our present functioning.

[10] We need to be clear that to follow Christ involves death of self and spiritual birth of God. We do not merely follow some actor's script of the life of Christ, as an actor would immerse into a role being played out in a production. Our engagement and participation in the real existing Christ involves more than a metamorphous. Our lives are not changed. We come alive spiritually from God breathing life in us. We do not act. We become and in becoming transform our temporal existence. Following is not a distant enactment. It is an immediate being of and becoming of God in our essence and existing.

Christ and Christ lifts us into God. Through Christ, we become spiritual creatures of God. Being and existing of God, here and now, is to be holy and to live with God's holiness in spirit, mind and heart. Why we choose to follow Christ does not matter. What matters is that we follow and in the following, God through Christ spiritually generates us spiritually. This is 'the Way' of Christ as presented in scriptures.

Gripped in bondage to *horrendous carnal fear of carnal non-existing* , people in early 'christian' communities looked away from and set aside both the instructions from Paul (1Cor 15) and Christ (John 3 and 1). Instead, like the people at the base of Mount Horeb, they construed carnal beliefs enabling illusions of enduring carnal living in one guise or another. They quelled their carnal fears and anxieties so met their carnal needs. Further, in fashioning doctrines and denominational frameworks, they devised means of controlling and managing people, effectively becoming self-serving politicians.

All too often the 'way' of the churches fell and falls short. This is not true of only the Christian churches. As Paul reasoned out in Romans, salvation has always been at hand and will be at hand in the very nature of existence[11]. So too, 'religious' organizations and people who stood up to lead people from whatever part of the earth, fell short and fall short. At the root of the shortfall are the enduring appeal of carnal power and the use of carnal power and influence to control people. It is not just that church leaders

---

[11] See Romans 1 and 2.

fell short, but the leaders had followers who followed to meet their flesh and blood needs, aspirations, bigotries and prejudices. In regards to the Christian churches, the shortfalls triggered protestations throughout the last two thousand years including the Protestant Reformation. The reformation replaced the authority of churchmen and church traditions with the authority of scripture, as it understood scripture at the time. The emergence of a scientific world view and the historical critical method of understanding scriptures destabilized the reformation's use of scripture as authority. The 'way' of institutional churches and churchmen continues to fall short.

.

In that shortfall, people are left naked as it were, encountering existence and reality personally on their own. Each is left alone, with the existence and reality of God, Christ and the Word of God in us and in existence before us. We are left personally alone with God. We still have access to the Gospel message, to the scriptures, to church tradition, to Christian leaders and thinkers. More than that, we personally have access to our experience and experiments of the reality of Christ, as well as access to other spiritually alive people's experience and experiments of the reality of Christ.

We are left alone with God, but with the Paraclete calling to us alongside us. Therefore, we have firm ground on which to establish and sustain faith and belief, from which we secure salvation and pursue holiness. Put simply, the Way of spiritual being is being of God in human terms, which is being of the reality of Christ and the Way is here and now for us to personal walk.

In the beginning…

"In the beginning…" involves more than one beginning. Christ tells Nicodemus (John 3:6) that: flesh gives rise to flesh, spirit gives rise to spirit. There is a beginning arising from the world after the flesh and a second beginning arising from the world after the spirit. The second beginning is housed or tabernacled in our temporal carnal body and carnal mind, but it is substantively and essentially different from the vessel that houses it. In effect, we experience two realities or two kinds of existing but simultaneously or co-incidentally.

To use some biblical wording, we actually experience, intelligibly sense and come to intelligibly know different realities that generate our person: a reality from *the world after the flesh*; and, a reality from *the world after the spirit* (of Christ). These two realities are exclusive of one another. They generate different kinds of existing: one temporal and finite in time and space; the other eternal and infinite not limited in time and space.

While there is a single Existence and Existing, there two kinds of experiencing Existence and Existing. Existentially we experience a non-essential existing according to the world after the flesh, which has no trace of the essence and properties of God. Within that non-essential existing, we can experience birth into a life in which existence and existing actually involves the essence and properties of God manifest in human terms in Christ after the spirit. This is the theo-philosophical core of the book of John, the authentic letters of Paul and Spinoza's life work.

Existential thinking can start with the existence of individual persons who themselves decide how to exist and in so doing determine their existence and existing. The existing is determined by the finite carnal individual person and is limited by the limits of the finite carnal individual person. The existing is experienced through bodily senses as things or objects existing external to the individual person. This existential thinking happens in a carnal paradigm, which is the world after the flesh.

Existential thinking can start with Existence and Existing itself, in which the individual exists in God of and from God indwelling forming their spiritual person according to Christ after the spirit (i.e. the world after the spirit). Existence and Existing is immediately and directly experienced from within the person's essence or spirit in God of and from God being formed according to Christ after the spirit. This existential thinking happens in a spiritual paradigm, which is the world after the spirit.

There are then two kinds of existential experience, one carnal the other spiritual. Each entails different existence and existing. The crux of *existential Christology experienced carnally* is the decision to follow Christ after the flesh, as far as can be known. The crux of *existential Christology experienced spiritually* is actively formationally-following Christ after the spirit in spiritual birth and life as generated by God indwelling forming our spiritual person according to the distinctions and specifics of Christ after the spirit, which we know in our engagement of union with God indwelling our person. Formational-following involves our assenting to and affirming our existence in God, of and from God indwelling forming our spiritual person according to the spirit or essence of Christ.

What distinguishes carnal and spiritual existential Christian existence and existing is *ultimate existential* significance meaning and purpose. The carnal Christian's significance, meaning and purpose is based on the individual person; carnal existence as the person encounters it; and, the decisions the carnal person makes about how to existence carnally. It is 'ultimate' in relation to their carnal person and the limits of personal carnal existence, which relation and limits extinguish ultimate significance, meaning and purpose. The spiritual Christian's significance, meaning and purpose is based on the essence and properties of God in human terms (i.e. Christian terms), spiritual existence as they encounter it, and their formational-following. This existence and existing is 'ultimate' not *in relation to* God but *in the union with* God which union provides God's essence and properties in human terms (i.e. Christ distinctions and specifics) as the essence and properties of the spiritual person. The spiritual person's significance, meaning and purpose is ultimate because there spiritual person manifests the essence and properties of God given in the distinctions and specifics of Christ after the spirit.

We actually experience, sense and come to know, in biblical terms, the world after the flesh and our carnal person in it; and, the world after the spirit and our spiritual person in it. The carnal reality we experience is a world of 'objects'. Our person is an object that experiences other objects and from that point of view is called a 'subject'. We can also actually experience, sense and come to know spiritual reality in union with God (Existence --- "I AM."). Union with God is intuited from the experience of union by means of which there is experience of the essence and essential properties of God. With intuition of God comes intuited distinctions of the properties of God, which are manifest in Christ after the flesh and which determine the mind of Christ in Existence and determines our mind when we take on the mind of Christ.

Carnal reality is external to our personal essence, existing or being in God, of and from God. This is the reality of the world after the flesh, which is manifest in terms of the flesh, into which we are born in the flesh, of and from the flesh. We have birth and life and live according to the world after the flesh. Spiritual reality is internal to our personal essence, existing or being in God, of and from God. It is the reality of the world after the spirit of (in human terms) Christ. The spiritual things of God are determined by the essence and properties of God manifest in human terms in Christ. Our spiritual person is manifest in God indwelling us actually spiritually forming us according to Christ after the spirit, which experience we sense and know. In this spiritual formation, our mind is also formed to conform to the distinctions and specifics that make up the mind of Christ.

People mistakenly set a mediator up a medium between themselves and their immediate and direct experience of Existence or their experience of God. The medium or mediator supplants the role of God. Prevalent among such mediators or mediating devices are theologies of religion and theories of science, with their accompanying priests and scientists. While these can useful in a limited way, they are absent real ultimate existential significance, meaning and purpose. Theologies, theories, priests and scientists supplant God to the determinate and 'fall' of the person.

Radical Christians are radical not because they are extreme in denominational terms, rather they are extreme in experiencing and knowing God immediately and directly in union, which is without any mediator or medium between them and God. Radical Christians find God only in union with God. God or Existence and Existing is not an object, which as a subject a person can experience in things external to the person. Experiencing, sensing and knowing in the subject-object paradigm is altogether different from experiencing, sensing and knowing the essence and properties of Existence and Existing in distinct and specific terms of personal union with God. The latter is in the realm of the infinite and eternal. For example, we cannot simply apply the cause-effect relation in finite and temporal, subject-object experiences to experiences involving infinite and eternal things internal to our person.

Of the world after the flesh, we experience a reality made up of '*objects*'. In the world of objects, we are personally a '*subject-object*'. Our person is a subject-object that experiences other external objects.

Of the world after the spirit, we experience, sense and come to know the reality of union with the essence of

God indwelling. Union with God is intuited from the experience of the union by which there is experience of uniquely existing as persons involving the essence and essential properties of God. With intuition of God indwelling in human terms, comes intuited distinctions of the properties of God in human terms, which are manifest in Christ after the spirit. The distinctions and specifications of the heart, spirit and mind of Christ in Existence determine our spiritual forming and our intuitions of the experiences. These intuitions are not derived from experience of objects external to our person. They are present by our personal actual being in God of and from God.

The reality of the world after the flesh is *manifest in terms of the flesh,* into which *we are born in the flesh of and from the flesh.* We have life and live according to the world after the flesh. This reality is *external* to our spiritual essence, existing or being in God of and from God. In this 'worldly' reality, things exist as objects external to our person's internal spiritual essence. In this reality we have both knowledge of our self as an external subject-object and of other things as external objects.

The other reality is *internal* to our spiritual essence, existing or being in God of and from God, *while the essence and properties of God is indwelling in us* in Christ-specific human terms. In this reality, we have spiritual life and we live spiritually according to Christ after the spirit. The spiritual things of God are not determined by mere objects of existence or their relation to one another; they are determined by the nature of Existence itself in its essence. The spiritual things of God that are relevant to us are determined by the essence and properties of God manifest in human terms in Christ indwelling our spiritual person. In union with God, we manifest the spiritual things of God indwelling us, actually spiritually forming us according to Christ after the spirit. *We actually experience this manifestation, from which experience we intelligibly sense and intelligibly know it, clearly and distinctly*. Our experience, sense and knowledge of these spiritual things are *immediate and direct experiencing, sensing and knowing of reality in Existence itself.* And, it is clearer and more certain than is our experiences of things external to our person, which experiences are artificially presented to us by our body's senses and perceptions.

Birth and life in the flesh comes with needs, concerns and desires of the flesh. But, accompanying or seeded in our creation is the germ of spiritual life, whose presence is experienced as an ultimate existential need, concern and desire for significance meaning and purpose. Life comes with ultimate existential concerns, which cannot be addressed by things of the flesh, regardless of any sophism or appeal of the things of the flesh, be they in religion or science. Ultimate existential concern is addressed by union with God and by nothing else. The subject/object paradigm has been useful, and it is useful for certain things. But the limitations of the subject/object paradigm have also generated abstracted obstructions and abstract distractions that have kept, keep and will keep people from discerning God indwelling forming them.

Union with God indwelling forming our spiritual person is the fundamental and common basis of true authentic existential Christian religion, as found in the book of John, Paul's authenticated letters and in Spinoza's work. This union involves knowledge of the experience of union. When we experience union with God we also know we are united with God.

John's Gospel separates the world of subject/object (the things of the flesh), from the world of union with God indwelling forming our spiritual person according to Christ after the spirit (the things of the Spirit). In his authenticated Epistles, Paul follows suit. Spinoza for his part, separates the things of imagination and reason (things of the flesh) from things if intuition (the things that follow in us from idea of God). All three sources have a similar grasp of reality and of what constitutes ultimate existential being and our experience of such being.

We have two beginnings.... We are born twice, and we experience two realities. We are born in the flesh of and from the flesh. While in the flesh, we are born in God of and from God according to Christ after the spirit; or in the spirit of and from the spirit of God in human terms. In our second spiritual birth are our personal ultimate existential significance, meaning and purpose. While this view is significantly pronounced in John 3, Paul gives it substance in 1 Corinthians 15. A close look at Paul's 15th chapter of 1 Corinthians, reveals that being born a second time into spiritual life is fundamental to his thinking and puts Paul on the same podium as the writer of John 3. Chapter 15 sheds light and supports Paul's other writings, for example Romans 7 & 8.

Paul starts chapter 15 by establishing that Christ was supposed to resurrect, that Christ did resurrect and therefore continues to exist. Paul then establishes that carnal death came through a man of flesh and blood; and that 'resurrection' came through a man of the spirit. The resurrection is defined as *coming alive in Christ*. The resurrection is not a resuscitation of carnal living in a modified form. Paul continues and establishes without resurrection or coming alive in Christ, there no point to his doing God's work. In effect Paul writes that unless there is more than carnal flesh and blood life, in various variations, then there is no salvation or holiness to be had. Paul then broaches the crux of the matter concerning salvation and holiness based on resurrection or living in Christ.

Like John 3, Paul does not allow for the temporal, mutable, perishable flesh and blood body which we familiar with, to exist spiritually in any form. The flesh and blood body is essentially different from the spiritual creature that comes alive in Christ. According to Paul we are first born of and from the earth, but once born and living in the flesh, when are then comes a spiritual birth, a second birth in "a life giving spirit", who is Christ. Like John 3, Paul is clear the flesh and blood life is "first" and "after" comes the spiritual. While we are "yet in the flesh" (perishable and mortal), we are born in the spirit (imperishable and immortal). We experience two kinds of existing at the same time: one mortal and perishable; the other immortal and imperishable. The latter existing is in Christ, of and from Christ and shares the infinite and eternal essence and properties of Christ. Paul's position is that the temporal carnal entity lives and dies, while once coming alive spiritually the spiritual entity exists in eternity and is not subject to carnal, temporal death.

In effect, as Paul writes at the beginning of his letter to the Romans, Christ is eternal and existed before we existed and exists while we exist, and will exist after we die carnally. While Christ died carnally, he did not die spiritually. The juxtaposing of the temporal and the eternal is the basis of experience of Christ resurrected, (including Paul's personal experience). He also makes a strong statement in keeping with John 3, concerning second birth and clearly associates this spiritual birth or coming alive in Christ with spiritual life after carnal death or 'resurrection. Paul catches this juxtaposition when says that "We will not all sleep, but we will all be changed— 52 in a flash, in the twinkling of an eye…" (1 Cor 51-52). Some will change into "sleep", some will change through a second birth that will carry their essential person into eternity and it will *irrevocably* come to pass in the twinkle of eye.

People, who carnally die without having come alive spiritually in Christ, perish in mortality. They have no infinite and eternal spiritual existence in God, of and from God.

Spiritually our person is not like the temporal subjects and objects of flesh and blood reality. Spiritually, we do not stand apart as subjects or objects. *There is no subjectivity or objectivity in spiritual reality.* We participate in eternity and infinity by union with God through Christ. In our spiritual forming, our mind is also formed to conform to the distinctions and specifications that make up the mind of Christ or the 'mind' of God in human terms.

Objects of existence, in themselves are subjects that are distinguished by how they differ from other objects of existence, and as subjects they interact with other objects of which they are not the subject. To a subject, other 'things' (including other persons) are external objects. It is the case that the subject is as much an object to him or her self, as are the things obviously external to the subject.

Life and living involves all existence (i.e. God) and experience of the essence of all Existence, including sensing and knowing the essence of Existence in itself indwelling our person. Experience and knowledge of external objects and subjects is not a complete experience of all existing and all existence. In itself, each object carries the nature of existence *according to the object's determination.* Sensing and knowing determined objects in existence is sensing and knowing external objects, which we are not a part. We sense and know those external objects apart from ourselves as subjects.

A subject-object can, from its subjective perspective, misconstrue other objects, their relationships, and the subjective knowledge of those external objects. The 'subject' knowledge we have is like the knowledge we have of other external objects. Subjective knowledge *contrives* illusions and mistakes of perceptions and conceptions, which have no objective reality. We contrive objects abstractly and subjectively projected them as 'reality'.

Some people set up media or a mediator between themselves and their experience of Existence or their experience of God. Often the media or mediator supplants the role of God. Prevalent among such mediators or mediating devices are counterfeit carnal theologies of religion and abstract theories of science. While these can useful in a limited way, they are absent real ultimate existential significance, meaning and purpose.

The abstract construction of false knowledge and illusionary knowledge is reflected in misconstrued, mistaken and inadequate knowledge of objects and their relations to one another. Reasoning about, perceptions and sensations of the external objects and about relations between external objects, generates only inadequate knowledge of the things of God, that is the essence and the essential properties of God manifest in human terms.

There is ample demonstration that we have accumulated and have lots of useful of knowledge of external objects and their relation to one another. However useful the knowledge of objects and their relation to one another is, the knowledge is not direct and immediate knowledge of existing or being. Religion founded on knowledge of things or objects external to our person cannot address the most fundamental matters of existential concern for life and living. Ironically, when religion does purport to do so, it is our knowledge of objects external to our person (i.e. science) that makes such claims untenable. Such religion bound in temporal objects fails its adherents, in regards to matters of ultimate existential significance, meaning and purpose.

A subjective illusion is anthropomorphizing God in abstraction. This presents God as a limited object that chooses as people choose, or acts as people act, or causes things as people cause things. God is not an object. God is not a person who does what a person does. "God's ways are not our ways.' While it be helpful in some situations to present God as a person, it is wrong to consider God as a limited person. Thinking of God as a person misdirects religion and misleads people in search of salvation and holiness.

To a subject as a subject, God can only be another object external to the subject. Our authentic encounter by union with God is not an encounter with an object external to our essential self. God is not an external object. Cast as an external object, God is presented as an idol. The experience of ultimate existential significance, meaning and purpose does not arise from external objects, the differences between objects or the relation between objects. Nor does such experience arise from subjective contrivances.

There are a number of bankrupt pillars of the failed and failing subject/object paradigm of reality that previously shored up some religious views and have up until now sustained certain religions within the subject/object paradigm. For example defining a person today in terms of a body object is no longer tenable given the knowledge we have of the body and its relation to our person. There is such a variety of human body objects, that it is difficult to see how our bodies can define us persons. With advent of genetics and eugenics there will be such profound changes made to body objects that bodies will be completely divorced from any notion suggesting that a person 'is' their flesh and blood body (and, that the object of religion is to secure a flesh and blood resurrection of object bodies from their flesh and blood death).

The human body will be redrafted to meet climatic and meteorological conditions of distant planets, as well as our own changing planet and the circumstances of oceans' deep. Increasingly we will ascertain that we are not defined in essence by our object bodies that carry our spiritual person as a vessel might convey a cargo. How are we to be defined and from what are to be defined? The answer is that we are being defined in union with God indwelling us forming us spiritually according to Christ after the spirit. This answer needs comprehending to properly read and grasp the core of the book of John; Paul's authenticated letters; and, Spinoza's work.

As standalone subjects, we are challenged to comprehend and understand objects that we encounter because though actually before us they are apart from us. How then, can we comprehend and understand external objects that existed once upon a time but no longer exist before us now. We are separated from those objects of the past by extended time and place. How are we as standalone subjects in the present supposed to comprehend significance, meaning and purpose from past objects and their interrelations lost in time and distant places? The encounter is illusionary. In pursuing such efforts, we chase illusions that cannot respond to our present hope.

We encounter objects before us, merely as ink on paper, which in themselves as ink on paper carry no ultimate existential significance, meaning or purpose. We want from our encounter with these ink and paper objects that are not part of us, to acquire comprehension and understanding of other distant objects that we have never actually encountered. If we did comprehend and understand those distant objects, we would still lack experience of actual union with God out of which is our salvation and holiness. Knowing past events or objects, does not mean we have assumed existential significance, meaning or purpose.

Theologies and science theories arise and fall in a parade that does not advance responses or solutions to the most fundamental concerns of life and living. At the root of this failure is the flesh and blood subject/object paradigm of reality, which cannot adequately speak to ultimate existential concerns or matters. In modern times, both religion and science have failed to address the most fundamental matters of ultimate existential concern for life and living. Over time, both have been distorted and disturbed by subjective superstition and fanciful magic. The superstitions and fanciful magic in both arenas persist and continue to disrupt religion and science as religion and science in themselves. Mistaken superstitions and mistaken fanciful magic are imposed on both religion and science by confused or mistaken but self-satisfying creatures of the world after the flesh.

Whether cast as theologies or science theories, or as superstition or fanciful magic, the subject/object paradigm is not fashioned to address matters of ultimate existential significance, meaning or purpose. In that regard, the subject/object paradigm of reality is a failed paradigm. Besides not being able to address matters of ultimate existential concern such as significance, meaning and purpose; the use of subject/object paradigm readily misconstrues external objects and the relations between the objects. In addition, people as subjects can subjectively supplant the reality of objects external to them and impose fanciful creations of the imagination in the place of that reality. This how people create idols and attribute god-like attributes to the idols they erect.

The dismantling of the subject/object paradigm of reality by philosophy and science has undermined and bankrupted theologies and religions founded on the subject/object paradigm. The only viable reality concerning ultimate existential significance, meaning and purpose is the reality of union with God indwelling our person.

Existing spiritually is the experience of God indwelling us forming us. The experience of that forming is experiencing Christ after the spirit. What we truly know of God, we only know because of our forming spiritually according to Christ after the spirit. In spiritually forming we experience, sense and know God through Christ after the spirit. Christ after the spirit is God present in existence in specific human terms, by means of which we are formed spiritually and by means of which experience spiritual birth and living. We are in God of and from God, as God indwelling forms us spiritually in Christ-specific terms that allow us to participate in the essence and essential properties God.

In seeking, finding and being in the Light within, Quakers have struggled with the subject/object paradigm for some 400 years now. In the process, they refined a "waiting" or "listening" to discern the voice of God and "see" the Light within. They have practiced and acquired the ability to "thresh" and separate the subject/object paradigm from their experience of union with God indwelling, as well as their intelligibly sensing the experience of union with God indwelling according to Christ after the spirit. But they are not alone in such knowledge. We can clearly find, see and understand descriptions of such experience and such knowledge in the book of John, the authenticated letters of Paul and the work of Spinoza. The Light has always been present to people as long as people have been and will present to be people as long as people are and will be.

In regards to God and the spiritual things of God, that is in regards to the essence and essential properties of God's significance, meaning and purpose, union with God manifests a reality that is not any object or any relationship between objects; but, it is a reality that is experienced, sensed and intelligibly grasped. The spiritual things of God manifest in union with God indwelling forming our person according to Christ after the spirit. The spiritual things of the reality of union with God are not found in the subject/object paradigm of reality that we have spent, spend and will spend so much effort to comprehend and understand.

The subject/object paradigm of reality comes out of existence and has its (flesh and blood) use; likewise the reality of union with God comes out of existence and has its (spiritual) use. There is experience of both from which we sense and acquire knowledge and understanding of:

- existence itself
- objects external to our essential person
- our flesh and blood person as an object, (our person as a subject-object, and,
- our spiritual person united in God of and from God indwelling our person forming us according to the essence and properties of God manifest in human terms, according to Christ after the spirit.

Spiritual birth in God of and from God is not merely the absence of the subject/object paradigm. In the absence of that paradigm and *in the absence of spiritual birth and life, there is nothing* in regards to our person.

Experiential evidence of spiritual birth and life is in our personally manifesting the fruits of the spirit of God. Being as Christ would be provides sensible experience of existing in Christ-specific terms so that the things of God are intelligible to us. In this intelligence we have or we put on the mind of Christ.

In the book of John, Christ calls for 'leadings' of such knowledge and understanding for people, so that they can personally enter into the Kingdom of God. In Paul's authenticated letters, Paul claims personal spiritual experience of Christ and claims that the experience is *intelligible*. He suggests that this *distinct or intelligible knowledge and understanding of the spiritual things of God is to be most highly prized.* Spinoza undertakes to explicate and demonstrate this sensing and intelligence of the mind of God in human terms, which is to say according to Christ after the spirit.

Ultimate existential significance, meaning, purpose are lodged in union with God; and, ultimate existential concern is addressed only through union with God. Righteousness, justice, mercy and God's love are in union with God. These things of God do not exist apart from union with God from which come spiritual birth, life and living. The spiritual things of God do not exist in the objects of the subject/object paradigm regardless of the aspirations of any theology, religion or theory of science. Empirical experience of and knowledge of the things of God is not in empirical experience and knowledge of the objects of existence. Only empirical experience[12] of existing in God of and from God provides knowledge of the essence and essential properties of God and knowledge of our spiritual person being formed according to Christ after the spirit.

Union with God (i.e. existence) is sensed and results in knowledge of being in God of and from God and being so in Christ-specific human terms. The knowledge is not objective nor is it subjective. The knowledge is direct and immediate knowledge of actually being or actually existing. This is not knowledge cast in subject/object terms. God is not an object that a subject can experience as an object. God is not an object that a person in union with God can talk to. Talking requires a subject and an object. It is not possible to talk God while in union with God. Worship

[12] Empirical experience of the things of God is the basis for experimental knowledge of the things of God.

requires a subject and object. God is not an object that a person in union with God can worship. In either example, there is separation and distance between a subject and object. For people to be able to worship God or for people to pray to God, God must be 'out there', and the following cannot be:

> ...you will see me. Because I live, you also will live. 20 On that day you will realize that I am in my Father, and you are in me, and I am in you. (John 14:19-20, NIV)

> Remain in me, as I also remain in you. No branch can bear fruit by itself; it must remain in the vine. Neither can you bear fruit unless you remain in me. "I am the vine; you are the branches. If you remain in me and I in you, you will bear much fruit; apart from me you can do nothing. (John 15:4-6, NIV)

> I have given them the glory that you gave me, that they may be one as we are one --- I in them and you in me --- so that they may be brought to complete unity. (John 17:22-23, NIV)

The temporal Christ may seem confusing. Christ talks to God even though Christ is the Word of God, experiencing and knowing God immediately and directly. Christ used his words to 'talk to' God for the benefit of the disciples, who did not understand what Christ understood by direct and immediate experience and knowledge. They looked for God outside themselves in the carnal world of external objects. They required *appearances* they could relate to through their bodily senses. For the benefit of carnal people (disciples), Christ provided modelling of an exemplar of *Christ after the flesh.* Why does Christ tell people to pray (see Mathew 6:5-9)? It is important to follow Christ in word and in deed. Prayer helps to cognitively reorganize the world after the flesh to approximate or reconcile to the world after the spirit. Approximating the things of the spirit in the flesh sensitizes our recognition and cognition of experiences of our own spiritually forming by God indwelling according to Christ after the spirit.

In union with God, there is no alienation or separation, nor any need for reconciliation. The same holds in union with Christ after the spirit, which union is brought about by God indwelling forming our spiritual person according to Christ after the spirit. The experience and the knowledge of the experience are not cast in subject/object terms. Christ after the spirit is not an object that we experience as subjects from a distance. When we talk to Christ, we are talking to an abstraction generated subjectively by us. If we are in union with Christ after the spirit, we cannot 'talk' to Christ --- nor is there need to 'talk' as though we were separate from Christ.

In union with God and Christ after the spirit, knowledge is intuitive and emerges from the union itself. In union with God and Christ after the spirit there is knowledge of the essence of God and knowledge of the essential properties of the essence of God. Such union with God in Christ-specific terms is union by means of which we acquire the essence and essential properties of God common in the union, (including existential significance, meaning and purpose). The experience of union with God and Christ after the spirit is experiential and therefore empirical. It is experience of a different kind than empirical experience of objects. Knowledge of union is in the uniting, sensed and intelligibly grasped by our personal spirit being spiritually formed.

In union with God personal spiritual birth and life has essence and properties in common with the essence and properties of God as manifest in Christ after the spirit. Such birth that carries what Christ after the spirit has in common with God into our existing or being is spiritual birth in and of the things of God. Spiritual life and living is sustained by God indwelling forming us spiritually according to Christ after the spirit. Knowledge of spiritual birth, life and living does not come from the objects of existence but comes from existing itself. The human character of God manifest in Christ after the spirit is the human character of the essence and properties of existence manifest in Christ after the spirit. The knowledge is present in the spiritual existing.

Radical Christians know by the experience of spiritually existing or being, that neither God nor Christ after the spirit are mere objects. God and Christ after the spirit are in the very nature of existence and existing. Radical Christians start with this experiencing and measure everything else in religion against this fundamental experiencing of existing and existence.

Union With God: Christ's Teachings Concerning the Kingdom of God

The Kingdom of God (or heaven) as a phrase, is consistently and coherently used by Christ throughout the New Testament. The evident consistency and coherence is too striking in substance to be accidental. The parables are illuminated by John chapter 3 *and also the rest of John's Gospel*. This becomes clear when we revisit all the teachings, fully aware that the phrase Kingdom of God is what we are spiritually born into and of which are an active part.

Outside the framework illustrated by Christ's teaching to Nicodemus in John 3, the many references to the Kingdom of God were open to misunderstanding by people at the time. Before Pilate in John's Gospel, Christ disowns the kingdoms of this world or the apocalyptic comings of this world's histories. The Kingdom of God teachings in the Gospels are Christ's teachings about our entering into union with God and living in union with God; and, doing so through Christ.

Bodily or carnal healing and miracles are not relevant in the parables about God's kingdom, in regards to understanding the teachings about the Kingdom of God. Flesh and blood healing and miracles are of carnal worldly things, the teachings of the parables are spiritual things. Just as the physical flesh and blood body is not part of the

Kingdom of God, the miracles or healings that are simply of the flesh are not part of that Kingdom.

Relating Christ's teachings about God to Old Testament notions of God coming in physical, earthly power to defeat carnal enemies; misses the meaning of the words and the points of Christ's parables, concerning the Kingdom of God. This approach to the teachings of the parables about the Kingdom of God, while sensible and reasonable in terms of the flesh do not support a worldly apocalyptic 'end times' approach the Kingdom of God. From this approach none of those teachings reference any coming carnal or physical kingdom on earth or events in history.

In John 3, Christ that people who are born in the flesh need to be spiritually born from above in order to 'see' or 'enter' the Kingdom of God. Such spiritual birth and life is distinct and separate from being born from a mother's womb in the flesh. It is clear from the rest of that Gospel, that such birth is union with God through Christ. The phrase "the kingdom of God" (or heaven) is found in many, many places in the Gospels and also is found in the Epistles. We learn from the Gospel parables concerning the Kingdom that the kingdom of God is the spiritual realm of God, which we are a part of and enter into or become a part of through birth from above, distinct from our bodily birth.

Union with God is not simply God inside us objectively alongside our person, as the many other 'things'[13]

[13] Sensory images and memories for example are inside us alongside us.

that are inside us alongside us. Union with God is God existentially indwelling the whole of our entire actual existing person. God indwells our person according to the essence of Christ or Christ after the spirit. The presence of God through Christ is the Word within us shaping, forming and sustaining us spiritually. Inner Light 'causes' us to personally intuit sense and know God. Our experience of existence is experience of our selves in God of and from God. As such, we are spiritual creatures of God, who live in every way as Christ would and does live in the Kingdom of God. Christ's Gospel teachings concerning our union with God (that is our being in the Kingdom of God) can be found in the many parables of the Kingdom of God in the Gospels.

If a person has knowledge of their union with God from being born from above, in God of and from God, as described in Christ's teaching in John 3, then Christ's teachings in all four Gospels (and also the apostolic writings in the Epistles) about the Kingdom of God (or Heaven) fit into the framework of that union. Christ's teachings about the Kingdom of God are strikingly consistent and coherent, if we understand that entering the Kingdom of God is spiritual life from above into God's Kingdom, in eternity.

The Kingdom of God exists apart from the existence of the temporal world. It is no more like the temporal world than the temporal world is like the infinite and eternal world of the things of God. *The Kingdom of God which we can enter is established by God according to Christ after the spirit.* The things of the world have no place in the Kingdom of God nor do the 'powers and principalities' or the forces of the world of flesh and blood have any lave in the Kingdom of God. Christ's parables are not parables about the world of flesh. They do utilize things of the flesh to illustrate things of the spirit for people after the flesh. The parables of Christ are illuminated by John 3 and they should be read in that light.

Entering or rather being in, of and from the Kingdom of God is union with God, by means of which we are spiritually in God of and from God. Because we are in God of and from God, God has 'dominion' of us spiritually but has dominion from *within us*. Because we are personally in God of and from God; we through God in us, personally act spiritually by God indwelling according to Christ after the spirit forming us. In our hearts, minds and souls, we become the means of God's 'dominion' over us because we are in God of and from God.

Prima facie by existing, we are being the "fact" of our existing. Prima facie, by existing we are also the 'fact' of God existing apart from our union with our bodies or the bodies themselves. Furthermore, prima facie our existing in union with God is the fact of our union by way of birth from above, or by way of entering the Kingdom of God. The facts are prima facie knowledge we immediately have in our actually existing. Union with God is also 'felt' bodily, as is the union of our selves with our own bodies. In our union with God, we sense God's indwelling presence, no less than we sense the presence of our bodies as a result of our union with our bodies.

Epistemontological: Existential Christology

Existential Christology is a Christology that considers Christ as *an accessible reality that is actually, presently existing and being*. Existential Christology does not reduce or limit Christ to merely flesh and blood historical, temporal Christ of 2,000 years ago. Existential Christology is about Christ actually existing in the existence in which we exist here and now; and, existing human terms enabling intelligibly interactions. Christ is essentially relevant to us when we are being forming spiritually according to the distinctions and specifications of the essence and properties of Christ.

Epistemology and ontology are usually represented as separate. Epistemology is about knowledge or understanding. Ontology is about being. An existential or spiritual approach to both ontology and epistemology calls for the synthesis of epistemology and ontology into '*epistemontology*' in which to be existent or having existential spiritual being is a synthesis of being, and knowing that being from its being. Epistemontology is existence that knows it is existing. In other words, understanding is immediate and direct in actually being. The knowledge is inherent in the being and the being is inherent in the knowing. Epistemontological can more narrowly be expressed as existential.

In a person's being and existing, experience of existence and knowledge of existing are grasped by the person in one action. In this existential act, knowledge is not abstracted cognition or reflection of existing: it part of the actual existing. Existentialism, at this protean level, transcends carnality and idealism. The act of experience and knowing by being or existing is singular: the ontology and the epistemology is one. In being and existing, the person exists and knows he or she exists in existing or being. This epistemontology makes existentialism distinct. It applies to carnal existence and spiritual existence. We know the things of the world in our bodily or carnal being; we know the things of the spirit in our spiritual being. Spiritual being does not come from nor is it of the carnal. Spiritual being comes from spiritual things.

Spiritual praxis (religion) is different from spiritual practice (piety).The latter (practice) are things we do because we know how to do them and we want to do them. The former (praxis) are things we do because of who and what we are. Spiritual praxis does not involve choosing or deciding to do things. When we are in God of and from God according to Christ after the spirit forming our person, we simply do what we are by being what we are. We do not chose or decide to manifest the fruits of the spirit, when we are in the spirit of and from the spirit after Christ, any more that plants (vines) choose or decide to manifest fruits.

Our fundamental existential or epistemontological being or existing, in regards to our personal selves, to God, to God indwelling according to Christ after the spirit is the foundation of existential Christianity, and the basis for an existential Christology. Some people, fleeing the world of the things of flesh feel a freedom from bondage to the flesh.

This *freedom from* the flesh is not the *freedom to* live to the spirit. Indeed many materialistic existentialists, to their horror, have found that *freedom from the flesh, without spiritual being*, creates a personal empty existence of absurd insignificance, meaninglessness and purposelessness. Being free of the flesh may provide an experience of 'personally empty oneness', but this is not the experience of being in God of and from God according to the specifics of Christ after the spirit. The latter is actually being in eternity; the former is an experience of 'nothing'.

In our actual existence, we are personally and intimately involved in epistemontologically experiencing and knowing God according to the Spirit after Christ. Our personal absence would extinguish our actual personal experience of God, the Spirit as well as Christ, out of which personal significance, meaning and purpose actually comes to be. In our actually existing in the Kingdom of God, we are entered into union with God and in this union; we prima facie have knowledge of God and the spirit of Christ manifest in us. We also have prima facie knowledge of our spirit being in God of and from God indwelling through the spirit of Christ What we know of God, we know because we exist; and, what we know of God, the Spirit and Christ as distinct from our selves, we know because these are in the forming of our personal being and existing..

The study of God, the Spirit and Christ are theology, pneumatology and Christology respectively. Within Christianity, theology has a single focus, while Christology is several foci and pneumatology is many foci.

God is one. Christology concerns the Word (as Christ), the temporal Christ, and the infinite and eternal Christ. Pneumatology, on the other hand includes the spirit of God, the Holy Spirit, the spirit of Christ (both temporal and infinite and eternal), as well as the spirit of Truth. All three have been described as living and as persons; but not as persons in the usual sense of that word and not living in the usual sense of that word. We have human specifics explicating God only in the reality of Christ accessible within us in God indwelling us according to Christ after the spirit. We are connected to God and Christ by the indwelling spirit, which at the same time gives us life in our spiritual forming and spiritual maturity.

. The working of the spirit generates or forms spiritual being or life. Such working may be evidenced in effects or sensations that some have described as breath-lie or wind-like. Some people mistakenly described the spirit as a breath or wind. But the spirit is not the evidence of the spirit; it is neither breath nor wind. The spirit gives us spiritual life, housed in our temporal bodies, which spiritual life we internally experience and sense. We experience evidence of its generation and movement like a breath or wind. We experience and see the effects or works of our spiritual person. From that we can rationalize and abstractly view the effects of the workings of the spirit in us.

In the Gospel according to the book of John, a number of things are described concerning the spirit. The spirit is the source of spiritual life; it flows like an endless stream of water from within spiritual being. As a result of the spirit's workings, we are born from above. Birth of and from the things of the world, i.e. carnal things of the flesh, is not a birth until a carnal person of flesh emerges. Birth of and from the things of the spirit is not a birth until a spiritual person emerges.

We experience the spirit and we also experience evidence of its workings. In a similar fashion, we experience the wind and evidence of its blowing being driven by forces within nature. John the Baptist saw the spirit like a dove descending from heaven and remaining on Jesus. Whatever John saw, it was not the spirit itself. Like the wind in John 3, the dove John saw appeared as evidence of the spirit's presence, it was the spirit itself. In a similar vein, Elisha did not know God from earthquakes or winds, but from a voice. The voice is not just a sound or noise, but what made it a voice are the words (the logos). The sound is evidence of the presence of the spirit. What intelligibly spoke to Elisha was a voice distinctly and specifically articulating words, not just a sound. *The spirit's communion was in the Word* not in the sound.

The historical temporal Christ had a spirit, which was at times moved and troubled; and which was given up on his temporal death. In our spiritual being, we communicate or commune with God with words (i.e. logos) which are discerned spiritually not by way of perceptions, sensations and conceptions of the flesh. Worship is in spiritual being or living. True worship is not a temporal event (i.e. like attending a church service); it is part of actually being or existing spiritually. It is all too facile to speak of the spirit as a bodily person, like the persons we encounter in the flesh. The Holy Spirit is not a bodily sensation, emotion or feeling. It is not a euphoria of the body. It is not merely a 'person' as we know people.

The present existential Christ is not the historically existent Christ caught up in temporal flesh during a short life on earth. The existential Christ exists beyond time and space, or temporality. The existential Christ is infinite and eternal. The existential Christ is God existing within human terms but beyond merely temporal being. God is inherent in our personal being or in existing. God is inherent in our being or existing. The creator or creation is inherent in our creation and in our being or existing. All of which is to say that God is within us as Light, as the Word, as the Spirit (of God) in our spiritual creation and being.

God within us is Lighting, Wording and Spiriting our mind, spirits and hearts. The specifics of God within us working in us are God in distinct and specific human terms. It is Christ infinite and eternal in human terms that explicates God. Our communion of God is in the reality of Christ. Within the Christian framework, it is Christology that informs both theology and pneumatology by making God practical for us as people.

We experience knowledge in different ways:

- *In perception*: perceiving forms our perceptions, and in our experience of the formations, we know what we perceive. Perceptions are caused by forces external to our person. We are passive in knowing by perception.
- *In conception*: conceiving forms our conceptions, and in our experience of the

formations, we know what we conceive. Conceptions are cause by our person. We are active in knowing by conception.

- *In utilising (using):* using forms our utilization (usage), and in our experience of the formations of our usage, we know what we do. This knowledge is caused by our doing. We can be passive or active in what we do: some things we do are externally triggered or caused; some things we do are internally triggered or caused.
- *In being*: being forms our being; or in existence, existing forms our existence, and in our experience of the formations of our being or existing, we know what we are. This knowledge is cause by our person being active.

In 'following' Christ indwelling, we form in Christlikeness because we are being formed by the 'hand of God' within according to the spirit of Christ. But this following is active, not passive. It is formational from within.

A distinction was made above between praxis and practice. Spiritual praxis involving the specifics of Christ is formational. When we are formed by God indwelling we do not lead. God leads and forms us, therefore we follow. But we are being formed spiritually. Therefore we have *formational-following*. This is not the same as what happens when we follow in the flesh by way practice triggered by things external to our person. Piety is triggered by things external to our selves, including our representations and reflections of what we sense of God within us. Discerning a true plan of living from a model of Christ and piously but passively following that plan and exemplar is an important part of our pursuit of salvation and holiness.

A true plan of living is our plan to work to do God's work. Having and being obedient to a true plan of living is piety. The discernment and practice of a true plan of living based on what we know of Christ cannot be under estimated. The discernment emerges from a blend of intelligible sensing of God indwelling our person according to Christ after the spirit on the one hand; and on the other hand, what we know from the flesh about the manifestation of Christ in the flesh, including in the manifestation of Christ in other people in the flesh. Both sources provide experience by means of which we affirm Christ indwelling, forming us according to the specifics of God in human terms. With experience comes experiment to discover and to refine true experience of the flesh and of the spirit.

When the following is *formational-following*, the following is an active affirmation of God in one's person, existing or being. Spiritually we are not formed…we are forming. Active f*ormational-following results in our spiritual forming, here and now*. That *we have been formed is not* the work of God at hand: that *we are being formed is* the work of God at hand.

We can formationally-follow specifically in perception, conception, usage, and in being or existing. In following, our spirit forms of and from the reality of Christ. In forming spiritually, our existing of and from Christ intentionally grasps and possesses us. Christian forming is a spiritual forming that comes to be by God's grace and by our following Christ. Our following coalesces into becoming and being. Those who follow other things form of and from other things.

The reality of the infinite and eternal Christ and our being through that reality, speaks to a Christology that is existent or existential. The scope of being Christ is all that is presently done within Christ. In Christ there is no quantity, no great or small, only quality in which the smallest is as much as the greatest.

Spiritual Flight From Carnal Snares

We are born into the world with only the possibility of salvation and only the potential for holiness. Along with that possibility and potential, we are also born with the capacity to do evil. In any case, we are born wanting and needing. We are born with hands outstretched --- reaching for fulfillment on several levels. We have biological wants, needs and urges from the moment we take our first breath. Psychological, cognitive and emotive wants and needs follow. All these emerge to form us into bodily or carnal persons. We emerge on the stage of each area of need forming and developing. We are also born with spiritual hands outstretched - reaching for the most potent fulfillment: spiritual fulfillment. By far and away, this fulfillment gives us our place in the infinite and eternal theatre of existence, the universe of goodness and our place in God. We are created with an inner Light that, as Spinoza suggested, "lights itself and the dark". The infinite and eternal spark of God ignites our hearts and minds to create us to be more than mere flesh. It creates us to be existentially significant, meaningful and purposeful.

In terms of flesh, there is nothing holy about us. The strong prey on the weak and eat their flesh or use them as play things for distracting amusement and entertainment. In terms of the flesh, all things, including the spiritually perverse, are permitted to the strong. In all their strength in the flesh, they remain perverse and depraved in spirit. All the while there is something from on high that calls out alongside and within for ultimate existential significance, meaning and purpose. This may be blinded in the slavers and predators possessed entirely by their flesh, as is any beast that does not see, hear or understand the spiritual things of God. We are born into a world of flesh that naturally generates slavers and predators, which exploit and devour us. We enslave and prey on others in gross ways and quantities; but we also enslave and prey on those near us in small ways and quantities. The latter is no more acceptable than the former. In either case, in the end the world after the flesh offers existential self-destruction.

Apart from wanton flesh, the spiritual yearning in people is core to their being. It is powerful, overwhelming and not to be denied without severe consequences to us as individuals. Its power is pervasive and extreme. Its demand for fulfillment may be snared in 'mere flesh,' confusing and misguiding existential efforts to find spiritual fulfillment. Under this perspective, we can understand the origin and influence of spiritual deprivation and depravity. Bodily or carnal well-being, while fulfilled carnally, can still house spiritual deprivation. We understand sin and sinfulness as separation from or the absence of spiritual salvation and holiness. We can understand that people give up, surrender in spiritual passivity and collapse into bodily or carnal comforts. We surrender ourselves short of our spiritual potential, in return for temporary satiation and a measure of temporal security and benefit. The demands of spiritual fulfillment do not evaporate; instead, they force a deprived, dissonant alignment of the carnal world. Not understanding our spiritual nature, and suffering deeply in profound spiritual loneliness, separateness, and isolation, we ourselves condemn carnal life and find fault with our carnal selves. In response to those views, we create a transient carnal foundation and build on it pseudo-spiritual lives to be free of fear, anxiety, loneliness, isolation and the demands of our spirit, for existential peace and rest. We may free ourselves from evil, but not find the freedom of holiness and of being in God.

Are we made like God as a part of God having God indwelling? Are we created with the Spirit of God central to the very core of our existence and existing? Is the Word of God in us active by God sparking our spiritual birth? If so, then we are essentially good, and through Godliness can find salvation and pursue holiness. Do we inherently have the Light of God in our hearts and shining on our minds? We can understand, as it was with Jacob's redefinition into Israel (Genesis 32:22-32), that people will 'wrestle all night with angels' not letting go until they are victorious and are blessed - until we become more than servants, until the fruits of our striving leaves us as "friends" and off-spring of God.

Are we essentially evil and therefore unable to find salvation and holiness? If so, then we could do nothing to find salvation and holiness. Imagine for a moment that people did not have that activating spark of God in them. We would then be utterly desolate. Then we would be, as some say, completely fallen, beyond the reach of salvation, completely sinful and separate, with nothing of God in us. If it were so, God could not work through us, because of the innate depravity. In such deprivation, we seek forgiveness for 'existing without God' in God's universe, even though we are not the source or cause of such deprivation.

Even before we were born, God had fashioned us in the 'image' of God, with the Word in us, for us to become holy. Before we were born, God was reconciling us to Himself through the spirit and mind of Christ. God's justice, righteousness, mercy and love understand that God does not abandon his spiritual offspring, but creates them and their world so that they find atonement and spiritual fulfillment. Therefore, we know that, while we sin and are sinners, God is nonetheless in us all the while. While we seek forgiveness and atonement for our sins, God is in us through it all. God works through the Spirit in us, first calling us to salvation, then to holiness, and through holiness to further repentance and forgiveness.

In Christ, the Christian finds the way to salvation and the path of holiness is made clear. Spiritual life for the Christian begins with the call of Christ: "Follow me." Christ provides Light through which we can "see" the Kingdom, and direction by means of which to "enter" the Kingdom. We do not find that Christ came saying "You can do nothing; therefore I have come to pay for your sin with my death." Christ came in effect saying: If you want salvation, "Follow me." Christ's disciples followed him to salvation and holiness, because of that, they repented. The salvation proclaimed by Christ was simple *and at hand*. It did not demand an acknowledgement and recognition of essential depravity and sinfulness on our part. It did not depend on a blood payment by any bodily death. God freely provides the promise of peace, fulfillment, comfort, shelter, and a home for us in Himself. It is this great formational love, which is in the nature of the Spirit of God that shines through God's holy people, by way the Christ after the spirit, to Light up salvation and the way of holiness.

Christian salvation is *the decision to*:

- ✓ *do* as Christ does
- ✓ act as Christ acts
- ✓ think as Christ thinks
- ✓ *be* as Christ is.

Christian holiness is practising and actually:

- ✓ doing as Christ does
- ✓ acting as Christ acts
- ✓ thinking as Christ thinks
- ✓ being as Christ is.

Christ was bodily born into the temporal world, bodily lived and bodily died in it. Bodies are only carnal vessels that 'tabernacle the spirit' in terms of flesh. The spirit and mind of Christ do not have the limitations of the temporal body of Christ. In reality, the mind of Christ was present to us in the form of the 'pre-temporal' Christ, which is to say the eternal essence of God in human terms. The mediating spirit and mind of Christ - that is the laws of God - have been, are, and will be directly written "on our hearts and in our minds" and so define us spiritually. The spark of God ignites spiritual life, the Light within illuminates and we manifest the laws of God in existing or being in Christ of and from Christ. The spirit and mind of Christ is present to us here and now as a 'post-temporal' Christ. The mind of Christ guided God's people. It helped them to know God. It helped them prepare the old and new scriptures. The mind of Christ guides God's people today, helping them to know God and to read and understand the scriptures.

We are in God of and from God however we are not God: we are different from God and cannot know or grasp God as we know or grasp created things. We are spiritually in God of and from God through distinctions by means of which we are formed specifically in union with God. Our actual existing spiritual life is generated and sustained by what John calls the Word. The Word writes or inscribes God's laws on our hearts and in our minds. In existing our hearts and minds specifically manifest God in human terms.

Following the very lofty writing in the Prologue of the book of John, the writer tells of some announcements of John the Baptist, and then spends time clarifying the Baptist's role in regards to Christ. John the Baptist is a created person and as such, he can testify and point to the reality of Christ. He can only share what he personally experiences. He personally experiences Christ and shares his personal experience. He cannot share Christ's experiences. He is not Christ. To believe that what John says about his experience is true, does not actually contribute to our salvation. The writers of scripture, have their purposeful expression of the Gospel as known to them from their experiences; given to us in their writings and ideas that they more or less understood; that their audience more or less understood; and, which we in our time more or less understand. While we actually participate in the infinite and eternal being of Christ in the present, we do not actually participate in the past temporal being of the writers of scripture. At best, we can only read abstract words that point to what they may have experienced. Our participation in the authors' purposeful written expression of the Gospel does not begin to equate or approach the spiritual experience of participating in the reality of Christ here and now. In a similar way, we do not participate in the being of any other person. We do not participate in the being of John the Baptist or any other witness of Christ. In as much as we know anything, we know we are and are aware that *we presently and actually participate in the real being of Christ*. Through this reality, we know and comprehend God. We grasp, take possession and we are being in God of and from God, through the Word in us, which is the reality of Christ. Scripture, written by people with whom we did not and do not 'participate in', all the same affirms what we have in common with those people through the Word shared by witnesses and by us personally. This commonality allows us to read the Gospel, which was spoken to them and written to us.

To follow Christ and be in God of and from God, we must find, grasp and know 'Christ after the spirit'. How can we do this? How did the early Christians find and come to know Christ after the spirit? Of the several ways available to them and to us, the most accessible, immediate and direct way of knowing Christ is in participating in the reality of Christ by what we experience and what we do, as

Christ experience and do. What we discern can be affirmed by others, who are also participating in the reality of Christ.

Creating or Forming Spiritual Existence

Grounding and Framing Spiritual Existence

Genesis depicts the creating of bodily flesh and blood life. The Prologue in John is concerned with spiritual life. John 1:1-18 does not breakout into discourses on engineering or physics, chemistry or biology. It opens up to Life that is spiritual life, which is Light. There is Light and Life in existence and in existing. The discourse moves from created things in general to specific things being formed by the Light. This Light is forming our personal spiritual existence.

The Prologue in John's Gospels identifies the 'beginning' is with the Word. It is written that the Word and God are present to one another. The beginning is with the Word, it is not identified with God. If there was no Word, there would be no 'beginning'. Life was created in the Word and has its beginning in the Word.

What kind of Life was created that had its beginning in the Word? Light (i.e. the intelligible essence of God in human terms) is the Life (i.e. spiritual life) created in the beginning in the Word. The 'beginning' being discussed is the beginning of the eternal things in the Kingdom of God --- which in fact do not have a beginning in themselves. The beginning exists relative to our understanding or relative to our Light.

In our beginning, the "Word was". In our beginning, "the Word was with God". In our existing, all things that have been made, as far as we know, were made by God's Word indwelling our person. In our person, (spiritual) life was in the Word indwelling our person. The Word provided our spiritual person with "the light of men". This Light in us, which is our spiritual life, shines in us and that which dark in our existing (that is our person after the flesh) "has not understood" and does not "understand" the Light.

In Existence and existing, he Word exists as Light which the world after the flesh "did not recognize" and does not recognize the existing Light. To those who receive the Light and accept, assent and affirm the work of the Word indwelling forming us spiritual, spiritual birth and life is given "not of natural descent", "but born of God".

The Prologue delineates the foundation on which the Gospel presented by Christ in the book of John is set. In the Prologue of John's Gospel, the ground and frame of spiritual existence is called the Word --- Logos. Logos is not merely just creating or the created order. It is not just reasoning or reason. Logos --- the Word is being in God of and from God. As far as things in the world have spiritual being, it is formed in them by the Word. As far as we exist spiritually and our spiritual existence has meaning, we have this through the infinite and eternal reality of Christ. As far as things in the world (Kosmos) have spiritual meaning, it is given to them by the Word. The Word through the reality of Christ in existence drives spiritual becoming. The Word itself is meaning and being. God's love, justice, righteousness and mercy are in our coming to exist and our existing through *the Word 'Word-ing' in us*.

Light is from spiritual Life. Darkness is the absence of Life. Darkness does not have power over or influence on Light or spiritual Life. Light has power unto itself in itself, which derives from God and from no other source. No merely temporally created person is the Light. That is why John the Baptist could witness to the Light, but was not the Light. People can witness to the Light in themselves, and point to the reality of the Light apart from themselves, but none is the Light.

We find, based on Christ's teachings in the book of John, *a covenant inherent in existence itself and in our existence, between the reality of Christ and people born of God indwelling according to Christ after the spirit.* This is *the Christ Covenant*. It comes into effect, when we actively formationally-follow Christ. We commit to and actually follow Christ in our living and being. Christ acts to enliven the spirit of God in us. Christ is lifted up within our very core, then in illumination we see and understand. The Paraclete, alongside us calling, focuses our attention. We grow in Christ, and from God we become of God in God. God in us forms us to be in God. The Word that was with God in our person can cause our spiritual life to come alive in us in our communion with the reality that is Christ and our engagement in the 'Christ Covenant'.

The carnal world recognizes many things, but it does not recognize the Light. The powers of the carnal world have no influence on the Light itself. However, those born in of and from the Light can affect the carnal world.

Christ exists as a reality: a spiritual reality. People can exist as spiritual realities. In seeking salvation and holiness, it is important to know and understand that Christ does not exist because the scriptures exist. The texts exist because Christ exists. Yet for ease, we turn to the texts to know Christ, who all the while exists in us, immediately accessible to us. At times, some people have been overly preoccupied with texts and have not attended to existence and reality itself. Over time, they have been fixated on the words in the texts and been distracted from the existing Word. The historical critical method within its own terms is a good corrective. It does not direct itself to the reality of Christ existing. It does not direct itself to spiritual reality here and now. That is not its purpose.

The historical critical approach to scripture brings certain clarity to the sources of scriptures and to the shaping of its messages by its authors. The approach speaks to writings from the past. Writers reach out to us through their writings. We reach back to them, through those writings. We read scripture to help us find our way and to help us along that way. We and the writers of scripture have shared experiences of spiritual birth and spiritual living through the reality of Christ. It is this sharing of experience that allows us to read and be acquainted with the writers' experiences.

The ground of Christianity is shifting, how shall we stand? The scriptures are not what they have been made out to be, how then shall we grasp Christ? If scriptures are not what they have been made out to be, all the same they tower before us in their unique role. Scripture remains under the Light but in a different way. We are not alone in our faith. Faith stands because of what God does in us. As presented in the Prologue, faith stands because God stands; and, God is in us standing. For our part, through our spiritual birth and being, we stand in God. Both in God, and in God in us, there is the accessible reality of Christ, which brings God to us and us to God. Through the Word, God in us leads us into God.

We live spiritually though Christ not through our beliefs or views of scripture but only by Christ actively forming us. We are called to exist in God of and from God according to Christ, with the least amount of flesh and blood baggage as possible. We come together in the present and over time, as spiritual beings --- being formed in spiritual existence --- to find our way and to help one another along that way. If we have Christ in us, if we have the Light and the Word in us forming us and providing us with experience of God working within us, we can proceed in faith and in confidence. We exist in God and God exists in us. We are being in God of and from God according Christ.

Spiritual existence like corporeal existence has a ground and a frame. Unlike the ground and frame of a house, the ground and frame of spiritual existence have their being 'in God of and from God'. Always present, always alive, the ground and frame of created spiritual existence are always grounding and framing. We are spiritually formed from the grounding and framing of existing in and of the reality of Christ. Spiritual forming lives in aspiration to be actually and presently, in God of and from God, while living in the world. The process of spiritual forming alters our personal essence and existing in our actual existing.

When scripture tells us that that laws of God are written in our hearts and on our minds (e.g. Jeremiah 31:33, Ezekiel 36:25-27, Romans 2:15, 2 Corinthians 3:2 , Hebrews 8:10 and 10:16, and Psalm 37:30-31), it is saying that the Word is at our core forming our existence and giving meaning and purpose to our spiritual existing. The Christ Covenant is at once a promise and a presently existing accessible means of salvation and holiness.

The practice of Christianity shifts and moves because people insert themselves in place of Christ and shape worlds of flesh that appeal to the needs and aspirations of the flesh. These errant constructs emerge, change and pass. Whatever piety they may have carried, passes with them. Even now some respond to such loss by freezing into a world from yesterday that will have no place in tomorrow. Others blur the boundaries between the holy and the mundane and become mired in a confusing unrecognizable landscape, upon roads leading to nowhere spiritually. Because both the temporal ground and frame of Christianity is shifting, *the primary concern of John's Prologue*, which rolls out in the rest of the Gospel as the *Covenant of Christ*, is relevant now.

Theology in Human Terms: God as Christ-specific

All things are involved in Existence, including our individual personal self. The substance upon which all things are is God. As a thing subsisting upon God we can be in union with God as far as our existing is. Our union with God is limited to what we are or is limited to our existing, the essence and properties of our existing. By way of union with God we have the essence and properties of God indwelling in our existing. Our experience of God indwelling through union with God is delineated by the lineaments of our existing. Our knowledge of our existing in God of and from God with God indwelling in us is formulated through our existential lineaments. *We experience, sense and intelligibly understand God only in human terms.*

Theology is the study of God and for Christians it is primarily the study of God in human terms that is the reality Christ:

1) internally from within through the working of spirit of Christ in forming our spiritual person, or
2) externally from what is known about the historical Christ, and from Christ as observably manifested in others.

We engage God because we exist in God of and from God and in so existing we have God in us. This experience is ineffable. Although sensible and discernable, experience of God as Existence and Existing ("I AM") is not intelligible or understandable. There is nothing about us that can 'contain' God. In opposition to that, our empirical experience is that we in fact have intelligible understanding of God. We are aware of and know we understand the that the essential things of God --- the essence of God and the essential properties of God --- are intelligible to us in distinct and specific human terms that we can relate to. The Word of God makes the things of God distinctly and specifically framed as Christ intelligible to us. Theology is and can only be the study of God in human terms, which is the study of Christ.

As cause of all things, God creates or causes everything we experience. In particular and intimately, God causes or forms within us the spiritual things that we directly and immediately experience internally. We exist according to "Christ after the spirit"[14] and know spiritual things by intuition within Christ. Our formation, by God forming us through Christ generates our knowledge of God, our personal spiritual formation and our knowledge of our personal spiritual formation.

Human knowledge is rooted in human experience grasped by intelligence and sensation, and this includes our discernible understanding of God. Sensing is the means by which we intelligibly grasp experience whether it is as images through bodily organs (sight, smell, hearing, etc.) or concepts, ideas, intuitions, etc., through 'cognitive-emotional' modes of grasping our internal experience of spiritual reality. Through our sense comes knowledge of the experiences sensed. We personally actively participate in generating or causing internal experiences that we sense then intuit. But we only passively sense or receive external experiences caused by things external to our person.

The actually present infinite and eternal Christ or the spirit of Christ is "Christ after the spirit" immediately

[14]For example see Paul's letter to the Romans chapters 7-8, as well as 1 and 2 Corinthians.

and directly present within us. We intelligibly and sensibly experience both. The finite historical Christ and Christ is present to us in abstraction and so present to us through our bodies, is "Christ after the flesh"[15].

Paul set down a basic outline and framework for Christian spiritual life in his work as seen in Romans 7-8, as well as 1 and 2 Corinthians. Paul writes about "Christ after the flesh" and "Christ after the spirit". *We can live according to the spirit in two ways: we can follow Christ through our flesh* (which is to say passively follow Christ after the flesh) *or through our spirit* (that is, actively follow Christ after the spirit indwelling, from within our person). In either venue, we are 'following' a true plan or rules of living. Those born from above, live according to the spirit (the spiritual order of God through Christ or the spirit of Christ, from which by way of reasoning we abstract the mind of Christ). Paul's discussions about the distinction between the flesh in itself (i.e. the body in itself) and the spirit in itself, are in concert with Christ's discourse on the same topic in John 3, as well as the Gospel writer's discourse in John 1. They are also referenced by Spinoza in his various discussions concerning Christ.

For over 2,000 years, Christian theologians have been concerned to demonstrate that Christ is God and that God is Christ. It must be clear that God is not Christ and Christ is not God. God is being and is actually being. God is existence and is actually existing. As persons, we only experience and sense in human terms or within the terms of our person. What we experience and sense of God is limited because we are limited. What we perceive and conceive is done in human or person terms. Our experience and sense is 'ours'. If God, without Christ, can immediately

---

[15] Understanding "Christ after the flesh" is about understanding Christ and should not be confused with our understanding of our own flesh.

and presently be united and experienced *by us* and sensed by us in human terms, there would be no purpose, place or need for Christ. If Christ is God in human terms, then Christ existing or being God in human terms is necessary in our union with God and our experiencing that union. In union with God through Christ, we know God exists, Christ exists and we exist.

God is the cause or creator of our spiritual forming and sustains the existing of our formation. Our personal Christ-specific spiritual forming is formed in God of and from God's actually indwelling our person according to Christ after the spirit. Christ-specificity is an act of being which actually is or which actually exists in real people who have been spiritually formed in God of and from God indwelling according to Christ. The forming is not a re-presentation of experience or sensing of things external to the person; rather it is a presentation of the actual reality of the person's spiritual forming.

Christ is specifically or distinctly immediately and directly manifest as God indwelling our person according to Christ after the spirit in our personal spiritual forming which generates sensibility and intelligibility of God within us. This is the sensibility and intelligibility that activates us to be as Christ would be in what we undertake to do.

Christ is also manifest to us through our bodies or through the flesh as handed down historically or as presented and as observed by us in the actions of people spirited by Christ.

From both these sources we construct an abstracted plan for pious living to be obedient to God and we utilize that plan to do what Christ as does Christ does it. We set goals in our living from that plan. We measure the attainment of our goals against that plan, including its models, standards, rules, etc.

It is God who fashions or forms us to spiritually conform to Christ after the spirit. This is our personal spiritual existence. We sense it and know it. When we are distracted by the things of the world, doing in the flesh what Christ would do in the flesh lets us recognize our spiritual self as different from what we do. We traverse away from the distractions of things of the flesh and into the focussed clarity of things of the spirit that is, into the Kingdom of God into which we have been born. The cause of our participating in the things of the spirit is not what we do in the flesh. But what we do in the flesh lets us re-cognize what God is causing us to be and what we are in spirit.

When we are externally caused to follow Christ (e.g. following something we read, a teaching or doctrine, or because we contractually obligated ourselves to do certain things, or because someone else tells us to do certain things, etc.), we follow "Christ after the flesh", through our flesh. This means we are not living carnally according to "this world", but we live according to "Christ after the spirit". In following Christ according the flesh, we live according to the truths of Christ. The problem with following "Christ after the flesh" is that, miracles aside, we have an extremely poor and fragmented grasp from outside our person of the finite historical "Christ after the flesh". Christian history is replete with people and leaders who believed they were following "Christ after the flesh", but instead were being moved by "the spirit of this world", its powers and dark forces.

It remains that pious living brings us to the gates of the Kingdom of God where we knock and enter. The importance of a true plan or rules of living constructed according to the specific existential distinctions that are the character of Christ cannot be underestimated.

God indwelling internally forms us to be actively following the spirit of Christ within us. God forms or generates us spiritually through Christ. In actively and personally following internally, we our selves affirm Christ or God, and in this situation we follow "Christ according the spirit", by means of which we are born from above and live spiritually in God of and from God.

Whether we follow "Christ after the flesh" or Christ after the spirit", we obey the 'laws of God' framed in Christ after the spirit. We are taught by God's indwelling Inner Light or Word either:

a) through external rules or agreements, or,
b) through internal 'rules and agreements' of being or existing, written in our hearts and on our minds by God through Christ.

Holiness is more than passive obedience. Our spirit is forming by God indwelling generating our spiritual birth and life through the spirit of Christ. We affirm God in obedience. There is a Christ Covenant, (discussed below). It is in the very make up and essence of existence. God exists with the Christ Covenant in hand. In union with God, we affirm God through Christ forming us, and God affirms us by the very nature of God manifest in the reality Christ. We experience, sense and come know passive obedience to Christ according to the flesh. We also experience, sense and come to know active obedience following Christ after the spirit.

Being Spiritually Formed

The temporal Christ did carnal things, as we do, for example he ate food, enjoyed aromas and felt anger. What separates the carnal and the spiritual in the temporal Christ? How do we separate the merely carnal and the spiritual when we undertake to construct a human model or exemplar of Christ? If we consider the essence and common properties of Existence ("I AM.") or God, of the spirit of Christ and of the temporal incarnate Christ, we can separate the things of God from the finite, temporal things of transitory, carnal flesh and blood existing. Eating is not common to all three, therefore eating is not among the spiritual things of God. The spirit of Christ does not feel anger, therefore anger is not common to all. On the other hand, kindness and mercy are in the essence and in the properties of Existence or God, of the spirit of Christ and of the temporal Christ after the flesh. They are common to all.

The Prologue in the book of John does not make any appeal to bodily or carnal power --- not to carnal miracles, not to carnal signs, and not to carnal wonders. It does not promise relief from bodily or carnal pain or the provision of carnal pleasures of temporal life. The prologue can be associated with the Genesis description of the flesh and blood creation. That said, it separates itself from Moses and the written external law that governed how people should live carnally. As discussed above, the beginning as presented in John is the beginning of spiritual life, which is the 'Kingdom of God'. To be of God, is to be spiritually just, righteousness, merciful and loving. Christ comes alive in our spirits and minds forming us personally to image God. We see, hear, sense and understand. We grasp and form into essential and spiritual children of God made of the stuff of God's essence and essential properties of that essence.

The Prologue in John's Gospel has been and can be compared to the start of Genesis. Though the two beginnings are worlds apart. If the prologue uses the start of Genesis to make a point, the point would be that Genesis does not concern itself with spiritual life apart from the life we have when we are born bodily or carnally, or 'of water'(John 3:5). Genesis talks about the creation of the carnal world. The Prologue talks about creation of the things of the spirit of God in us. The Prologue is not a story of history. It addresses us here and now. It looks to the spiritual things that generate our spiritual lives --- the creation or beginning of Truth as we personally have it. In brief, the Prologue says through God and by the Word's forming, we have spiritual existence and being.

John's Prologue speaks to the ground and being of spiritual forming. In few words, it is set down that we are of God and having spiritual life, we exist spiritually. John 3 clearly describes separate bodily or carnal living and spiritual living. Two breaths are breathed into us: one giving a life of flesh and blood; the other a life of spirit. In Genesis, life is breathed in the inert body of Adam, who then exists bodily or carnally or biologically. In John 3, we learn how, while carnally alive and living, we are born again from above and given a second breath, through which we live spiritually.

Of particular in interest in the Prologue of the book of John are some twelve verses at the start of the book. Verses 1 to 13 are concerned with eternal things. Verses 14 to 18 concern the temporal flesh and blood Christ.

> [1] In the beginning was the Word, and the Word was with God, and the Word was God. [2] He was with God in the beginning.

The beginning referred to at the start of the book of John is our existential beginning. There is no reason for the writer(s) to be concerned about any carnal beginning, which is the concern at the start of the book of Genesis. At our existential beginning was the Word, with distinctions and specifics that make it the Word. Different from God because of the distinctions and specifics, the Word is all the same with God in such a way as to be God. There is union of Word and God.

> [3] Through him all things were made; without him nothing was made that has been made. [4] In him was life, and that life was the light of all mankind. [5] The light shines in the darkness, and the darkness has not overcome it.

The Word exists articulating God so that God can be 'heard' or 'understood'. The Word communicates intelligible being. There is no need for the Word unless there is a person to 'hear' and 'understand' the Word. Life exists in the Word's articulating, but not any Life. It is the Life that is revealed by the illumination of the Light "of all mankind", which spiritual Life that exists in the Word. In the Genesis account God created light then separated the light from the darkness. Creating Light caused a separation of a divide between the Light (the spirit) and the absence of Light (the carnal) which is darkness. The Light illuminates the spirit and reveals the carnal, giving understanding of the carnal (darkness) to the spirit. The Light does not extend any understanding to the carnal; hence the carnal (dark) cannot understand or comprehend the Light.

The separating of Light from the darkness creates or illuminates spiritual being or existing to generate knowledge and understanding of spiritual being or spiritual existence and existing. Because spiritual Life is in the Word then when the Word generates a spiritual birth and life, that spiritual life involves the Light of all humankind. It does not involve the carnality of all humankind, which carnality does not see, hear or understand the spiritual things of God.

There is a kind of life that is inherent in Existence and Existing and is inherent in the Word. Such Life is not carnal (sarx) life, it is spiritual Life. The Word was Life (zoe), that is essential or spiritual Life or Life of ultimate existential significance, meaning and purpose, not merely transient carnal life. The Word is God in action; hence all things that have been made were made through the Word. In particular God or Existence and Existing's ultimate existential significance, meaning and purpose is in the Word's act of creating mankind such that mankind can understand or comprehend spiritual Life (afford in union with God). Mankind comprehends or understands this Life in which mankind participates and the *experience of comprehending or understanding is Light*, which indwells the essence and the properties of the essence or spirit of the person's formulated mind. The Light of humankind gives understanding and comprehension; it reveals the essence and the properties of the essence of God to humankind. This Light (spiritual life) shines in the darkness of a person (carnal life). The Light knows itself and it knows the dark because it knows itself. The dark does not know itself and neither does it know the Light. Carnal life is blind (and deaf and without understanding).

The 'beginning' is not a simple matter. It is not either the Genesis account or the Johnnine account, but the beginning involves both. It involves water and spirit (John 3:5). Humankind is fashioned for carnal (water) life depicted in Genesis and the spiritual life depicted in John. The Johnnine account is not meant to correct the Genesis account, but to complement or add to that incomplete and inadequate account.

> … [9] The true light that gives light to everyone was coming into the world. [10] He was in the world, and though the world was made through him, the world did not recognize him. [11] He came to that which was his own, but his own did not receive him. [12] Yet to all who did receive him, to those who believed in his name, he gave the right to become children of God— [13] children born not of natural descent, nor of human decision or a husband's will, but born of God.

The true Light (the spirit of Christ) was coming into the 'water world' and its coming always was coming and always will be coming. The true Light is always coming into the world, but it does not 'settle' and actually exist in the temporal world unless it is recognized or received in assent and affirmation. The true Light is in and is coming to humans whose essence is the essence of the Word. Humans who recognize their spiritual nature receive the Light coming into the world through their spiritual person. The birth and living of the spiritual person is not carnal (sarx) or natural descent, it is not caused by carnal events such as people's decisions. It is caused only by God indwelling.

> [14] The Word became flesh and made his dwelling among us. We have seen his glory, the glory of the one and only Son, who came from the Father, full of grace and truth.

In the spiritual birth and life a person born a second time from above, the Word was coming and has become. The Word became flesh and becomes flesh in every instance of second spiritual birth. What needs to be kept front and centre is that the temporal Christ was not born again a second time, but existed as the spirit of Christ in eternity before being carnally housed in temporality, and it remains in eternity after carnal death destroys its carnal tabernacle in temporality. At the time of the carnal 'birth' of the temporal Christ was the spirit of Christ simultaneously existed. Christ becoming flesh had *no spiritual* significance, except that Christ could bodily interact with other people. The spirit of Christ by means of which we united with God and through which we have salvation and holiness, does not require a carnal body to spiritually interact with people. It is *we* who must be born of water and of spirit. Consequently…

> 18 No one has ever seen God, but the one and only Son, who is himself God and is in closest relationship with the Father, has made him known.

The twelve verses above from the prologue of John's Gospel (John 1:1-18) speaks to how we are 'of God' and what our relation to God is. It is clear in the Gospel that we are in God and of God. Nicodemus asked, "How can this be?" God is beyond us in regards to our comprehension and reach. God is infinite and eternal. We are finite and temporal. The answer is the very reality that exists between creator and creature; it is the Christ Covenant embedded in spiritual reality itself. The Word can be comprehended and grasped as infinite and eternal reality, and it can be comprehended and grasped in its infinity and eternity *while we are in finite and temporal flesh.* The reality of the Word is that it is with God; and, is *with us in us*. Our spiritual life originates of God through the Word. We existentially grasp spiritual birth in ourselves and live spiritual lives that are of and from God.

The Prologue says we received the law from Moses, that is the external law which we follow because we desire to do good and we do good things. This is given by grace of God not from within our person. The Mosaic or 'church' laws are given indirectly by things external to and apart from our essential or spiritual person. Then it says we received grace in *place of* grace *out of the fullness of Christ*. The grace in place of grace, is God indwelling spiritually forming us according to Christ after the spirit in which are made righteous from and of God. This line of thought is taken up by Paul in Romans.

The Prologue is clear that no person has seen God. We never saw and never will see God with our carnal human eyes. Only Christ who spiritually is God has '*seen*' God. Christ did not *see* God as an object for example a carnal image or carnal bodily presence. Yet the writer of the Prologue is clear that the Christ, who alone has *seen* God, has made God know to us (so that we too come to 'see' God not as an image of the imagination or an object of the bodily senses. Christ fully '*saw and sees or knows*' God because Christ spiritually is God, and Christ 'sees and knows' what he himself is. The mind of Christ fully knows God as a whole. The particulars that are the ideas of the mind of Christ are contained in the idea of the mind of Christ or the idea of God in human terms, which idea we have in our spiritual birth and which idea we have in our spiritual living. Our knowledge of God from Christ is given by the Light which is Christ being received by the person being born in God of and from God.

God is the substance of the carnal world; God is the substance of the spiritual world. These two worlds are different. In the beginning was the Word: the Word, which was with God, is the means of us grasping God because the Word is within us. We do not grasp God through bodily or carnal existence. This grasping is beyond our flesh and blood capacities. The essence and existence of God and the spiritual things of God are not comprehended by bodily or carnal flesh and blood bodies or carnal minds. In the end, carnal things have no essential existential value in themselves. Any existential value that carnal things acquire is ascribed to them by spiritual things.

The Truths of spiritual justice, righteousness, mercy and Godly love do not exist in or from carnal things. Those exist through the Word, which was and is with God. The Word is written in the forming of our spiritual hearts and on the make up our spiritual minds. It is alongside us calling us to realize that of us which is in God of and from God.

Our person is formed of the 'stuff' of actual existence. Our carnal person is formed out of finite temporal things, in time and space. As flesh and blood individuals, we cannot grasp or comprehend all the infinite number of finite temporal things and their relationships, which make up temporal existence. As flesh and blood individuals we do not cause our finite temporal selves. On the other hand, our spiritual person is formed out of the infinite and eternal things of God. As individuals, we can and we do grasp and comprehend the essence of the infinite eternal things of God. We can grasp and comprehend the essence and properties of God in the whole of Existence and Existing because God indwelling forms our spiritual person. Further, we recognize our experience of God indwelling as the Word immediately and directly forming us distinct and specific spiritual things in human terms, which are *intelligible* to us. All these are internal to our person: they are God indwelling being manifest through our spiritual person. We experience these things directly and immediately. We can shape our carnal lives according to these things, that is to say, according to Christ after the spirit.

In all this, God is the Word. We are not. We are spiritual of and from the Word, but we are not the Word. Spiritual life is with God, and God is spiritual life. We are of and from the spirit, but we are not the spirit. We are of and from the Light, but we are not the Light. We are not the Word or the Light, but we are of and from the Word and of and from the Light through our spiritual creation, in which we comprehend and grasp both the Word and the Light.

Specifications are the intelligible human discernments of Light. Specifics (what Paul called distinctions) are the intelligibility of the Word forming us according to the specifics and distinctions of Christ. Christ exists and comes from within us, imputing our discernment and intelligibility by way of which we have knowledge of God and our selves in God, of God and from God.

Bodily or carnal things do not comprehend or grasp spiritual things, but the spiritual can comprehend and grasp bodily or carnal things. In so doing, the spiritual can master the bodily or carnal, patterning them to echo the spiritual things of God. Existence without the Word and Light is personal existence in darkness of spirit. In personal darkness of spirit, the Light continues to shine and the Word persists. How is it that in our existence in darkness, we can still be born from above of God and be shaped by the Word, to see, understand through the Light within to choose to assent and affirm salvation and holiness? In Nicodemus' words, we are confronted by the carnal person's question: "How can it be?" It is because God is with us and in us, and because we are in God. The spirit of Truth, the Spirit of Christ through the Paraclete, is alongside us calling us to be born of the spirit, not merely 'of water'.

God incarnate is Christ, that is, God in human terms *apart from time and space*. Through the Word, we have access to this Christ, including this Christ's spirit and mind. The spirit and mind of God, shaped by the Word, shines in us, as Light within us. We recognize the things of God by God's grace and respond with birth from above into spiritual life, because we have the Light and Word in us. We recognize God through the present spirit and mind of Christ written into human terms on our hearts and in our minds. When we formationally-follow Christ, our spirit and mind is born of and from God and we live of and from God.

Jesus Christ proclaimed the Way, the Light and the Truth in finite *and* temporal terms. People could not hear. They could not spiritually see or understand, from their bodily or carnal view. They did not receive the proclamation and continued in darkness of the spirit. Those born of and from God actively follow the Way of the infinite and eternal Christ, heard, seen and grasped here and now. Those who formationally-follow Christ and are born of God are Christ incarnate here and now.

In created existence, carnal, corporeal life does not exist alone. We experience more than the merely carnal. We actually experience more: we hear more; we see more; we know more and understand more. Our existing and being is more than biological; we are also spiritual in our existing. Whenever and wherever people have lived, we find some reaching beyond merely carnal, corporeal, biological life. Among us here and now, we can find biologically alive people who do not seem to have spiritual yearnings and who do not seek spiritual things. We also find many biologically alive people with all their strength, reaching for and trying to grasp God, beyond their biological life and merely bodily or carnal existence. Created spiritual existence is not an alternate bodily or carnal existence. There is a single created existence that includes both a created carnal life and a created spiritual life. While these are exclusive of one another, they co-exist. Our spirit has the capacity to shape the world of the flesh in a symbiotic way. Spiritual life adds spiritual meaning and truth to carnal life. In doing so, it changes the very existing and existence of that life. This is done through the Word, through the reality of Christ, grounding and framing spiritual being into becoming a spiritual life and then into becoming spiritual. Simply put, we are engendered by God to be in God of and from God.

Understanding and knowing the things of God, for example, God's love, justice, righteousness and mercy, involves us becoming or being of God's truth. Such knowledge and understanding is experiential. It is acquired from spiritual experience. Our existing and being is in, of and from God; and, in that spiritual experiencing, comes knowledge and understanding on which our faith rests. It is said that demons have knowledge and understanding of God and of spiritual things, but they have not faith because their knowledge and understanding does come from them being in, of and from God through the Word and so experiencing God through spiritual birth and life in the reality of Christ. Christian faith and belief exists in actually being in, of and God, so being spiritually alive and actually living spiritually through the Word in the reality of Christ.

In our created existence, we can experience carnal, flesh and blood, biological, corporeal life and also experience spiritual life. Christ says as much in John 3. In created existence, we are born to live biologically as flesh and blood. We are born again to live spiritually in that same created existence, manifesting God's love, justice, righteousness and mercy.

Spiritual Forming, Sensing, and Intelligence: Experience and Cognition

Experiential learning with a focus on active and reflective critical thing is at the root of personal development. We experience ourselves as immediately connected to or united to our bodies: we sense this intuitively and in so doing formulate our carnal person through our flesh and blood body and its interactions with other external bodies. We also immediately experience ourselves as connected to or united with the *whole of existence*: that is God. We sense and intuit that union with God. We do not know that we experience union with God, nor sense or intuit that union through our flesh and blood selves. We are in God of and from God, while we are in the flesh but this union is not part of our flesh and blood or bodily experience. We sense and intelligibly grasp our union and the forming by means of which we have spiritual birth and existing. If the emergent entity is a 'body', it is not a flesh and blood body existing in time and space: labelling it a body is confusing. Our union with God is mutual and in union we share common properties of the essence of Existence. As we are in God of and from God, so God is in us spiritually forming us according to Christ after the spirit.

Our personal individual connection or union with existence or God involves our actual selves and our sense of our self united to our bodies. Our bodily limitations do not contain or limit our spiritual sense and intelligence. Our union with God is spiritual; involving the spiritual things of God. It is sensed in our actual existing, quite apart from the body and the limitations of the body's finitude. Our existential sense of union with God is self-evident or self-manifesting in our actual spiritual being, within our inner most person. We sense of the infinite and eternal and we sense our union with it. This intuition is directly immediately from God and of God. It has been describe within Christian thought in scripture and in Christian philosophy and theology, in several ways over many years, as the spirit of God or Christ, the Word of God, the Inner Light, God or Christ's indwelling presence.

Experiential learning begins with random sensory experience[16]. The randomness follows the ad hoc order of our experience during the course of daily living. As such, apart from reflecting the day's or the years' history, the sensing is without ultimately significant focus or meaning, purpose. Even when random experience is rationalized and ordered by reasoning, it remains ultimately meaningless and insignificant. Should the ordered somehow reflect an 'order in nature' that would be interesting but not of ultimate significance, meaning or purpose.

Though we actually experience it, spiritual forming does not come *from* our experience. The forming is not a temporal event. The birth is in the infinite and eternal Kingdom of God. We experience the forming separate from the forming itself. We experience what God forms, but we experience it as we are being formed. We do not form our spiritual selves. It may be that the forming and the experience are one. But the forming existentially precedes the experience of learning or having reflective knowledge of the forming. We know God is spiritually forming us as God forms us: we know immediately and directly.

---

[16] According to Spinoza, this was true of Christ. Spinoza held that Christ had immediate and direct "pure intuition" of the things of God. Ideas in the mind of Christ were not caused by other ideas, but each is intuited in Christ's intuition of God, without any mediating or intervening cause. Christ never had to reason from one notion to another, except in his efforts to teach.

God forms us spiritually according to a specific and distinct order: according to Christ after the spirit. The mind of Christ defines this order, by means of which our spirits, minds and hearts are ordered, created, caused or formed. Those who are spiritually ordered according to Christ after the spirit, undertake to order their daily flesh and blood lives accordingly, including the world about them. While we do not cause our spiritual formation, we do learn and know about our spirits. Out of such knowledge we can develop our carnal selves to change our daily living and to change the world around us.

Learning begins with the organizing of the sensory experiences. Such organized learning can be focused on reality itself, or some part of reality. Learning that is grounded in reality can function as an adaptive tool enabling the person to change to attain goals in this life. Once established as an adaptive tool, experiential learning is able to contribute to the quality of personal development (quality assurance given the targeted outcome or goal) and the improvement of the experiential learning process (quality improvement given the targeted outcome or goal). We can measure the efficiency and effectiveness of our learning. adapting or developing. The value, meaning or significance of attaining the goal and measurement of effort to attain the goal are established by the goal itself.

To survive (i.e. meet needs) and thrive (i.e. attain goals), organisms learn from an environment in which and to which they are functionally related. On learning, they adapt relative to a targeted outcome of surviving or thriving according to their purpose, be it according to "Christ after the flesh" from without, or "Christ after the spirit" from within. On the other hand, in actualizing spiritually, the forming conforms to the reality of God as manifest in Christ. The spiritual person forms spiritually, and then adapts their carnal living so that carnal life aligns with the spirit of Christ.

Most applications of experiential learning theory have concerned learning about things outside oneself, within one's setting or environment. Experiential learning theory can also encompass learning about things internal to one's self and not bound in time and space, for example one's spiritual forming. We can learn experientially "after the flesh"[17] or "after the spirit", and we can learn about Christ "after the flesh", i.e. the historical Christ; or about Christ "after the spirit", that is the actually present infinite and eternal Christ. We do 'good' in following either approach; and we are obedient to God either way. We can follow either after the flesh or after the spirit, but we are formed spiritually only in formational-following after or according the spirit of Christ.

People are born and experience through flesh and through spirit. *While the latter is 'in' flesh, it is not of or from flesh.* The flesh is bound in duration that is in time and place. Things of our flesh temporally begin and end. Things of our spirit are caused by or 'are being' by God in God of and from God. They are housed in God. These are also temporally housed in flesh though they are not of or from flesh because they are immediately and directly in God of and from God. Spiritually God causes us in God of and from God; and, our flesh is the temporal vessel *in which* our spirit comes to life apart from the shell housing it. Spiritually, we also are in the 'vessel' of the Kingdom of

[17] Following urges, instincts, and satisfying worldly needs to survive or thrive, is life after the flesh. We can choose to and actual follow the historical Christ after the flesh as best we can discern the temporal Christ. All such following is passive: it does not emerge out of our being or existing. Following after the flesh has its own righteousness, but it should not be confused with Formational Following the indwelling "Christ after the spirit".

God, which carries us spiritually in eternity, *while we are in our temporal carnal vessel*. As Christ says in the book of John, we must be born of water and spirit; that is born of flesh and spirit. We are not merely spirit.

By way of both experience of the flesh and experience of the spirit, we intuit our actual existing and being. Intuitions are not representational; they are intuitions of present and actual being and knowing: that is our present being and existing. (The intuitions as things in themselves, are presented and can be re-presented in reflective cognition.) By existential intuition, I am and I know I am. By existential intuition of God's indwelling presence, I know God is, and I know that I know God is. By existential intuition, I am in God and I know I am in God. These existential experiences are immediate intuitions, which we sense in our being what *we actually are*. They are the foundation of Christian theology; ontologically and epistemologically grounded in actual reality or existence. These are substantively and qualitatively different from cognitive constructs that reflect or re-present our direct experience of external objects.

By way of flesh, we construct cognitive presentations that re-present what our senses experience of bodily or carnal existence *and* of spiritual existence. These created abstract models become part of our cognitive functioning structure. Models allow our reflecting and adapting utilization the true but abstract information of the construct. We use these models in making and adapting true plans or rules of living. They are guides to pious living. Like a map, models give us a sense of the reality, but maps are not the reality they catch in re-presentation.

The model can be developed and refined based on the information that is true and the contexts of the true information. There are things of God that we know from immediate and direct spiritual experience of them, our sensing our experience and our knowledge of our experience and sensing. These are real and part of the reality of the mind of Christ. We know some of the ideas in the infinite and eternal mind of Christ, even if we do not know them all and their relationships to one another. These *real intuitions* according to the mind of Christ become *important points of orientation* in the development of a broader and more detailed abstract model or map of the mind of Christ, which map we can readily use to guide our daily living to be pious and holy.

Experiential learning theory explains how we learn from experience and in particular the learning from experience that results in personal coping and adapting. In regards to both coping and adapting the development of cognitive models that catch and reflect our experience of reality allows people to collect and organize information about themselves and their settings in cognitive constructs. These abstract cognitive 'spaces' serve as learning laboratories in which experience is stored, tested and critically reviewed. The information is easily stored and retrieved. Thought experiments can be conducted, safely and without risk. While experience itself is random and ad hoc, these cognitive structures are not. They are designed to reflect standardized abstracted realities approximating existence as much as possible. The abstract cognitive structure is refined by means of testing in thought or in action, then reflecting on the action and its impact and adding relevant information into the model.

Critical *action-reflection* applied to further and future actions secures quality assurance and allows for measured quality improvement of action. Active-reflective-active thinking is limited by what the model is representing. Active-reflective critical thinking is shaped by the cognitive model used as a standard through which to interpret experience. Abstract cognitive models may be constructed from sense experience caused externally and sensed through the body or sensed carnally. They may be constructed from sensory experience caused internally, which is directly and intuitively grasped. Models or exemplars may be constructed from both kinds of sensed experience.

People experience God according to Christ after the flesh and according to Christ after the spirit[18]. The two are different kinds of experience and from them we have two kinds of knowledge. Either way, the Christian's purpose is to follow and obey God through Christ. To be in God of and from God by following and obeying Christ and to exist as an ultimately existentially significant creature with ultimate existential meaning and purpose, we must spiritually be caused directly by God. Following and obeying any other created external entity deprives us of the salvation and blessedness experienced by union with God. Our spirit is born in God of and from God: as the sole cause of our existence in eternity and in duration. Our existing is also sustained by God as the sole causation of our actually being or existing. Being or existing of and from anything less, is to be deprived of God or be depraved.

Our minds are arranged according to the world of the flesh or according to the world of the spirit. Minds arranged according to the spirit of Christ actively share common properties with the mind of Christ. Commonalities of our minds and the mind of Christ exist in our personally having the mind of Christ. Through the flesh, we can grasp the mind of Christ in the abstract, and follow the abstracted

---

[18] Romans, 1 Corinthians, Galatians, John 1 and 3.

mind of Christ. In so doing, we follow Christ and live rightly, but in doing so we do not actually experience our personal salvation or holiness. In our bodily mind according to the flesh alone, we do not existentially personally possess the common properties of the mind of Christ.

We follow Christ after the flesh and in doing so bind ourselves to the Christ Covenant and its promise of spiritual life for those who engage in the Covenant. The Covenant is inherent in Existence itself, consequently is also in inherent in our existing.

When we actually experience salvation and holiness and when we personally have the mind of Christ through the indwelling spirit of Christ, then we actually or existentially share the common properties of the mind of Christ. We actually hold these in common with God through Christ in us, but we do not actually hold them in common with other people. Other people do not indwell us, only God actually does indwell us, through our union with God. While we can assume that other people also have the properties common to God and to our personal self united with God, it can only be assumed and not known know for sure. My experience of Christ is limited to my experience, as is my experience of red or of geometry is limited to my experience. Because God indwells, I immediately and directly know God, as I immediately know myself: God causes both. In causing them, God causes knowledge of them. I do not know others the same way. Others I know only through my flesh and blood body, with its limitations.

Spiritual Existence

We do not experience spiritual life apart from carnal life, though we might experience bodily or carnal life without spiritual life. This is reflected in the notion that darkness does not overcome or grasp Light, or that 'he was in the world' but "the world did not recognize him". Darkness of spirit is dominion over a person by that person's bodily or carnal life, bereft of the spiritual things of God. It is living with in passive response to the Word, the Spirit of Christ through the Paraclete, and the calling of Christ within. In the absence of dominion of the reality of Christ in a person's created existence, the person's human condition is deprived or depraved of Truth, Light and spiritual life.

While spiritual reality does not derive from carnal reality, we do not experience them apart. We experience bodily or carnal life simultaneously as we experience spiritual life. Spiritual life is not an 'out of body' flesh-and-blood-like life. In our single created existence, we have a created carnal life and a created spiritual life. Yet, ours is a single existence, at once temporal and spiritually eternal for some. These two very different kinds of existing provide two very different experiences of living and life.

Our pursuit and grasping salvation and holiness comes with noisy 'Strum und Drang' (Storm and Stress). In this life, a person finds scattered glimpses of spiritual intelligibility. Some people experience occasional momentary rays of Light breaking through dark clouds in stormy and threatening skies. Over the centuries, many have glimpsed eternity in moments of temporality. William Blake pondered such miracles and wrote:

> To see the world in a grain of sand
> And a heaven in a wildflower,
> Hold Infinity in the palm of your hand
> And Eternity in an hour[19]

In regards to ultimate existential significance, meaning and purpose, temporal moments are matters of life or death. They are our *only and fleeting* portals to eternity. While glimpses of eternity can be had, eternal salvation and holiness can also be had in our union with God indwelling forming us according to Christ after the spirit, in our being or existing in God of and from God, while we are in the flesh, but not of or from the flesh. Kierkegaard caught the terror that grips a soul aware of the transient yet existentially critical moments in which a person might find eternity, in a book calling people to faith. He named it: 'Fear and Trembling'. When the moment passes, eternity is lost.

Existential Christology holds that Christ is actually existing here and now, not in carnal flesh and blood, but in existence itself; and, that a person can exist in Christ and in so doing have Christ exist within their individual person. Christ exists in a distinct and specific fashion. Christ has a distinct and specific character or person which we recognize from within our person. The person or character of Christ is not in the flesh, but is infinite and eternal, in a distinct and specific fashion. Being or existing in God, of and from God indwelling according to Christ after the

[19] Auguries of Innocence.

spirit, is to exist having the mind, heart and spirit of Christ as our own mind, heart and spirit. For our part, in spiritual birth and life from above, we manifest Christ's distinctness and specificity in our person and character while we live in the flesh in our temporal life.

In the few moments that we have in this flesh and blood life, we find salvation into the Kingdom of God, in which carnal death has no place. We come to terms with carnal life because we come to know the essence of God in knowing our own essence from our experience of spiritual existing. In those few moments of transitory union, we glimpse life without fear or abhorrence of carnal death. In those few fleeting moments, we taste joy, love, hope, patience, and all the fruits of God's spirit. Then the fleeting stops --- by God's grace the union is not transitory. We personally come to stand in eternity when we are spiritually forming in God of and from God; with no beginning and no ending; manifesting kindness, forgiveness, as well as love and joy and the fruits of the spirit in our eternal existing and temporal existing.

The original human condition, that is bodily or carnal life, is lifted through the lifting of Christ within and without, into being spiritually born and in being spiritually alive. The deprivation is replaced with justice, righteousness, mercy and Godly love.

In the creating of a person's existence, there is both a life of flesh and a life of spirit. There is a point of viability or birth, when these two lives come alive. For people, bodily or carnal birth and life seems to precede spiritual birth and life. The flesh takes a breath and come alive. The spirit takes a breath and comes alive. They come alive at different points. Spiritual life does not derive from or originate in carnal things. Spiritual life is through the Word, directly of God. Spiritual life resides in the application of incarnation of the Word, and is manifest in spiritual birth and living so as to give ultimate existential or Godly significance, meaning and purpose to carnal life over and above carnal life.

Carnal life is real and we experience it carnally. Spiritual life is also real, and we experience it spiritually. These are realities: one is transient, without meaning, significance or purpose; the other exists in God of and from God spiritually forming things in that reality. Each has their place in our existence. We need to exist carnally to be formed spiritually. In merely bodily or carnal existence, there is nothing to recognize, know or receive the essence of God or the properties of that essence. As we exist bodily or carnally, we are called to seek spiritual birth and life. That part of us that seeks is spiritual, not carnal. No matter how much carnal knowledge and power we assemble, if this all we have we will remain in darkness, bereft of God. However, in the darkness Light shines. This is the Word of God in us. The Spirit of Christ through the Paraclete and the spirit of Truth alongside us, calling and testifying to the Light that cannot be overcome by the carnality of the human condition. The Light shows us the Way. We follow Christ and God is revealed to us. We know that we can know God and be in God of and from God. Through Christ, we incarnate the heart and mind of Christ. We do not incarnate Christ through the bodily or carnal world. We are born spiritually from above. We live and are of God through Christ, the Word of God forming us.

We are created with Light in us, but we do not breathe that life from existing carnally. We are created with the Word in us, but while that Word is passively written on our hearts and in our minds, the Word is not actively incarnate in our carnal person. We are without spiritual breath or life until we are born from above of God and come alive spiritually. In following Christ, we come into communion with Christ and experience union in the reality that is Christ. Our personal spiritual life is created in that communion.

In itself, carnal life has no meaning and no being of consequence. Spiritual life derives its meaning from participation in God of and from God. God was the Word; God is the Word. As God exists, so the Word exists. The Word was written in our hearts and on our minds. It was to be called into our being, and was to be comprehended by us by the Light of the spirit of Truth in us.

The Word is creating meaning, significance and purpose in created existence. Without the Word, existence is absent meaning. Existence without meaning does not grasp God. Spiritual chaos renders creatures, created to be spiritually in God of and from God, lost and fearful with carnal dread. Such lost souls, in their existential essence continue to seek salvation and holiness. Their being requires meaning which comes from the essence and nature of God. Our being and living grasps and acquires ultimate existential meaning through the indwelling spirit of Christ forming us spiritually.

God in human terms is the eternal reality Christ. This reality is not subject to time and place. It is not temporal. The reality of Christ is with us and is accessible to us today, here and now, through the Word, which is with God. The Word that was and is with God 'under-stands' and 'sub-stantiates' our personal spiritual existing. We are created to be spiritual and to live of and from God. We are not fully existentially complete till we are knowing and possessing the Word in our actual spiritual being. The Word became flesh and revealed the reality of Christ manifested in time and place in Jesus. Jesus was born, lived and died. During that time, Christ was present to us as a reality (God in human terms) incarnate in time and place, and as an *eternal reality* (God in human terms) *incarnate apart from time and place*. As Jesus, Christ incarnate spoke to his people, today, as the eternally present and real Christ speaks to us here and now as God's indwelling Word incarnating in our person.

'the Word became flesh' and 'the Word becoming flesh'

John 1:14 is one of the most important verses in Christian scripture. It is *a unique and singular wording*, in a unique and singular Prologue, in a unique and singular book of scripture. That contrasts to the *many* references in John and Paul concerning the separateness and substantive difference between the flesh and the spirit. Properly understood this phrase used only once, opens the exquisite workings of Existential Christology. The Word became flesh in the eternal Kingdom of God before our experience of time began.

Well intentioned, but mistaken and malignant out of context use of the phrase "became flesh", darkened Christology, reducing it to superstition and magic. The Word became flesh. It became *human* flesh; it did not become a dolphin, a snake, a fish, a bird, a worm or a tree or flower. John's statement is not a statement in support pantheism. The phrase means that the Word took on temporal definition that people can comprehend. It did so in Christ. Christ is God in human terms: after the spirit and after the flesh. In taking on temporal definitions, the Word in essence remained the Word but in temporal terms took on Christ-specific distinctions.

John 1:14, goes on to say that besides taking on temporal terms, the Word tabernacled or dwelt among us. It did so in the person of the historical Christ. It is clear throughout the whole book of John that the Word also 'tabernacles' in our persons and that the Word dwells among us through our spiritual persons. It should be noted that the Word was and is tabernacled in living flesh begetting our personal spirit, *at the same time our spiritual person is also begotten in God, of and from God.*

Like the historical Christ, we are flesh in specific and distinct ways. We are spirit in distinct and specific ways. Christ came in the flesh already spiritually alive, unlike Christ we are born in the flesh waiting to be born again spiritually according to Christ after the spirit. We experience not one but two births. Christ did not require the second is spiritual birth.

As the Gospel moved into the Greco-Roman world, it moved into a world of varied and confusing relationships between people and gods. The Greek gods easily and frequently incarnated. Some Roman emperors considered themselves having evolved into or become incarnate gods. These were not really outlandish views in the times. It was necessary for the early Christian communities to address the issue of God, people and Christ. The book of John addresses the issue of God manifest in people and in particular in Christ, at the start of the book. Then throughout the rest of the book the teachings of Christ are presented to demonstrate that although flesh and spirit are separate in essence, we, nevertheless, while yet alive in flesh come to be united with God in spirit.

The poetic presentations in the book of John seem to have been all too readily overshadowed by 'acceptable' idolatries after the flesh, constructed out of misunderstood and misconstrued recollections of Christ after the flesh. Within Christ's life time and within merely a few years of

Christ's death, Christians were destructively at odds with one another. Many according to their flesh and blood rendering of the historical Christ and his temporal teachings, attempted to comprehend and live the Gospel message of Christ within the limitations of their worldly comprehension of objects external to themselves. The history of organized 'church' Christianity quickly became a history of conflict and base self-aggrandizement. The focus was mostly on re-presentations of the tangible flesh and blood historical Christ.

The various accounts of Christ were construed from the sharing of imaginative stories. However inadequate or poorly grasped by people, Christ after the flesh was and is a mere reflection or recollection of events and people that no longer exist. Constructed from people's memories, this imagined Christ was lifted up to serve numerous and diverse organized Christian 'churches'. Those organizations were built on fragmented and incomplete recollections that could not, cannot and do not serve to save or to sustain spiritual life. The few people who lifted up Christ after the spirit from within themselves were lifted into the Kingdom of God by the hand of God. As people's knowledge became more sophisticated and 'scientific', Gospel interpretations, re-presentations and 'proofs', became more sophisticated and scientific. Regardless of being shored up by sophistication and science of things of the flesh, the 'church' organizations remained 'kingdoms' of things of the flesh.

John's Gospel says that the Word was in the beginning and that the Word was God. It also says the

Word become flesh and dwelt among us. It does not say that God became flesh. It does not say the Word itself transformed. It does not say the Word transubstantiated. Simply then, the Word became flesh. Apart from becoming flesh in eternity, the Word also tabernacled or dwelt among as a historical person and the Word dwells within us, therefore among us.

The Word (Logos) is existentially ultimate meaning, significance and purpose. The indwelling Word writing on our hearts and in our minds forms us spiritually to have God's meaning, significance and purpose. Following the Prologue, the rest of the book of John makes it clear that the Word *is among us*. The 'us' included the temporal flesh and blood Christ as is evident in Christ's teachings. The finite carnal Christ person did not and does not dwell in us, nor do we dwell in that temporal finite flesh and blood person. But the Word dwells in all.

We are flesh and we dwell among one another. Unlike the Word, we do not dwell in one another. Only the Word dwells in us and among us. The Word always was and always will be with us and among us, including the historical person of Christ , as well as born again spiritual persons who have been formed by Christ after the spirit indwelling them.

Does the Word becoming flesh mean that the Word was like a person? Each actual person in created existence exists uniquely. No person is existentially like any other. Each is unique. The Word being flesh, and dwelling among us would have its own unique existence of flesh. In regards to carnal life as an actual created person, the Word fully manifest in a person would in essence be unique and not have a common essence with any other created person. If the Word was a particular flesh and blood person, the Word would not exist as the Word which is in all persons and is common in them. The Word becoming flesh means it is tabernacled or housed in a actually existing flesh and blood body in a fashion that 'remakes' that body and its relation to other bodies according to a pattern of Christ. Personal essence itself is not common, but essential properties can be held in common by individuals who conform to the specific distinctions or patterns of Christ. In regards to spiritual life, the Word was in communion with each and every actually created person: not physically but spiritually.

The Word became flesh, but what is flesh? It no longer is what it once was thought to be. The questioning of faith, salvation and holiness has crossed a different threshold. In addition, the deconstruction of the biblical texts has eroded traditional straightforward literal or near literal reading of the text. Consequently the faith of many who relied on 'knowing' the texts as the basis of their faith has been cast adrift. The progress, in the last century especially, of the various kinds of textual research and criticism, our understanding of the texts of scripture, their accurate reflection of the original authors, and critical interpretation of their meaning, forces a rethinking of their role in authentic belief and faith. There is good reason why the information has been poorly absorbed by the membership of the established churches. It serves the purposes of the established churches to safeguard accepted dogma and doctrine, than navigate surer waters. Further, the old dogma and doctrine meets the carnal needs of the world after the flesh that so dominates most people's lives.

The great divide between the spiritual and bodily or carnal things, established in John's Gospel, informs us that bodily appearances are too easily misconstrued to be spiritual things. This is evidenced in the confounded Nicodemus. Nothing that we experience and know bodily or carnally will give us spiritual insight into spiritual truth, or spiritual birth and life. If we are to be born into and live in spiritual reality, the ground and frame of our spiritual life will not emerge from the created carnal world. If our ideas of what a person is, arise only from our experience of the body, that is our carnal life, then our ideas are grounded and framed by the flesh and they are limited to the body's limitations. We cannot use only ideas founded on subjective physical appearances to define what a person is or to determine what reality or existence is. A person is both flesh and spirit. What matters spiritually is not what the person is in flesh or in created carnal life. Spiritual insight comes from spiritual experiences of God.

Authentic Christianity is rooted in *real and present personal spiritual experience*. Authentic Christianity is not grounded in stories heard or read, nor our reflections concerning past historical events that longer exist in our time and in our place. Authentic Christianity is grounded in real, actual and present personal encounters with and engagement with God indwelling forming our person according to Christ after the spirit.

Authentic Christology is not about the, historical Christ. That is a matter of history. *Authentic Christology is not grounded or rooted in the past.* **Authentic Christology is about Christ here and now**. Christology is not merely about the Word becoming flesh in the past. Authentic Christology is about Christ being actually and presently manifest to us here now and being manifest in God indwelling our person forming our person according to Christ after the spirit.

The carnal death of Christ was initially an embarrassment to his disciples because they had not understood the relationship between the things of the flesh that are of the flesh and the things of the spirit that are of the Spirit, as taught to Nicodemus by Christ. Carnal death, which means so much to persons of flesh, has remained an embarrassment for those who aspire to enduring life in the flesh of and from the flesh.

There are stories told that the reason for the advent of the historical Christ and for his execution was that he came to replace the need for (culturally based) sacrificial offerings of propitiation. It was an established tradition that flesh and blood sacrifice was required for the forgiveness of sins committed by the person or by the person's ancestors. Sins against 'god' required a person's flesh and blood sacrifice for payment or ransom. Christ took on this 'requirement of God' by his own flesh and blood sacrificial death. As a result God no longer required flesh and blood sacrifices. Playing on people's 'natural' sense of guilt and using the death as a substitutionary sacrificial requirement has allowed the churches to instill a profound sense of obligation in people, which obligation is readily transferred towards benefits for the churches themselves. It is a confused Christology that casts itself in unnecessary contradiction as a result of wanting to explain the carnal birth and death of Christ in non-temporal spiritual terms. The historical Christ was forcibly killed by temporal forces.

It was the historical Christ after the flesh who was crucified and died. The pain was flesh and blood pain that carnally frightened and terrified the carnal people. The death was a flesh and blood death that carnally frightened and terrified the carnal people. The death on the cross evokes our carnal anxieties and fears. Those born in God of and from God according to Christ after the spirit are raised out of their flesh, or spiritually 'resurrected' while in their flesh. As outlined by Paul in 1Cor 15:50-55, in life that has experienced second birth, flesh and blood death loses its "sting". It does not fearfully or ominously lord over our existing and being. This view had been implied in Christ's teachings in the book of John, as was demonstrated by Spinoza in his work some 1600 years later.

The carnal, historical Christ was a person like any other person, but Christ was unique, because the carnal, historical Christ did not experience second birth according to Christ after the spirit; his carnal birth came with the actual spirit and mind of the spirit of Christ. When born in the flesh, Christ Jesus was essentially or in spirit in God of and from God. Indeed, when dead in the flesh, Christ remained essentially and spiritually in God, of and from God.

In regards to holiness, this was not something the person of Christ Jesus *acquired.* Christ did not experience salvation --- he was never without it. Christ did not acquire holiness; it was ever present with and in him.

For our part, God indwelling forming our person according to Christ after the spirit forms our person to have the properties of the spirit and mind of Christ in common with Christ as a result of that forming into union with God through Christ. Other persons, who experience second birth in union with God, also share the Christ distinct and specific commonalities in spirit, mind and heart.

Given that it is the work of the spirit of Christ to lead people to salvation and blessedness, we do not require knowledge of the historical Christ in detail, in matters concerning personal salvation and blessedness. We do not require a literal record of the life of the historical Christ to articulate an authentic Christology and the work of Christ in us here and now.

There is no need to generate a confused Christology that attempts to demonstrate that the carnal, historical Christ is directly responsible for the spiritual birth and life of persons born a second time at present by way of God indwelling causing the formation according to Christ after the spirit. The historical flesh and blood Christ existed 2,000 years ago in past time and in past place. The historical Christ is in the past --- not in the present. The existing Christ is in the present for us to spiritually encounter engage with through our union with God. In our lives we really encounter and actually engage the existing Christ, who forms us spiritually not carnally in flesh and blood terms.

The historical Christ was be characterized by race and gender, by particular skin colour and facial features, etc. *The existing Christ has none of those flesh and blood attributes* and *does not engage us in flesh and blood terms.*

Story Telling Meagre Echoes of Spiritual Existing and Spiritual Existence

Before Euclid and the dissemination of his work, people found and used geometric principles in practical applications. But in Euclid, practical geometry was lifted into an abstract but formally reasoned system or a synthetic system of knowing geometry and applying geometry. Today, I do not learn Euclidean geometry by studying stories or histories of Euclid. My grasp of geometrical Euclidean 'truths' does not depend on the fact that Euclid existed in the past. My grasp arises from my direct experiences in the present in actually reasoning from comprehended axioms and applying propositions, as well as applying those abstractions to real present experience.

The above also applies to the Gospel of Christ, which is inherent in the personal existence I experience and which I discern from personal experiences of my existing in God of and from God according to Christ after the spirit.

People construct different kinds of stories using perceptions, abstractions, sensations, and images as a response to the call from within for existential significance, purpose or meaning. The constructions are re-presentations of experience. In re-presenting experience people mostly re-present common everyday bodily temporal experience, caused by things external to their person. People use stories of past experience of temporal events external to our person. We also re-present individual experiences in existence caused from within our person or being and is not shaped by sequences of temporal life, but is formed and shaped by existence itself, without the limitations of transient events.

People may have and may appear to benefit from having strong dominating sensory images attached to powerful emotions and persuasive narratives or stories. Regardless of their strength and dominance, such imaginings remain things triggered and shaped external to our person. They can distract and derail our direct and immediate union with the essence of God, which is at the core of our spiritual existence or being. The stories are signage from outside, contrived according to the world after the flesh. They do not generate or form us in union with to exist in God of and from God according to Christ after the spirit. The externally generated images, signs and narratives do not make up the stuff of personal salvation and holiness, which stand on present actual but eternal experience of God, while we temporally exist in the flesh.

A story's purpose can be to lead and control people for better or worse. Leaders use stories with specific purpose and meaning to politically control others by fear mongering or instituting taboos; or to lead others to attain goals. Fictitious stories can shape our existence and experiences into depraved inadequate experience of living. Stories can falsely be the basis of our beliefs concerning the nature of reality or the actual existence of the objects of the stories and our part in that reality or existence. Stories are not authentic existence. They are reflections of reflections, and mere re-presentations. Left to themselves, existential beliefs based on superstitious are idolatrous accounts of existence and existing.

People use stories to meet real carnal, flesh and blood bodily needs for:

- Security,
- Comfort,
- Belonging,
- Significance,
- Meaning, and/or
- Purpose.

People also use stories to avoid bodily burdens and pain, such as:

- Anxiety,
- Fear,
- Isolation,
- Alienation,
- Emptiness,
- Guilt,
- Pain, and/or
- Death[20].

[20] In the end, we have come to understand that carnal life is an abstraction. Many, who purport to debunk religion as they understand it, are merely busy debunking those flesh and blood abstractions. Carnal death, like carnal life is something that we construe in our imagination. To our detriment, we then allow our abstract constructs of death to dominate our person. Spiritual life is not our creation and is not subject to the inherent meaningless, insignificant and purposeless of things of the flesh.

Stories help us to understand and successfully cope with life in carnal terms.

Stories can be used to provide satisfying explanations for things. Whether the story is true or not is another matter. When stories are connected or attached to powerful personal spiritual needs and experiences, their influence can be and often is disproportionately overwhelming. Persons of influence and power have exploited the power of stories as long as such persons have existed to control and manipulate others --- for better or more often for worse. Stories can be used to separate us from actual real things and used to generate superstitions and fanciful magic. Stories can take supplant or replace true foundations of spiritual meaning and purpose, including our direct experience of God.

It may be that the first stories were randomly recalled reflections and recollections. Once we attempt to include significance, meaning and purpose in telling stories, then we introduce the option of criteria or measures that allow for critical reflection and critical recollection. Stories are shaped by critical review to convey not only historical events but also the ultimate significance, meaning and purpose of actual real events.

In imagination, we experience stories we are told or we observe, but we do not directly experience the things those stories are about. We receive stories external to our person; even the stories we tell ourselves are received external to our person. Stories are not present actual sensory experience, but rather a re-presentation to our bodies of temporal bodily sensations of things, whether external to our person or internal to our person.

While grasping the meaning and purpose of stories can affect us deeply. Such grasping is not the same as existentially grasping God and God's significance, meaning or purpose, which we can only do in the immediate presence of God within our person. While we can impart abstracted significance, meaning and purpose through stories, these are meanings and purpose that come from us, not from God. On the other hand, personal experience of God which generates spiritual formation brings living existential meaning and purpose directly from God into our personal experience.

We experience spiritual things and then have evidence of such experience in the fruits of the spirit manifest by our spiritual selves. The fruits of the spirit may be noted by external observers. In the production of the fruits of the spirit, the spirit working within us also provides sensible or intelligible evidence within us. Our personal knowledge of God has several sources. The most direct, intimate and sure knowledge is God within our person immediately informing in our being and being spiritually shaped or formed in God of and from God according to Christ after the spirit. Personal active intuitive experience provides us with direct or immediate knowledge. This is not knowledge from a story that we tell ourselves or that others tells us in one form or another. This knowledge is personally active immediate intuitive experience that is at once experience and knowledge. Such experience and knowledge can be told to us as a story, and as such it is something external to our person that we passively perceive.

We engage and grasp God personally and we are of and from God in actual personal experience, not from hearing, reading or seeing stories of God. Even if the story development and the story telling is itself inspired, the inspiration belongs to the story teller. Even if the person hearing the story is inspired to hear it, merely hearing it is not actively being in God of and from God. We engage or grasp God through personal union with the essence of God, through which engagement or grasping God forms us spiritually according to Christ after the spirit.

The New Testament is filled with stories that have served and serve diverse, sometimes unintended purposes. The Christ birth stories are examples. The telling and writing of the different New Testament Gospels spoke to different traditions and communities. Some traditional stories and writings emphasized the legalistic aspects of the Gospels, and others traditions that emphasized the social justice aspects of the Gospels. This is well illustrated in the two distinct Christian birth stories in Mathew and Luke respectively. The original purposes of these two stories were conveniently and powerfully morphed over time into a single third story, fashioned with its own adapted or evolved purpose and meaning involving social justice affirmed by legalisms. Following the morphing, what has been handed down through different venues to particular communities was a third story that did not reflect original events, or reflect the stories about those events that had been initially told for decades after the emergence of Christian communities.

As far as we can tell at this time, the four canon Gospels appeared sequentially. Mark, our first documented Gospel, does not have a Christ birth narrative at all. Mathew, the second documented Gospel, has a Christ birth narrative to situate Christ within Jewish religious tradition and culture. It sets out a Hebraic framework to contextualize a very specific birth story that favours Jewish-Christian values of the Jewish-Christian communities at the time. Luke, the third documented Gospel, also has a Christ birth story, but it is contextualized within a value framework for Gentile-Christians and Gentile-Christian communities of the time. Luke's story has little in common[21] with Mathew's except the mention

[21] Mathew has no account of John the Baptist, Elizabeth, Zechariah, no trip to Bethlehem, no shepherds, no empty inn, no stable, no manger, and the angel spoke only to Joseph not to Mary. Because Mary and Joseph lived in Bethlehem not only was there no trip to Bethlehem, the Magi came to a "house" not a manger. (More problematic is John 7:42, which seems to indicate that Jesus was not born in Bethlehem at all.) Luke has no Magi, no guiding star, no reference to King Herod, Old Testament prophesies or the killing of children in Bethlehem, and no escape to Egypt. In Luke the angel spoke to only Mary not to Joseph. Mary and Joseph went from Nazareth to Bethlehem for the birth, then to the temple in Jerusalem after the 41 days required for purification rites, and finally went home to Nazareth. There are two distinct stories. As these were told and retold orally year after year and decade after decade, an as they were set down in text then transcribed over and over, as they were written and transcribed decade after decade and century after century, the stories were 'tidied up' and synchronized so as to present them as compatible. Over the years a third birth story has emerged which combines Mathew's and Luke's and in so doing creates a story with its own third meaning and purpose. This third Christmas story can deprive the other two stories' of their original message, meaning and purpose. In all three, we have to ask what was left out and why; what was put in and why? The reason was historical evidence or accuracy.

of Bethlehem. John, the forth documented Gospel, does not have a historical birth narrative at all.

John does not have a temporal, historical Christ birth narrative; but has a creation story concerning personal spiritual birth or spiritual formation and being. John lifts the Gospel of Christ out of history and temporal events and sets it down in reality itself as it is present to us. In effect, in the book of John, the historical birth is not relevant in regards to the salvation and holiness of individual persons. What matters is a world created to allow for personal spiritual birth and holiness and the message call us to be born in God of and from God.

Stories, even inspired stories, and textual representation of those stories bring with them all the fallibility that comes with storytelling and transmission of stories from person to person, group to group and time to time. Stories, however useful and how ever powerful their impact on us, our beliefs and values, remain mere stories that at best can only be represented in meagre fragments of real personal experience from other times and in other places.

As set down in the Gospels, the disciples *had or heard only stories about salvation.* The Gospels reflect Christ's disappointment that his disciples had not actually experienced second birth during Christ's ministry. *At the time, they had knowledge by story, not knowledge from personal experience of union with God.* The disciples were converted, but they had yet to be born from above according to Christ after the spirit. For that reason, we see they continued to behave according to their temporal bodily understanding. Stories re-tell *only the experience of **the effects** of the Wind or spirit of Christ, they do not tell about the Wind itself or spirit of Christ itself.* The spirit of Christ can only be known in our personal experience while the spirit of Christ actually blows or rather actually shapes our spiritual becoming and being to be in God of and from God: *we experience the work of the spirit and the effects of that work.*

Paul seems to be the only writer of the New Testament that tells 'stories' about his personal spiritual experience of spiritual forming and spiritual being. We find this for example in his epistles to the Romans and in 2 Corinthians. Paul clearly says he knew Christ after the flesh. He likely did not encounter Christ in the flesh, face to face. But though his body he had a bodily vision of Christ on his way to Damascus. In being told stories by witnesses, he heard about Christ through his ears. He may have also seen Christ manifested in certain people, for example in Stephen. In all these experiences and encounters, Paul knew Christ after the flesh. Like the stories of the disciples in the Gospels, Paul's 'Damascus' conversion concerns bodily events: hearing, seeing, becoming blind, emotional and psychological trauma.

None of his bodily flesh and blood experiences are what Paul speaks about in his epistles when speaking about his union with God through Christ after the spirit forming him spiritually and sustaining his spiritual being.

At some point, Paul experienced Christ not through his bodily flesh, but through his spirit being formed by God indwelling according to Christ after the spirit. What Paul experienced was Christ after the spirit: that is the experiencing of Christ in personal spiritual forming, as presented and taught in John's Gospel. Paul personally experienced, then told and wrote about his personal experience of spiritual forming and being according to "Christ after the spirit", from within his bodily "jar of clay", for example in 2 Corinthians 5:15.

When we read the book of John or when we read Paul's spiritual confessions, we are still only reading about such experience as recorded in those stories. If what we read remains only the reading of someone else's stories, then what we read can at best be meagre, incomplete, unclear knowledge of a distant shadowy echo of the reality which we are personally called by God to experience directly in our spiritual forming and being, shaped by the hand of God, that is by Christ after the spirit.

Besides the reality of factual error, historical accounts will never speak to our personal spiritual condition as we actually have it. When it comes to spiritual birth and spiritual existence, all that matters is our personal experience and our immediate and direct knowledge of our experience, inscribed in our hearts and on our minds.

What is the Gospel of Christ?

The Gospel of Christ is written in fabric of existence itself. In so far as we exist, it is before us and in us in our existing. It is an Existential Covenant between God (as all existence, of which we are a part) and people's actual personal existing. It is activating in an individual person's spiritual birth, life and living.

To fully appreciate the Gospel of Christ, the question of why was Christ killed needs to be examined and answered. Christ was not crucified because he was trying to prevent a violent crime, or free someone being trafficked. He was not crucified because he was feeding the hungry or providing life skills to the ignorant. Christ was not put to death trying to curb or stop extreme extortion. Christ was not crucified because he was leading a revolt with 'soldiers' and military might. Christ was not crucified because his community wanted to offer a blood sacrifice or make a guilt offering. No one ever stood to say someone has to pay God for our sins. No one claimed that God had been offended, and as a community we must offer a blood sacrifice or make a guilt offering, therefore let us offer Christ as such a sacrifice. No one argued that God's offence cannot be assuaged by anything an ordinary person can do; it will require the death of Christ who being God will suffice as a sacrifice for God. These rationales may have been used by redactors to explain in flesh and blood terms the reason why, if Christ were God, that Christ endured a human flesh and blood death. But this was certainly never called for by any person or character in the documented Gospels.

Christ in his time could have put together an aid organization to feed hungry people and starving children, he did not. Christ could have assembled a group to help people secure justice within their justice system, he did not. Christ could have established healing communities to provide help and healing to the sick and broken people. He could have gone 'global' with his organization, he did not. Christ could have started a group to help free slaves and protect the weak from extortion, he did not. Christ could have started a group to acquire military might to defeat oppressive state powers, he did not. Christ could have established a church of sorts and created disciplines to generate righteous actions in its members, Christ did not.

What Christ did do is present existence and reality and a person's place in such reality and existence as ultimate existential significance, meaning and purpose, of which Christ is the definition and delineator. Christ was put to death because he put forward a view of reality that was irreconcilably opposed to the established religion or rather the established theo-political powers of his community. That these leaders responded with a death sentence is reasonable and to be expected. Christ's call to his reality challenged the establishment flesh and blood 'churches' and provoked his death sentence. Christ challenged the very reality and existence of people. In particular, Christ's Gospel challenged (and challenges) the theo-political leaders' carnal existing and carnal reality that had been, and often continues to be, framed in flesh and blood terms. His challenge was about people's lives as they live them, but also about people's afterlife as they imagine it. Christ's challenge was on the one hand incomprehensible, as reflected in Nicodemus. On the other hand, it dreadful to those snared or 'owned' by their carnal flesh and blood living.

Christ was crucified because of the Gospel he preached, which was a Gospel about reality and existence and in particular about our spiritual reality and personal spiritual existence. The reality and existence preached by Christ was at odds with the prevailing realities in, of and from the world according to the flesh that was prevalent in Christ's community. (And, which remained prevalent in the succeeding 'christian' church communities. Historically, there are all too many parallels in the established church that Christ encountered in his community, and the established 'christian' churches people have encountered since.)

Because the presentation of his view of reality in his discourse and conversation, his teaching and parable-izing concerning the Kingdom of God and personal entry into that Kingdom, Christ was put to death by those in 'authority'. They were people in the flesh, of the flesh and from the flesh. They responded in carnal fear and under carnal threat. They dealt with it by way of the self-righteous condemnation and the destructive violence of the world after the flesh. Christ was distasteful to the theo-political leaders in his community. They did not recognize his message or its meaning.

All that transpired and afterwards, people followed Christ not after the spirit but after the flesh. *Theirs was a god of carnal flesh and blood.* The son of their god of flesh would also be of the flesh. How can the powerful son of god be killed by ordinary people. How could the son of god actually die? The son of god (like any 'worthwhile' god of flesh) would come exercising worldly power, to secure worldly rewards for his faithful adherents. These people required and they got a revised history and a redacted rationale for the death of Christ. Various rationales, theories and explanations emerged to undo their confused disappointment by providing a worldlier account of the temporal death of Christ than the simple truth. What emerged included rationalizations like magical foretelling forced out of the old scriptures. Or, for example, a resurrection story that though Christ died, Christ returns from carnal death in the flesh *to live again in the flesh with fleshy splendour exercising power according to the world after the flesh for all time*.

There seems to have emerged what might be called a carnal 'confusion of the cross' that encouraged some carnally variant gospels other than the Gospel of Christ. In Christ's historical carnal death by crucifixion, Christ gave definition and specificity to spiritual reality for people going through temporal life. Christ in effect put carnal death in the flesh in its place in relation to spiritual life.

Christ was crucified for simply preaching spiritual birth and life in God of God and from God, then describing how this would play out when people generated fruits of the spirit of God. Christ was put to death for teaching, preaching and conversing about the Gospel of Christ. The Gospel of Christ concerns existence, the nature of existence and our part in that existence, including our birth from above and our spiritual life in the Kingdom of God. It was his active expressions of the fruits of the spirit, outside the established rules and tenants of worldly theo-political laws that violated the religious leaders' sense of propriety to the point of Christ's condemnation and death. The Gospel of Christ is not acceptable to the world after the flesh. Christ was not crucified by nasty brutish and violent thugs, though it has been represented in such a way. Christ was put to death by the established and *respected* theo-political systems of his own community, following procedures that were commonly exercised on many ordinary but condemned people.

The Gospel of Christ, unlike the gospels of the disciples and apostles, is not written in words on paper. The Gospel of Christ is in the very nature of existence that makes up spiritual reality. It is written by the hand of God in the very essence our spiritual hearts and onto the very make-up of our spiritual minds. The Gospel of Christ is 'spoken' in our spiritual forming without words but with specific distinctions. We know the Gospel of Christ because we are spiritually alive.

The Gospel is God's message concerning God: God's Word spoken to us in human terms giving us ultimate existential significance, meaning and purpose. This is God explicated in Christ in our actual present existing or present living. The Gospel is given to us in our very spiritual make up, because we have God in us, active as the Word and the illuminating Light. The Gospel message is that we are created able to grasp, possess, adhere to and realize God in us. The Word of God is the meaning of God --- it is what we in human terms grasp of God. The Gospel of Christ is not an abstract text referring to a theology or a history: it is the reality of Christ here and now. We are existing to manifest God in human terms (that is the reality of Christ), through our being in God of and from God. Such manifestation through the very reality of Christ is an incarnate manifestation of Christ through our being or living.

The Word of God today does not temporally exist except through the being of an actual living person or actual living people. We can reach for, grasp and manifest the mind, the heart and the spirit of Christ through our being in God of and from God. God is present in us and to us in human terms, as Christ. Christ is an eternal reality[22] therefore exists here and now and as such is present to us here and now. The Gospel is that the eternally existing reality of Christ is present to us and through that reality, God is actively in us and we are actively in God. This understanding of the Gospel predates the temporal Christ of history. The evidence for the eternally existing reality of Christ stands apart from any transient evidence for the temporal existence and temporal work of Christ. This is not to take away any significance from the temporal existence of Christ or any documentation or text concerning that temporal existence.

---

[22] The temporally incarnate Christ is the Christ that was born, endured and died. The eternal Christ as reality is part of the world we experience and is accessible to us in our existing or being.

What is our source of understanding the meaning and significance of the Gospel? This is an important question. God's message is not limited to or constrained in a few 'human' texts, that themselves defy clear reading despite the temporal value of the texts. God's revelation is as broad and deep as human existence itself, including the infinite and eternal presence of Christ in us: in mind, spirit and heart. One may understand through the text, but seekers who have God at hand and God within, are not limited to and are not constrained by the limitations of the texts or their understanding of the texts. This is good news. The texts help, but the Word of God is more, much more than the mere texts. With or without the texts, the Word is *real and present*, here and now.

In the realities of our existing and the existing of others, we have existential evidence that Christ is a reality of which we are spiritually born and in which we spiritually exist. The *Gospel of Christ is the Christ Covenant* and was present in the temporal Christ and was voiced at that time. Since the passing of temporal Christ, the Gospel of Christ has been 'spoken' in many, many lives, through which it was given voice[23]. The reality of the Gospel of Christ is present today, to be voiced in our time in you.

The good news of Christ is Christ. The Gospel of Christ is not the message of the disciples, the apostles, the church fathers or anyone else since the emergence of the

---

[23] Not all leaders and organizations authentically voiced that reality, which is clear from the history of those claiming to follow Christ but were following their personal needs and wants and cultural preferences.

Christian Church. Though they may all present the message to us, they nonetheless present it impersonally and indirectly. Christ presents the Gospel to us immediately and directly, here and now. Other presenters diminish the Gospel message because of the limitations of the witnesses and their biased means or media of communication. Unfortunately, such biases are present in the texts and recordings of the accounts of the experiences of witnesses.

The actual present and real Gospel as given directly by Christ to each of us personally is not founded on temporal historical events. It is not founded on evidence of past events. Personal salvation and holiness does not depend on past temporal history or historical evidence of past temporal events. If we can find and grasp our own existence, we can find the Gospel --- it is embedded in our being. The Gospel is more present to us than we are present to ourselves. In so far as we exist, we can choose by selecting and affirming salvation in God of and from God. We can choose spiritual life and choose to do the work of God by discerning, finding, selecting and affirming our formationally-following Christ from within our person.

The Existential Cross of Christ: Explicating God

There are two powerful messages or revelations about the Cross of Christ in the Gospels. First, Christ tells people that they should pick up their Cross and follow him[24]. Second, Christ bodily dies on the Cross at Calvary. The Cross, as taught in the Gospels is a symbol representing choosing from the great divide or watershed of reality in which and of and from which we are to be. "Jesus answered, "Very truly I tell you, no one can enter the kingdom of God unless they are born of water and the Spirit. Flesh gives birth to flesh, but the Spirit gives birth to spirit.[25]" Between the water and the spirit the Cross of Christ separates the water and the spirit and enables the spirit to overcome the water.

Christ called people to follow him, not to follow the prevailing forces of the carnal world about them. The call was not to replace one set of carnal rituals, rites, ceremonies, superstitions and magic, with another set of carnal rituals, rites, ceremonies and magic. In the end, the prevailing powers of this world dealt with Christ and his ministry by crucifying him in the flesh and destroying his carnal life in order to protect their carnal religiosity.

---

[24] Notably, Christ did not say pick 'my' Cross and follow me. Christ after the spirit requires that we do his work. Christ requires that we do our work in Christ, of and from Christ.
[25] John 3:5-7 NIV

The Cross exists to *deny and negate the absence of existential value in the world after the flesh*, into which we are born and live as creatures of flesh and blood. The Cross stands to lift our person out of that existence to one which manifests the essence of Godliness.

Without flesh, there is no Cross. Without Spirit there is no Cross. Without flesh housing or tabernacling Spirit there is no Cross. The Cross is where the spiritual distinctions or specifics of God in human terms, that as Spinoza wrote, Christ after the spirit takes on, human nature[26] actually existing with a birth after the flesh and a second birth after the spirit[27].

As a person, Christ wielded the Cross in his life and death. We wield the Cross in this life when we piously choose to lift Christ or the Light within. As persons born from above in second birth, Christ within us wields the Cross lifting us into the Kingdom of God. We pick up our Cross when we lift Christ by doing what Christ would do or when we piously, willfully and intentionally follow Christ. Christ within our person picks us and lifts us, through the Word of God forming us spiritually, to be as Christ would be. In this mingling or union, is in our atonement with God and in God atoning our person.

Incarnation existentially explicates God in human terms. Flesh and blood bodily death does not un-explicate God. As far as Christ actually exists, the Cross exists

---

[26] Spinoza, Benedictus de, 1632-1677, *A Theologico-Political Treatise and A Political Treatise*, 1951. Dover. pp. 18-19.
[27] See John 3:5

separating the things of Christ from the things of this world.

Christ was passive in his carnal death. Flesh and blood people were active. It is important to note in regards to Calvary, that as a flesh and blood person Christ did not embrace death. All evidence is to the contrary. Christ tried to avoid his bodily death. As a flesh and blood person, Christ loved and chose life. But Christ loved and chose spiritual life above carnal life. The life Christ chose was lifting the Cross not into death, but into spiritual life. Christ was arrested, imprisoned, scourged, and bodily put to death. Despite bodily punishment and death, Christ was spiritually triumphant --- from Bethlehem to Calvary. Christ picked up his Cross:

- what he saw, he saw through it;
- what he heard, he heard through it;
- what he understood, he understood through it;
- what he felt, he felt through it; and,
- what he spiritually lived, he lived spiritually through it;

explicating God in specific human terms.

The existential Cross of Christ[28] is the touchstone of Christ-specific spiritual forming. When we choose to

[28] To know existentially is to know by being or existing, which is to say by experience. Knowledge acquired by some means other than existing it, is not *personal existential knowledge*. Impersonal knowing about something, for example to know about our existence as reported to us by someone else, is for us to *personally know nothing about our actual personal existential being*. But, knowing about

follow Christ, we choose spiritual life and in lifting Christ, we are drawn by Christ to Christ. Once we pick up the Cross, we either destroy Christ or with personal affirmation we let Christ live in us and through us. The existential Cross is in the make-up of the existing Christ. We lift Christ through the Cross of Christ and in turn, we are lifted by Christ so that in union we commune with the Creator and the Creator communes with us. The existential Cross is where and when God touched Christ in this life. It is where and when Christ in this life touched God. For our own person, God touches us and we touch God through Christ. Such is Christian existence established by the Cross of Christ.

The death at Calvary was a finite and temporal event. The significance of the carnal death does not extend into the infinite and eternal things of God. The carnal death of the historical Christ was not or is not an eternal and infinite thing in the Kingdom of God, where it has no standing. Calvary was a significant temporal event, but the Cross of Christ is something infinite and eternal, at the heart of the significance, meaning and purpose of Christ in existence. The Cross has been a very compelling

---

something that we are being is to personally know something about our personal existential reality. This is true in regards to our spiritual existence or being.

Some writers separate Hebraic and Hellenic as viewpoints, referring to persons of faith on the one hand and persons of reason on the other hand. But in thinking the philosopher experiences and is existing, just as much as the person of faith experiences. Philosophers experience God and have knowledge of that experience. Persons of faith, for their part experience philosophizing, rationalizing and creating abstractions. Persons of faith reflect on and think about their experiences. The Hebraic Hellenize; the Hellenic Hebraize. Existential is experiential and intelligible.

phenomenon in Christian experience. All too often, the Cross has sadly been reduced to things of the flesh appealing to the flesh snaring us by the power of the flesh.

The Gospel of Christ is that God in human terms *serves* people. In particular, God serves people spiritually. *The flesh and blood Christ served people in tangible ways and in so doing shone the Light of God into the world after the flesh. Christ after the spirit serves people spiritually, enabling them to also shine God's light into the world. We are most Christ-like when we are enabling others to let their Light shine into the world.* Those who follow Christ, for their part serve God by serving people. Like Christ, they suffer for others. Like Christ, they sacrifice for others. Like Christ, they take on the burdens of others. Like Christ, they pursue righteousness, justice, mercy and Godly love. In so doing, they take up their cross and formationally-follow Christ. Like Christ they spiritually serve God, being in God of and from God. God in turn serves them by housing or tabernacling their personal spirit within God. The Word became in order that we personally become spiritual.[29]

The existential Cross was with Christ in every step he walked from the first step he took. It was also in Gethsemane, in the trials, in the scourging, and on the cross of the crucifixion. With every breath and step, Christ chose to do the work of God and fulfill God's will. The Cross we bear is our choice for spiritual life within our person as well as within our actual existing and being here and now; all

[29] The flesh itself does not become spiritual, but we personally apart from the flesh come alive, live and exist spiritually in God of and from God.

while dying to the world. Christ himself carried this kind of Cross from Bethlehem to Calvary. It was at the centre of his mind, spirit and heart. Christ's temporal death makes Christ more human, than does Christ's incarnation on its own. Dealing with temporal death is part of existentially taking up one's Cross and following Christ.

From centuries of bondage snared to the flesh, carnal religiosity retains power to obstruct our eyes, ears and understanding. Our seduction by the flesh to value things of the flesh and honour them keeps enticing and luring our weakness for carnal comfort, satisfaction and security. History teaches that we remain entangled by efforts to salvage the familiar carnal religiosity of ritual, rite, ceremony, superstition and magic. While being born spiritually the sinews of carnal religiosity hold fast calling for remnants to survive the birth. The Cross of Christ continues its work in such contorted and confusing circumstances, separating water from spirit.

The notions that Christ's death was a sacrifice for sin, a payment for an offense or a payment to redeem captive people, projects much, perhaps too much of bodily desires and bodily propensities onto God and the makeup of created existence. Confused people caught up in the flesh and thinking that a substitutionary flesh and blood sacrifice is required to free people from bondage and captivity are the flesh are confused. The required death is our personal death to the flesh that we can then live to the spirit.

In order to live spiritually, one must die to this world. Christ carried his Cross in every breath he took.

Christ calls for us to do the same. We each personally carry our Cross in every breath we take. With each breath, we decide to be alive spiritually or not. We decide to express or manifest Christ or not. Christ is present through us, or we do not affirm Christ, in which case Christ is not present to us and through us. Christ himself carried this kind of Cross from Bethlehem to Calvary. It was at the centre of his mind, spirit and heart.

The existential Cross exists in the Word 'become flesh', be that in the historical Christ of 2,000 years ago or in Christ, here and now. The Cross is present in the Word becoming flesh or having flesh become Christ-like. When Christ tells people to take up their Cross and follow him, he did not and does mean that they should be subversive, be sentenced to crucifixion, and then be crucified. In his teachings about the Cross in the Gospels, Christ was not referring to a Cross that would be made by a soldier, on which the person would actually be crucified. Temporal death did not and could not destroy the Christ reality. Many were crucified in the Roman world. Many died terrible deaths and experienced great suffering. Many simply died into death; Christ died into Life. In the teachings, Christ was referring to being spiritually born from above and living spiritually.

When did the Word become flesh? It was not merely a transient onetime event in human history. That is clear from reading the Prologue in John 1. The Word became flesh in the eternal expanse and in the eternal instant. The Word became flesh in the infinitely large and infinitely small. The Word became flesh in created existence. The Word is inherent in the makeup of created existence. The Word through the Spirit of Christ through the Paraclete is 'alongside creation, calling creation into being', which is the meaning of the word Paraclete (John 16:7). The Spirit of Christ through the Paraclete was with people in Bethlehem and Calvary and in all in between. The Spirit of Christ through the Paraclete is present to us calling alongside us now. The Word became (and becomes) flesh... the Cross became (and becomes) a reality when the Word became flesh and when the Word becomes flesh. The Cross links God to us and we to God. In a manner of speaking, God 'suffers' tangible specification when the Word is made flesh.

We have a present living connection with God through the Word of God, manifested in human terms in Christ. Christ is in us allowing our communion with God. In our creation, the Word is inside us, alongside us calling us. If the Word did not become flesh, the gulf or chasm between God and people would not and could not have be overcome. We would have *no present living personal connection with God.*

When the Word becomes flesh, the Cross is present --- the essence and meaning of the Cross is present. Where ever Christ is, the Cross is. Following Christ and living according to "Christ after the spirit" has Christ as the essence of being, giving personal essence to our being or existing. Wherever the Cross is, Christ is dying to this world and rising spiritually victorious. The infinite and eternal Christ exists and subsists; and darkness does not comprehend nor does death overcome that reality, of which we are a part through birth from above. For our individual, personal part, in taking up our cross and following Christ, we actually express Christ and we actually spiritually live through Christ.

In not expressing or manifesting Christ, the Christ we would have expressed or manifested does not live temporally through us. In effect, from the perspective of our temporal existing, Christ is destroyed or dies. We cannot go back and do what we did not do at the time. We actively lift the Cross and are drawn to Christ. Or, we nail Christ down on the Cross and lift up that action of destruction and are lifted into personal destruction.

When Christ taught the beatitudes, he was teaching what he had learned from his experience of existing in the flesh but of and from God. He was not setting down laws from on high, as was done for and done by Moses. Christ existed, and in existing knew of what he taught from his personal human experience. Christ personally experienced the beatitudes directly. Each day Christ picked up his cross. Each day he carried it, and worked it to serve others. Each day Christ learned from his existing. Christ's experiences of the beatitudes were shaped by his carrying his Cross each day. His teaching was shaped by his Cross. And, so it is for us. One might imagine that Christ continued to experience existence and learned from his experience in Gethsemane, his trial, scourging and crucifixion. Each day, Christ picked up his Cross and carried himself into Life. At Calvary, Christ also picked and carried his Cross into Life, triumphant over temporal death.

As Martin Luther might have said it, we know the Cross by living it. To know the Cross any other way, is to not know it at all. We do not know the cross because we know the details or worldly causes of the temporal death at Calvary. We know spiritual life by being spiritual.

The existential Cross exists when an individual personally lifts it; destroying their individual, personal manifestation of Christ or affirming Christ coming alive and living within. The existential Cross exists when a person picks it up to follow Christ and actually carries it in his or her personal existing or being. At the core of one's heart, spirit and mind, that existential Cross of Christ draws the individual person into death or into Life.

Calvary is history; we are not. Calvary is an echo of the existential Cross carried in all created existence by Christ. The Cross that we carry in following Christ is at the core of our hearts, spirit and mind. It feeds the heart, spirit and mind with the blood and body of Christ making us in Christ of and from Christ. Christ's Cross was carried long before Pilate or Calvary, and it is carried today. The Cross of the Gospel of Christ is a Cross of service to people calling them to Life. The suffering of the Cross is that where there could be Life there is destruction and death. Christ is reality. Existing in, of and from Christ, is existing from the Cross lifted to Life.

The Cross and Our Existential Atonement

The Call of the Cross

The Cross is God's promise of life, lived, of Light shining, never to be overcome. This is evident in the Gospel throughout the book of John. The Cross is a sign of the culmination of Christ's temporal ministry and work. The message of the Cross is the temporal message of the Gospel, which Gospel is given to us in eternity through Christ in us. The message of the Cross is that Light shines in darkness and darkness does not overcome the Light *within us*.

The Cross as a sign of Christ's life (not his death) is a sign of righteousness in a world absent righteousness. It is a sign of justice in a world absent justice. It is a sign of mercy in a merciless world. It is a sign of Godly love, in a world absent love for one another. The Cross stands to say that despite temporal bodily destruction and death, Christ lives and as Christ lives, so righteousness, justice and mercy prevail, along with the love of God for existence and for us as spiritual creatures existing.

As Christ in us is lifted[30], we are drawn to Christ, and we are lifted. Through us righteousness, justice and mercy prevail because Christ exists and lives in us and through us. Notably, the Cross stands to tell us that in our

---

[30] This is apart from being lifted in crucifixion at Calvary.

world righteousness, justice, mercy and Godly love are frail and are seemingly easy to destroy and kill. The Cross tells us that in our world, Christ can be manifest and expressed in our existing, but *it is not a sure given that Christ will be temporally manifest or expressed in our present temporal world.* We are individually and personally responsible to give temporal life to the existing eternal Christ through our being in God of and from God while we live. In chapter 8 of the book of John, Christ speaks about the world of spiritual things, as opposed the world of carnal things. He teaches that when he is lifted up, people will be able to see because spiritual light will illuminate their seeing. People will learn and understand when the spiritual things of their existing are illuminated by the lifting of Christ within their person. The reality that is Christ generates us into a different being and existing when we experience life through that reality.

Christ reveals that righteousness, justice, mercy and love are not merely between God and each person. Rather, righteousness, justice, mercy and love are between *each person and God in other people*. Righteousness is between me and God in my self. Justice is between me and God in others. Mercy and love are given to affirm existence in God of and from God. I am merciful to myself, as well as to others. Christian righteousness, justice, mercy and love are in the very make of God. God is such that we in God, experience the essence and properties of Christ in us. We recognize the face of God as righteousness, justice, mercy and Godly love because we know Christ in specific human terms in our existing and being.

There is more. Through Christ and forgiveness in Christ from within us, we experience and know forgiveness in regards to righteousness, justice and mercy. In the face of failed righteousness, justice and mercy, forgiveness opens up righteousness, justice and mercy to be restorative or redemptive. Forgiveness leads us to God. In and through the reality of Christ, we can forgive failed Godliness. Because we are in God of and from God, we can personally restore or redeem people who fail God in us. In Christ, we have our measure and standard against which we measure ourselves. This we do through the active presence of Christ and the Cross in our existing and being. As the application of mercy and love transforms and lifts righteousness and justice to a new level, so the application of forgiveness to the failings of our selves and the failings of others lifts righteousness, justice and mercy and love to a new level. Without forgiveness, failed righteousness, justice, mercy Godly love cannot be redeemed or restored. Just as without mercy and love, righteousness and justice cannot ascend to the height of God's Kingdom.

Righteousness and justice without forgiveness and mercy are extremely harsh taskmasters that break and destroy people and their souls. Christ's ministry called each person to forgive and to have mercy, in order for them to be truly righteous or be truly just. The message of the Cross is that Christ lives. The Cross changes the world: our relationship to one another changes and our relationship to God changes. The Cross changes or differentiates our understanding of the mind, spirit and heart of Christ. It is the heart of the Gospel of Christ. The Cross lights our understanding of righteousness and justice by infusing them with forgiveness and mercy and Godly love. The Cross is forgiveness and mercy and Godly love for creatures of the Spirit. That is clear from the crucifixion stories.

In reality, nothing we do can 'offend' God. *We do not have such capacity.* Giving offense is a carnal thing that carnal people get caught up in. If we could offend God or Existence, the offense would result in immediate and complete destruction or annihilation of the supposed offender, even before the offense is committed in in finite, carnal time. Neither the offense nor the offender can exist in light of the nature of God and existence. *Christ and The Cross tell us that our offense to God is in our offenses to one another.*

We can offend God *existing in human terms* that is the spirit of Christ that exists in real, living people. There is no compensation for such offense. Once we offend, we cannot redeem our failing. The only remedy is forgiveness and mercy from the people offended and forgiveness and mercy from our selves, both in Godly love. We forgive and we have mercy and we manifest Godly love only by God's grace in us that is only by Christ existing in us. We forgive and have mercy towards others and towards ourselves, because we are born from above and we are existing through Christ in us. This is also the source and substance of our love for one another and for ourselves as children of God. In being or existing in God of and from God in human terms, we are able to forgive and to have mercy and being so enabled, we can act or be loving, righteous and just.

We have experienced and come to understand the above through the Spirit, not merely through scripture, *where there is scant reference to underdeveloped notions of forgiveness or mercy*. The notion that we should forgive others does not loom large in the recorded words of the writers of scripture. Forgiveness and mercy, on which justice and righteousness stand, are critical, seminal, and necessary to Christian living. Forgiveness is key to the teachings of Christ. The meagre and impoverished treatment of forgiveness is noteworthy in scripture, especially noticeably absent in the writings of the Major and Minor Prophets in scripture[31]. After the crucifixion, we are left with the eternally living Christ, the Cross and the message of the Cross: be merciful and forgive one another: love one another as God loves each of us. Through experience of the Cross, we have a different grasp of righteousness and justice, which are infused with the kind of mercy, forgiveness, and love which comes with Christ indwelling forming our person spiritually. As recorded in the Gospels, the message of the existential Cross was not understood during Christ's ministry. This is evident from the response to the parables as told by Christ, and retold by people afterwards. Even the message of the Cross in the

[31] Roughly speaking and applied by relevance the words forgive and forgiving as applied to people forgiving one another are not in either Major or Minor Prophets' writings. There are 2 appearances in Acts and the Epistles. In the book John, there is only 1 reference, and 1 reference in Mark. In Mathew there are 5 instances, and in Luke 3. Again, roughly speaking and applied by relevance the words mercy and merciful as applied to people having mercy to one another are not in the Major Prophets' writings, and of the minor prophets there is only 1 reference in each of Hosea, Micah, Habakkuk and Zechariah. There are 0 uses Mark, John, and Acts. In all the Epistles there are instances. In Mathew there are 6 instances, and in Luke only 2.

bodily death of the *forgiving* Christ was not fully understood at the time of the crucifixion.

A lone voice from within us alongside us has called and does call out for the forgiveness of the people in whom the spirit of Christ slept and sleeps. People led by the spirit of Christ, turned away from the world, as the resurrected Christ of eternity emerged to lead people from within themselves. As Christ was lifted, his ministry and death illuminated his followers so that the blind did see, the deaf did hear, and those who were captive were freed into the Kingdom of God.

Over centuries of confiding with the Spirit of Christ through the Paraclete, and through existing through Christ in us, some in Christian communities experienced and came to understand the forgiveness implicit in the work of the Cross. We grasped this personally and we have grasped it collectively. We have it by two thousand years of personal experience and trial, as well as by our communal experience and trials in the present and actual existing Christ.

Before the Cross, offense and sin in scripture required a carnal, flesh and blood sacrifice to God, to assuage God's being offended by the mere existence of people and their frailty. The law according to the flesh required some kind of payment for compensation. With the explicit emergence of Christian mercy and forgiveness, as well as Godly love for one another, and Godly love for one's own self; the notion of blood or guilt sacrifice or offering lost all value, meaning and significance. God requires mercy not sacrifice. Christian atonement is in real, existing forgiveness, mercy and Godly love, not in any kind of blood or scapegoat sacrifice.

The Cross stands to say, it is for us to follow Christ and assume personal responsibility in our existing and being. The Cross stands to say that despite the infinite and eternal presence of the Word of God in us and in existence, *it is we who are personally responsible for not piously following Christ*. It is we who are personally responsible for the temporal absence of God in our existing and being. The Cross is where we choose and where we are chosen. The message of the Cross is for us to realize that we, ourselves, are personally capable of letting Christ shine through us. In a life of darkness and death, Christ and all the glory of God is in our hands ready, when we follow, to temporally become and be manifest through us.

We effectively destroy and kill Christ here and now, by lifting the darkness of the world, which in turns lifts us into darkness. We negate or destroy our potential to have Christ alive through our living. Alternately, we realize the potential to have Christ alive through us. By lifting Christ, we are lifted into Light. In simple words, we are responsible to realize Christ in us or to destroy Christ in us as much as this is in us to do and be. The 'call' is for us to personally pick up our Cross provided by Christ, which is the Word activating the Light within through the spirit of Christ, and follow Christ wielding his Cross.

The Work of the Cross

What prevents Christ coming into our temporal existence is simply our personally not responding to the Light in us. We are spiritually created to respond to the Light or Word in us. We negate our spiritual being by destroying or negating the Light that exists in our essence and core. In our created world, it is we who generate good. Evil is that we do not generate such goodness. The Cross stands to reveal what we do with the life we have. Our light shines. Even in the face of temporal tribulation, destruction and death, darkness does not comprehend or understand this, and neither can it overcome it.

To understand the work of the Cross, we need to appreciate the difference and the connection between the temporal world and the infinite and eternal world, or between this world and the Kingdom of God. These two phenomena connect *in our existing*: in our birth, in our death, and in our life in between. Within those phenomena emerges our reality, for better or worse: with ultimate existential significance, meaning and purpose; or, not.

Within a carnal framework, the resurrection of the historical Christ has been represented that after bodily dying, Christ temporally rose from his carnal death with a type of carnal body of flesh. That is, Christ lived in the flesh, after dying in the flesh. Some suggest that the resurrected body of flesh is different bodily or different carnally than the pre-resurrected body of flesh. For example, the resurrected body may not decay. Those who are focused on the god of flesh[32], find reassurance in such an enduring resurrection of the flesh. In any case, within that limited framework, Christ died, and then rose from his 'biological' bodily or carnal death in a 'biological', carnal way.

As described in the scripture texts, the resurrected body of Christ was a carnal body. It was an object external to persons. It was present in space and time. The disciples could touch it, see it, hear it, and interact with it. It excited because the disciples and followers were able to bodily sense it as an object external to their persons. As described in the scriptures, the resurrected body did nothing spiritual for anyone present or for anyone after. It did calm the carnal anxieties and fears of those people. It enabled them to set aside the carnal death of Christ, because here was Christ existing carnally despite having earlier died carnally. Their hope was that they too could continue to exist carnally despite having to 'temporarily' die carnally. Carnal death is merely a temporary obstacle, to continuing to 'live' carnally. This perspective causes people to latch onto and stay attached to their carnal person. It does nothing spiritual for anyone present or for anyone after.

Within the testament of the scriptures, it is never suggested that Christ died spiritually. As there was no spiritual death, there was no need for spiritual resurrection. In reality, the eternal Christ lived and lives still. In eternity, outside the limitations of time, there is no death. In the framework of flesh, people focus on and attend to the

---

[32] This idea of the God of flesh is discussed in the next chapter.

temporal transient carnal resurrection of the flesh. This fixated obsession is largely driven by our biological or carnal fears and anxiety about carnally dying. *When Christ bodily died, he died to us, not to God.* The resurrection of flesh would be of no interest to God.

Our temporal existence is the vehicle of the spiritual birth and life while we exist in the flesh. In our carnal existence, the eternal and the temporal are mixed in one gestalt: like an active, impressionist art piece, with some active dots being carnal and other active dots being eternal and the mix experienced as a single whole experience. If the carnal dominates our attention and then the neglected spiritual 'dots' are not attended to, and, they do not come alive. When the spiritual is attended to and becomes ascendant, the spiritual awakens and comes alive through the reality of Christ being lifted within us and through us.

In carnal life, focus and attention are 'naturally' drawn to the nearby carnal stimulants and the 'truths' of carnal forces that confront us in our daily living. While there are powerful natural carnal attractions of the flesh, there are concurrent natural attractions of the spirit (i.e. we have God within us calling us). Focus and attention are also naturally drawn to the eternal or spiritual, and to the truths of spiritual life. As set down in John 3, the two kinds of dots do not dissolve into a homogenous substance. They are apart and remain apart within our single person. In existing temporally, we are not two, we are one of and from the flesh or of and from the spirit.

Temporal bodily or carnal existence is transient; but it is also active and activating. It is present to us in our bodily or carnal life. It is powerful in its luring and its demanding. It is shaped by the meaningless, insignificant and purposeless but strong forces of bodily or carnal life. Ultimately, we were not created to be merely transient bodily or carnal creatures devoid of meaning and authentic purpose. Existing does not have to be primarily a 'bodily or carnal pleasing' solution to temporal fears, anxieties or bodily inclinations for enduring carnal life. The bodily or carnal framework of temporal existing and being, can be recast. While we have carnal bodies, our purpose and end is spiritual. The birth from above framework provided in John 3, selects for ascendancy of spiritual things in such a way as to recast or rework carnal things.

Because God is eternal, spiritual existence in God of and from God is eternal. Spiritual existence is also active: it is Light and as Light it shines. This active spiritual existence is in our spirit, in our essence and core of our being. We have been created to be spiritual, that is to be in God of and from God's Truths. As living entities, we experience and choose the Light in us, that is to say, we select for or choose the spirit and mind of Christ to personally determine and define us. It remains then, for us to work out our salvation and holiness by the grace of God, which we have been endowed in our creating.

Through the reality of Christ we are reconciled to and atoned with God. The real and eternal spirit and mind of Christ, that is the Word of God in us, can be manifest through us in our spiritual being and existence in our daily living. The spirit and mind of Christ, which is God and is of God, manifested in our spiritual being and spiritual existing informs our bodily or carnal life, whether we live for 100 seconds or 100 years. As the active Word of God in us, the spirit, mind and heart of Christ, shapes and forms our life into an existence of reconciliation with and atonement with the created existence of God. The result is personal temporal holiness reconciled to the things of God. Still it remains that in this life, the way of holiness is humbled by its frailty.

Because the eternal, real existing of Christ is present here and now, Christ's faith and belief in me and in you, is actually present in our existing. This existential faith and belief is immediately from and comes directly from God. It is in the nature and make up of being itself that both being and existence has unconditional faith and belief in ascendant spiritual life. Existence itself has unconditional faith and belief in spiritual creatures born from above while housed in temporal bodies, which express or manifest Truth.

Christ wept before Jerusalem. Christ wept in Gethsemane. Christ wept from his Cross. God through Christ continues to weep for the lost. In the absence of our realizing Christ in us, Christ is temporally destroyed and killed. Christ wept for what could have been. It is in the makeup of the reality of Christ to unconditionally affirm people's existing, even to the point of weeping. When Christ's faith and belief in people was not realized through them --- Christ wept.

The call from the Cross is for us to actively realize or actualize Christ through our existing, and to temporally have Christ come alive and live through our existing.

Christ's unconditional faith and belief in people is spoken loudly from the Cross within us. The message of the Cross is encapsulated in the faith, hope and charity issued by the Cross. In the process of dying carnally, Christ pled for people to be forgiven because they did not understand or know what they were doing. Christ was speaking out in forgiveness of righteousness, justice and mercy. Christ knew then and Christ knows now that people without Light act; and, in their actions, they destroy and kill Christ within their person. It is the make-up or the face of the Christ-reality to affirm people's existence, at the same time to sorrowfully weep for those lost in the void. All creation groans for the lost, as it were.

In the end, we can only destroy Christ within our person, as Christ lives in us here and now during our transient temporal life. We cannot destroy or in any way affect the infinite and eternal Christ, God's Word in human terms. We cannot in any way affect the infinite and eternal faith and belief that God affirms through Christ. We may not turn to the Light of God in us, but we cannot destroy or kill the presence Spirit of Christ in our being. The resurrection is that although we can destroy Christ through our temporal lives, in reality Christ always lives in us. As Christ rose and as Christ rises in us, so Christ triumphantly celebrates the Word of God in us coming to fruition.

Since the crucifixion, the issue of bodily death has permeated people's thinking concerning both the crucifixion and the resurrection. Carnal people captive and bonded to carnal lives have always been pathologically pre-occupied with their carnal death and finding a temporal extension of carnal life in the flesh. Such people are alive in the flesh, but dead in the spirit. They hope to become the 'living dead' in order to secure enduring lives after the flesh. What value does temporal resurrection have for God? Is the Gospel message that the dead historical Christ of flesh was temporally resurrected as a body of flesh? Is the message that because the temporal Christ temporally resurrected into an unending temporal body of flesh, therefore we too will resurrect into a temporal body of flesh that endures forever? Is the Gospel message only that we can personally live forever? If so, then consider that Satan lives forever. The Gospel message is that we are in God of and from God and that we have ultimate existential meaning, purpose and significance existing and being in God of and from God according to Christ after the spirit.

The Gospels do not reveal anything extraordinary in their accounts of the death of Christ. Christ felt abandoned ("my God why have you forsaken me") and expressed relief when death came ("it is finished"). Christ held fast his unconditional faith and commitment to people ("forgive them they know not what they do"). Christ's temporal death was not an extraordinary bodily or carnal death. From the scriptures, we find that Christ went through and experienced death with considerable forbearance and grace. What matters about the temporal death of Christ was not the bodily or carnal death and its significance, but the undiminished emergent spiritual life of Christ in existence. The world cannot destroy or overcome the reality of Christ. Salvation is from God --- it is infinite and eternally present. Through God's grace, we who have God in us are in God.

Our purpose is to be holy --- as God is holy, so we are created to be holy.

Born in the flesh and lifted into the Kingdom of God, our lifting atones our existing and being. Atonements played in the flesh that are of and from the flesh are offerings and needless sacrifices that offend God in their insignificance, meaningless and purposelessness. The atonement generated through the work of the Cross, atones our very existing and being, which in turn generates direction in our daily living.

Spiritual Forming: Atonement Through the Cross

From time to time, some people posit that we personally create our own existence. They suggest that we choose existence in this or that fashion and in doing so we shape reality. The meaning or significance we have is the meaning or significance we impart to our selves. We do not shape reality, nor do we create meaning and significance. We do not frame God or Existence. We may choose to participate in ultimate existential significance and meaning, but we are not the authors of such significance or meaning. Existential philosophers in the 20th century demonstrated that existentially the carnal person's actual existence is rationally absurd, void of ultimate significance, meaning or purpose. Given the painful losses and suffering that a person endures when actually existing, a rational person would conclude that death is better choice than life, as Job concluded in the book of Job. Trapped within carnal, flesh and blood experience, and absent ultimate existential significance, meaning and purpose, pathetic efforts endeavoured to salvage carnal people living absurd, insignificant, meaningless and purposeless lives, using the fiction of personally creating ultimate existential significance, meaning and purpose. The effort was and is existentially false and it fails.

At the very root of existence, heart of existence knows that, as Pascal put it, 'the heart has its reasons that reason knows not of'. The heart of existence has knowledge of the spiritual, quite apart from the carnal. The heart experiences the ultimate significance, meaning and purpose of actual existing, which experience is not absurd or void, as our merely carnal existence is. Furthermore, the Heart's experience of ultimate existential significance when grasped in distinct and specific terms enables the person to arrange their carnal life according to the laws or rules of the Word of God. Such re-arrangement 'atones' carnal life to spiritual life, which itself is atoned to God.

The great divide delineated by Christ in John 3 and discussed below in the next chapter, changes the purpose and meaning of sacrifice. Under the great divide bloody and terrible bodily or carnal sacrifices are replaced by sacrificial offerings of the spirit. The sacrificial offering of our spirit or essential existing involves appeasing God by joining with God in union with God to manifest God and the work of God; rather than appeasing God by killing a carnal life.

Regardless of which day and regardless of which culture; whether it is a food or blood offering, animal life or human life; whether it is a fragrance or a burnt offering: God does not ask for or want these rituals, rites or ceremonies. God 'wants' that Christ be lifted up in our minds, in our spirits and in our hearts, so that God becomes manifest through us as manifest expressions of righteousness, justice, mercy and love. In following, we are given spiritual life and we become of God through God in us. The terms or specifics, within which we realize spiritual existing, are the terms of the existing infinite and eternal Christ. From the beginning, Christ was the Word by means of which we are being spiritually formed or created; and, by means by of which we are being sustained. Those sustained by the flesh are destroyed with the flesh; those sustained by the spirit live in the Kingdom of God.

People can and people do destroy the reality of Christ within themselves. By their actions in the temporal world, they destroy Christ's being alive through their personal existing in this world. Throughout his temporal, historical ministry Christ called people to 'atone' --- spiritually or to not destroy the spirit of Christ in their existing. If this is a person's intention, that person will undertake, as far as they can, to live out a personal carnal life according to Christ after the spirit.

People are born again in, of and from the spiritual things of God; and, the ultimate existential concern of their being is realized in their spiritual being. This was Christ's gospel message: this was the message of the Cross. Born in God of and from God according to Christ after the spirit, the spiritual person is atoned to or with God and is enabled to shape their carnal existence according to their spiritual person.

Origen, Augustine, the Eastern Orthodox, Anselm, Abelard, and Calvin all used the same scriptures to understand atonement. Each took from scripture different and individualized understandings. Yet, all were people of God, focused on righteousness. What matters is not whether they understood atonement. What mattered was whether they "followed" Christ. In following Christ, they did the work of God[33]. Atones comprehended and

[33] The work of God that we do when we follow Christ, is not the kind of legalistic, liturgical works referred to by some of the protestant reformers.

understood in the experience of actually following Christ, not in the dissection of scripture and its 'legalisms'.

The bodily or carnal death is a backdrop in which God's Light shone all the clearer. The Cross stands to demonstrate that in human terms God's nature is to unconditionally affirm God's faith and belief in people. The Cross stands to say that Light transcends darkness as illustrated in 1 Corinthians 13:4-8.

The crucifixion of Christ as described in the gospels, demonstrates Christ's unconditional affirming faith and belief in people existing as children or creatures of God. This fundamental love for people did not falter or fail, despite temporal destruction and death of the historical Christ. As recorded, Christ did not request bodily or carnal assistance from other people or from God. There was no call for retribution or punishment. There was no call from Christ concerning justification for any offense. The only call from the voice of God was a plea from Christ asking for forgiveness on behalf of the destroyers. The crucifixion is witness to an act of righteousness, justice and mercy from Christ.

As far as people have choice and make decisions, people in their lives can choose or people can decide to temporally let Christ live in them and through them, or temporally destroy or kill the Christ in them. What temporally destroyed and killed Christ, is as vibrant today as it was 2,000 years ago. The influences and powers that acted then, act now. Christ is as crucified in the present as in the past. Christ is crucified within us; Christ is crucified by us in what we do. The Cross reveals that: people are capable of and people do destroy and kill God in human terms. The Cross stands to say that we can destroy or kill Christ; the Cross also stands to say we can have Christ living in and through us. The Cross then stands to signal atonement and redemption through the reality of Christ.

In the present, Christ is not some kind of bodily or carnal cross somehow being temporally crucified by in an ongoing fashion. Consider instead that within you there is Christ. Within you, in your heart there is a kind of cross. Consider that it is you who are crucifying the Christ in you. Consider that, from that cross within you, Christ unconditionally continues to believe in you and your Godliness. Consider that the Christ in you while on that cross in your heart, weeps for you and calls for you to be forgiven, because you do not know what you do. Consider that even through you act to destroy Christ, Christ continues to stand and resurrecting within you Christ lifts you through the power of God. The lifted Christ alongside you calls for you to follow the Light. Consider through all this that you choose and you decide. You crucify Christ in you or you 'put on' Christ in you. Consider that your spiritual forming, freely given by God through Christ, is in your hands acquiring spiritual life or negating it.

Some think that Godly righteousness and justice is a 'higher' kind of carnal righteousness and justice. They start with justice as understood in carnal terms, defined by carnal or biological sense. Then they elevate that worldly justice by 'perfecting' it, as it were. The idealized abstractions become what they then call divine justice. From such thinking emerges the need for sacrificial offerings to angry gods to pay for offenses and sin, as well as assuage guilt. Out of such worldly-bound thinking emerged amongst other ideas, notions of penal substitution and ransoms or purchases with bodily or carnal goods, including bodily or carnal blood and death. Such things may serve the purposes of governing leaders, but they are not what God is or what God wants. Christ did not and does not come into the world for such things. Understood as a merely a historical event, the crucifixion confuses those without Light.

Bodily or carnal atonement does not carry any 'benefit' into the eternal; it is a temporal event with temporal limitations. Temporal blood sacrifice does not generate spiritual birth or sustain spiritual life. Christ cleared the temple of those engaged in such carnal offerings. Despite mistaken efforts to appease God, for example the burning so called witches, Christ's call to clear the temple of biologically life offerings and sacrifices, has been heeded in practice.

Despite the spirit of the Gospel message, some seem redactors incline their reading and understanding to person centred Old Testament covenant approaches to God, as well as its anthropomorphic tendencies. They tend toward similar bodily or carnal aspects of the old scriptures, which inform their understanding of sin, atonement, redemption and carnal justice. Such approaches require religious observances of bodily or carnal offerings and sacrifices to 'even off' a carnal or temporal sense of balance or requirements. They call for carnal penalties to make up for carnal and temporal offences. For them, there is no need for and no searching for the message or Gospel of Christ as presented to us here and now and as presented to us in scripture. Consequently, they go forward not seeking or finding the ministry of Christ, and they remain captive to the flesh.

For Christians, sacrificial scapegoat slaughter ended when Christ cleared the temple[34]. Historically across numerous cultures, and notably, for this discussion, in the 'holy land', animal sacrifice and offerings, and, both voluntary and involuntary human sacrifice and offerings (including children) was a known practice for many different religions. It may be that some people misdirected Christian thought and theology by using these bonds of the flesh to entice or engage people to follow Christ.

The Cross sees and tells of plaintiff, pitiful groans and suffering sobs of persons of flesh, alone; helplessly immersed in darkness and pain and detached from God. Such woeful enfeebled creatures are resigned to the abandonment and deep hostile violations of flesh and of spirit. They plunge in an endless bathos of utter despair; weeping tears that none see; and, crying with disembowelled voices, at each inhuman blow from the forces of darkness beating down on them, blow after blow after blow. They are numbingly conscious of faint, meagre, impoverished feelings of pending spiritual existential defeat and death.

---

[34] The practice of animal sacrifice for offering or scapegoating did not catch on in Christian 'churches'. Certainly it did not survive the destruction of the temple in 70 CE.

The people of the Cross know of the hopeless, faithless and merciless condition of their forlorn fellow creatures. Having being lifted out of the flesh by Christ, the people of the Cross emerge with triumphant spirits and with the strong arm of God lifting and holding them in the Kingdom of God. The Kingdom of God is our union with God through our being born in God of and from God. The message of the Cross is that those who have Christ within and who have lifted Christ in their inner most being, will not be bereft and abandoned to suffer in ultimate dark isolation, at the hands of the world's powerful forces of darkness. In response to the call of the Cross, they emerge out of darkness growing spiritual pinions, as eagles renewing themselves in flight, being touched by the hand of God.

When coming to terms with atonement, we need to be clear that in the final analysis and discernment, people always and in the end will always aspire to God. It is in their make up or in their creation. This aspiration plays out in existential conciliation and reconciliation. Carnal atonement satisfies carnal urges and sensibilities. Some pursue and find worldly atonement in carnal 'justice'. Those who follow Christ engage in and find spiritual atonement that aligns their existing and being with the existing and being of God. Spiritual atonement triggers a realignment of temporal bodily or carnal life according to spiritual determinations. In our atoning, we must be clear whether atonement is applied to spiritual reconciliation of the flesh or to carnally binding people to the world after the flesh.

The God of Flesh: *the pursuit of temporal immortality*

From within the actual essence of our existing, God emerges present to our being in God, of and from God indwelling forming us according to Christ after the spirit. Light's beacon shines within us while we actually live. All these truths are tabernacled in our actual carnal, flesh and blood bodies. We experience two realities: the world after the flesh; and the world after the spirit.

Our initial experiences are driven by our personal efforts to avoid the biological experiences of carnal pain and carnal satisfaction. After these, our experiences are driven by personal efforts to endure in the flesh for ever. In our efforts, we imagine and construe gods of flesh. These gods of flesh, which are create by our carnal person, which we sustain to which we impart characteristics of their creators. The look like we do carnally, they are motivated by what motivates us carnally and they behave as persons according to the world after the flesh behave. They are anthropomorphic creatures of our making. They are idols without reality and do not actually exist. While those false gods shrivel in the Light, they hold sway over the flesh. At best they are perilous. They are potent to snare our carnal person and hold us captive in what we see, hear and understand.

Unlike gods of the flesh, God or Existence is not our carnal creation. In relation to God, it is we who are created both carnally and spiritually. We in our being know God or Existence is: the biblical "I AM". In our actual being we know that we exist in God or Existence and that the essence of God or Existence is in our person. God or existence is present to us in terms that are common to God and to our person or God is present to us in human terms that we grasp and hold. Beyond human terms we do not know God or the things of God. Though we create gods of flesh, we are not creators neither of God or Existence, nor of the essence and properties of God or Existence, nor are we creators of God in human terms. What we personally individually cause or create is carnal and imaginative at best.

The Christ Covenant[35] manifested and expressed by God in human terms, structures Godly salvation and holiness for those who formationally-follow Christ and do the work of God in their very existing. In regards to living according to the things in the flesh of and from the flesh, we can *do* the things of God by following Christ after the flesh. But *doing* the things of God is not our *being* in, of and from the things of God.

The Christ Covenant does not provide a way to live temporally in the flesh forever. The spirit born from above is not of the flesh. The spirit is housed[36] in flesh; it is not of or from flesh. The ways of the Spirit of truth are not the ways of flesh; that is, the ways of merely bodily or carnal or biological life differ in substance from the ways of the spirit of Truth. It is one thing to follow "Christ after the flesh", that is the historical temporal Christ, and in so doing live a pious life. It is quite another thing to follow the

---

[35] The Christ Covenant is discussed in detail in a later chapter. For now, consider it the implicit agreement between God and person, put into place when the person follows Christ.

[36]We could say the born from above or born again spirit is "tabernacled" in flesh.

forces of this world as conveyed to us through our physical bodies adrift in the world's churnings.

As Paul suggests in his discussion concerning the law and righteousness in Romans, those in the flesh of and from the flesh are not subject to the 'law' as given by Moses, (nor is any other flesh and blood creature in nature is not subject to such law). Neither are they righteous by default. The righteousness of God manifest through those born from above is in God of and from God, it is not of and from the flesh. This righteousness of God that is in those born of the spirit is not a righteousness that comes from any denominational doctrine, law or rule. God's righteousness is not a thing of the flesh nor is it derived from things of the flesh.

Those who are in God of and from God indwelling according to Christ after the spirit, regardless of any church membership, are a law unto themselves. They manifest God's law as it is written in their minds and on their hearts in their spiritual forming

There is a 'carnal person' in our flesh and blood living that wants to endure forever in time and place. To orchestrate this, the carnal person invents an imaginary god of flesh to provide them with what they are unable to get from reality itself. The god of flesh born of human imagination is to provide, health and enduring, comfortable living. If these things are provided, then some illusion or empty promise will suffice. Their imagination devises is a flesh and blood God that seemingly controls the flesh and blood world, in terms of flesh and blood. The contrived god of flesh is portrayed with similar properties as our carnal flesh and blood bodies and living. The carnal flesh and blood urge to endure in the flesh, is not the urge to salvation and holiness, but it does drive and confuse people in regards to spiritual being and living. The god of flesh may resolve temporal needs, but it denies the person eternal salvation and holiness.

Though the flesh exists without meaning or truth, bio-emotional needs and drives generally prevail in our flesh and blood bodies when left to themselves. Whether a person exists for a year, a hundred years or a hundred thousand years, such existence endures but it does not incarnate Truth. To attain salvation and holiness in union with God, we must look 'outside' and beyond our temporal biological carnal selves. A person has ultimate existential significance, meaning and purpose, which derives essence only from God, and not from the bio-emotional needs or drives of our carnal body or carnal imagination.

Being born from above from outside our transient and temporal body generates ultimate meaning, purpose, and significance in our existing. There is within our person, but outside our bodies, an entire Kingdom --- the Kingdom of God. The urge within us to be of and from or be in union with God, is more *existentially primordial and real* than the carnal urge to endure in the flesh forever.

Though being in God of and from God is the most primal existential urge within us, that urge does not "grab" our immediate attention as much as we are "grabbed" by alluring sensory and perceptual excitations and actions stimulated by the body and the imagination. Once that primal urge to be of and from God is awakened and brought to life and to our personal Light, everything changes. There is no satisfying our existentially urgent need to fulfill ultimately meaningful existing, except in our actually being in God of and from God in terms that are intelligible, that is in human terms or according to Christ after the spirit.

We do not follow Christ and do the work of God for personal bodily or carnal reasons or for reasons that emerge from the flesh. Such obedience and service is idolatrous. It is not pious. Existentially we are called to follow Christ and to do the work of God. The response to this call is spiritual birth and life. From the Light we have from such birth and life, we fashion our temporal, carnal lives informed by our Light. Where our Light does not reach, we use our reason to construct a Christ after the flesh. Be it from history or be it from our knowledge of the Light from others, or be it from the fragmented and partial Light we our selves possess, we gather what we can and we fashion a plan of living life that we discern to be Christ-like. That plan of living is an external guide or road map for pious living. When we follow the Christian plan of living, we do what Christ would do and we do the work of God because we choose to do so.

We can know Christ within us "after the spirit" and we can know Christ external to us "after the flesh". Christ "after the flesh" is the historical Christ. Knowing Christ "after the flesh" should not be confused with us living "after the flesh". If we live 'after the flesh', we do not follow God indwelling through the spirit of Christ: we do not formationally follow Christ. If we passively follow the external "Christ after the flesh", we follow Christ. When we actively formationally follow the indwelling "Christ after the spirit" we follow Christ in being.

Followers of Christ after the flesh follow Christ after the flesh with the risk of their efforts being infiltrated, diminished and redirected by the forces of denominational culture. People's natural temporal preferences for the things of the flesh are powered by our biology, culture and carnal forces of this world. From out of the flesh and driven by carnal forces, idolatrous 'gods of the flesh' arise.

Religious leaders employed the 'ways of flesh' to control flesh through promising punishment of flesh on the one hand, and carnal rewards of enduring life-of-flesh on the other hand. People accepted 'ways of the flesh' to have facile solutions to their flesh and blood anxieties, fears and desires as well.

What can be more important to a Christian than denominational community? The reality and accessibility of Christ in any person spirited by Christ into spiritual community of and from Christ is more important. The denominational church is raised through people; those spirited by Christ are raised directly by Christ. Denominations and temporal churches commune: earthly temporal body to earthly temporal body. There are no denominations in the kingdom of heaven; nor are there denominations in the Kingdom of Heaven on earth. Communities of people spirited by Christ commune primarily and directly with the spirit of Christ within. They then share their personal experience in community but only abstractly body to body, with all the limitations of bodies of flesh.

Our historical understanding of the incarnation has been muddied by the yearning of the flesh for things of the flesh to satisfy those yearnings. Biologically we want to live as we are in the flesh forever: this is a yearning of the flesh --- and a very powerful, overwhelming yearning at that. In addition, in order to exert its influence and control incarnation has misused, for example in the now defunct doctrine of transubstantiation in the Eucharist ritual. At a time when this doctrine was full blown with the winds of magical superstition, Spinoza wrote the following in his Letter 76 (December 1675) to a former student:

> O youth deprived of understanding, who has bewitched you into believing that you eat, and hold in your intestines, that which is supreme and eternal?[37]

Such statements could easily have induced civic and religious condemnation and sentencing to death. Even more, consider that it was not just that a person would be physically ingesting God into their bowels, but that before that, God would have been put into a piece of inanimate bread and into some inanimate wine, for no knowable reason --- except to 'puff-up' an ordained priest with undeserved authority. Similar issues surround incarnation theories of the historical Christ, and more so the resurrected Christ.

Spinoza distilled true Christianity from Christianity of the "superstitious kind"; he certainly dids not dismiss Christian faith according to "Christ after the spirit".

---

[37] EP76

Spinoza's close and intimate Christian friends (Collegiants) did not count themselves "superstitious", as illustrated by Simone de Vries' letter of 1663 (EP8)[38], 7 years before the publication of the *Tractatus Theologico-Politicus* and 12 years before his 1675 letter EP73 to Oldenburg:

> "But although we are physically so far apart, you have frequently been present in my thoughts, *especially when I am immersed in your writings and hold them in my hand.* But since not everything is quite clear to *the members of our group* (*which is why we have resumed our meetings*), and in order that you may not think that I have forgotten you, I have set myself to write this letter.
>
> As for our group, our procedure is as follows. One member (each has his turn) does the reading, explains how he understands it, and goes on to a complete demonstration, *following the sequence and order of your propositions*[39]. Then if it should happen that we cannot satisfy one another, *we have deemed it worthwhile to make a note of it and to write to you* so that if possible, it should be made clearer to us and *we may, under your guidance, uphold truth against those who are religious* ***and Christian*** *in a superstitious way*, and may *stand firm against the onslaught of the whole world.*"[40] (my italics and bold)

"...those who are religious and Christian in a superstitious way" *are not like the members of this group* de Vries refers to: i.e. 'those who are religious and Christian' but *not* in a

---

[38] *Spinoza Selections*, Ed. J. Wild, Chas, Scribner's Sons, N.Y. pp. 88-9

[39] This may be a general wording of references to the KV; or, it may a version of the KV drafted in geometric form.

[40] Spinoza Benedictus, *The Collected Works of Spinoza*, ed. and tr. by Edwin Curley, Princeton University Press, 1985.

superstitious way. What the group was reading would allow them, the non-superstitious Christians, to "stand firm against the onslaught of the whole world", perhaps that of persecuting Calvinists and Catholics. The writings that de Vries was holding in his hands and that the group studied was likely lost writings given to him and the group by Spinoza. The draft likely emerged out of Spinoza's *Treatise on God, Man and His Well-Being*, believed to have been written in the early 1660's. There is a reference to such a treatise in Spinoza's 1662 letter to Oldenburg[41]. In that treatise, Spinoza wrote "…we may say in truth that we have been born again. … but this our other and second birth…" which alludes to the book of John chapter 3. The draft in hand also was in effect early versions of parts of the *Ethic*. Again, it is critical that we keep Spinoza's life purpose in mind: he was not doing philosophy as an end in itself. The Ethics was being prepared in the service of personal salvation and blessedness; to think otherwise will confuse the message in Spinoza's work. Simone de Vries was a keen follower and supporter of Spinoza's work, along with a number of other local Collegiants, whose 'Christian' credentials' are overt and solid[42]. De Vries here describes Spinoza as the guide for this group whose purpose is to "…uphold the truth against those who are religious and Christian in a superstitious way" and who "…stand firm against the onslaught of the whole world." It seems that not only did Spinoza attend this Collegiant 'college' as a member; according to de Vries he was a *guiding* leader or a kind of minister, (in so far as Collegiants had ministers), of a very motivated 'church' group. De Vries, like his mentor Spinoza, was in search of true salvation and blessedness *free of superstitious ways*. De Vries followed Spinoza and also support him

---

[41] EP6

[42] See the writings of Jelles, Balling, Meyer and the others.

financially. In his will, De Vries left Spinoza a considerable sum of money. Why? Was De Vries solely smitten by Spinoza's learning? Perhaps, de Vries thought Spinoza's views on Christianity were important and significant enough to warrant financial support.

Some spiritual church leaders and people of God populated the same flesh bound churches. Those attempted to counsel and guide towards spiritual birth from above. They espoused and lived the things of the spirit and manifested being in God of from God. Despite the dead weight of those who primarily pursued the things of the flesh in "superstitious ways" , spiritual life has been championed and presented as a legacy for us by *those ever present protesters and prophets.*

Personalizing God in spiritual human terms (that is according to Christ after the spirit), allows us to have a spiritual relationship with God. Personalizing God in terms of flesh will not allow us a born again spiritual union with God. If we read the scriptures with eyes of flesh and understand scripture in terms of the flesh, we will only derive things of the flesh from scripture. We must be careful and we must be concerned if and when God is reduced to bodily or carnal life-of-the-flesh presentations or character. The things of the spirit are of the spirit and not of the flesh; and, the things of the flesh are only of flesh and not of the spirit.

We do not follow Christ to extend our biological life of flesh and to deal with biologically driven feelings of fear and responses of anxiety to bodily or carnal death of the flesh. Yet to extend our biological life is a primordial and powerful flesh and blood instinct of the body. Many times over, people demonstrate that they will do almost anything to avoid their biological death. Amongst all the bodily appeals, this bio-emotional urge stands alone in scope of power and pervasive drive. Little wonder that over the years people have given so much to raising up the God of flesh and serving that idol with mind, spirit and heart to secure enduring rewards of the flesh. Through Christ, we participate in eternal life. Through Christ, we do not secure enduring lives of flesh, as we know the flesh. Through Christ, we follow Christ and do the work of God and are of God here and now.

It should be kept in mind that Christ did not intend that we should turn his temporal, historical life into an idol. He positioned his ministry in reality itself, in which reality we presently exist. He instructed his followers to follow him, in his temporal absence, not by going back but by going forward and engaging the infinite and eternal mind, spirit and heart of Christ within their person and manifesting this engagement into spiritual birth and life.

Those who follow Christ rightly surrender their bodily person to their spiritual person born from above. *They do not surrender the ascendant spiritual self.* It does not further one's salvation or holiness to surrender one's bodily person to some other carnal thing even if that thing is 'dressed up' in pretense to spiritual things. Surrendering one's self to carnal things is idolatrous: surrender should be only to God and the things of God, which we know through God in us, not through our bodily or carnal senses. Such action is *not surrender into passivity*, it is activating fulfillment. We are called to follow --- not to surrender. Our surrender to God means nothing to God, but our following assents and affirms God. There seems to be a natural inclination for people to surrender their needy carnal selves to some other 'greater' carnal thing. In the process of that surrender, they become spiritually passive. Surrender to the God of flesh, is an impediment and obstacle to spiritual birth and wellbeing. In their need and to their spiritual detriment, people have mistakenly surrendered themselves to priests, churches, dogmas and legalisms to the carnal benefit of such people and institutions.

We find references in the Old Testament, to an external God of flesh described in terms of worldly powers to which people surrendered in awestruck passivity and self-depreciation. Such surrendering into passive submission, without any Living Spirit from within, is surrender into nihilistic and absurd emptiness fraught with voided significance, idiotic meaning and aimless purpose.

We create the God of flesh: then we look to our own creations for a solution that provides us with enduring temporal life. This distracts us from the reality of temporal death. This created God of flesh often serves our craving to exert bodily or carnal power and satisfy our bodily or carnal appetites. People generate different kinds of idols and think they have God. The God of flesh is a God created by human flesh. In the end, there is nothing eternal, infinite or glorious in religiosity rooted in created gods of flesh.

The flesh has a preference for itself and it drives us to see and understand in terms of the flesh. The flesh's fear of death defines most peoples' lives. They recreate their world in opposition to carnal death. It is reflected in their values. It drives their formulation of worldly meanings to fill the otherwise empty living of the flesh.

Redemption is freedom into spiritual life. Redemption is the work of Christ --- given freely by God. Redemption has no price as price is understood in worldly terms. The actual price or cost of redemption from the carnal snares that captivate people is the 'death' or destruction of their carnal person, which allows the gestation of their spiritual person in the flesh but not of and from the flesh. Spiritual generation or formation is spiritual action in a carnal world. Because salvation is in God of and from God, it cannot be 'paid for'. It is grace freely and unconditionally given by God to those who receive it through Christ.

Imagine that there was no life-of-the-flesh afterlife. Those who are born of God from above would still follow Christ and do the work of God. They would pursue righteousness, justice and mercy all the same. Spiritual redemption is freedom from spiritual bondage to the carnal God of the flesh raised up for fear of death and for the appetite to endure biologically forever in bodily or carnal wellbeing. Those born from above, with thriving spiritual lives think of bodily death in the carnal terms in which it is cast, but their thinking is framed in the context of their spiritual being. They are grounded in God and are spiritually formed of and from the reality of Christ. Bodily, temporal death and all its baggage is revealed to them for what it is. Bodily death is dealt with, as Christ would deal with merely bodily, temporal death.

A True Plan or Rules of Living

The reality we existentially 'take' or 'grasp' in our existing forms us personally. In the infinite order of infinitely finite things and their relations, carnal persons fade into nothing without any real ultimate significance, meaning or purpose. Real ultimate significance meaning and purpose exist only in the essence and properties of the essence of God or Existence itself. The eternal cast into the temporal or cast into *human terms* is the reality Christ having distinctions and specifics that are infinite and eternal, as well as accessible while we temporally actually exist in the flesh. While we are born of water or in the flesh, we can also be born of spirit or be born in God, of and from God in union and sharing the essence and properties of God in human terms. The Christ Covenant inherent in Existence is that we have second birth in selecting or assenting and affirming to our spiritual forming. Carnal people who, while in the flesh, do not choose or select for Christ, are not obedient to their inner Light in either spirit or action. They die and fade without significance, meaning or purpose, into the absurdity of nothing. We know these things because we have God indwelling our person forming our spiritual essence and essential properties according to the distinctions and specifics of Christ after the spirit, which we grasp and hold.

Through the actual temporally existing body we grasp passively and are personally formed by world according to that world's absurd, random chaos. We experience and know that we can be formed through the body in a pattern or according to a plan of living that is aligned with *Christ after the flesh* according to our knowledge of Christ from our experience of the world after the flesh. As creatures made in the image of God or made in God, of and from God in human terms, we exist obedient or in accord with our spiritual nature either because we actively formationally-follow Christ or because we passively follow Christ after the flesh fashioned according to our grasp and understanding of Christ after the spirit. Apart from these two righteous kinds of existing, we can exist temporally as merely carnal creatures according to the world after the flesh, manifesting nothing of significance, meaning or purpose.

Our existing according to Christ after the spirit is in the hands of God. We exist according to the world after the flesh in abandonment of our essential existing, falling into ultimately randomized and absurd, as well as insignificant, meaningless and purposeless living. *This fall and fallen condition is arrested, reversed, prevented and amended in the use of a true plan or true rules of living.*

If we were totally spiritually depraved, we could still live pious lives following Christ after the flesh as understand Christ after the flesh. But people are not totally spiritually depraved. People have God indwelling providing some Light to their person. Though the flesh does not beget the spirit, the flesh lived according to the Light to an extent fosters spiritual development. While such piety reduces obstacles to spiritual growing, it is not to be confused with *being* spiritual.

Radical Christians are committed to following Christ. But a person is in the process of being formed spiritually by God indwelling, what does the radical Christian do while being formed spiritually from within? The answer is that *radical Christians devise plans or rules to follow based the Light they presently have*, any complimentary enlightenment that comes from other people, or from other people in history. The plans are rooted in God and the things of God, as far as the person experiences and grasp those things. Such a plan constructed from what we grasp of God and the things of God as a reference external to a person, that serves as a standard and guide by means of which to organize and act so as to be in concert with the essence and nature of God or Existence. Such a plan, in so far as it is of and from God in human terms, allows us to do the work of God, even when we are still forming spiritually.

The sources for the determining the true plan or true rules are twofold. One source is the person being in God of and from God according to Christ after the spirit; that person is being immediately and directly caused by God to act in Christ-specific ways in their personal existence and existing. The other source is our grasp of Christ after the flesh, be that from history or from other people born from above manifesting Christ before us. This source makes use of the abstracted character or model of Christ, as an exemplar. It allows us to measure and manage our responsibilities and obligations, as well as our actions. This process assures us that we are doing good in our daily living and allows us to undertake to improve the good we do in our daily living. The plan is an adaptable guide. The methods and means of experiencing and experimenting outlined below, are merely tools to help in discerning what can make up the plan, then to help in the construction of the plan, and to support the development and adaptation of the plan.

God is reality. We can grasp that reality because we are in it in human terms and it is within us in human terms. The grasp is in essence whole; or, it is merely a partial grasp that leaves us confused and deluded by illusions of reality by which we are misguided to live as counterfeit creatures absurdly without ultimate existential significance, meaning, or purpose. A true plan or rules of living founded in the reality of God can be utilized to navigate the counterfeit world after the flesh.

What we existentially 'take' or 'grasp' of reality forms what we know as our person.

1. a) By way of our flesh or bodily senses, we grasp the world after the flesh in itself and according to that world we are formed absurdly, randomly and chaotically. That is the world without Light of Chris's distinctions. Spiritually we are less than passive, *we are spiritually still.*

   b) By our person being carnally formed by Christ after the flesh when we apply our reasoning and critical thinking to what we know of Christ after the spirit and are obedient to that knowledge. Our personal actions are Christ-specific. We are spiritually passive; but *the spirit of Christ is present in what we do.*

2. By God indwelling through the spirit of Christ actively forming or generating us; and, in forming or generating us, *activates our grasp of existence and of our person in existence, according to Christ after the spirit*. Our obedience is immediate and direct; it is not reflective. We are spiritually active or alive in second birth from above. Our 'natural actions' are Christ specific.

Christ after the spirit is not Christ after the flesh. The former is externally manifest to us in the latter. We know Christ after the spirit by way of union with God indwelling immediately and directly forming us according to Christ after the spirit. In regards to Christ after the flesh, if we have the actual living temporal body of Christ before us, we can know Christ through our faulty senses, as an external thing. If we do not have Christ in the flesh before us, we can only know Christ after the flesh through evidence from others or through our actions in the external world. Both of these kinds of sensory observations are effects or evidence of Christ after the spirit, which we ourselves cognitively connect.

The book of Isaiah speaks about people with evil plans (drawn from the world according to the flesh) and people with true plans or rules for living, 32:3-8 (NIV):

> *Then the eyes of those who see will no longer be closed, and the ears of those who hear will listen. The fearful heart will know and understand, and the stammering tongue will be fluent and clear. No longer will the fool be called noble nor the scoundrel be highly respected.*

> *For fools speak folly, their hearts are bent on evil: They practice ungodliness and spread error concerning the Lord; the hungry they leave empty and from the thirsty they withhold water. Scoundrels use wicked methods, they make up evil schemes to destroy the poor with lies, even when the plea of the needy is just. But,* ***the noble make noble plans, and by noble deeds they stand***[43]*. (my bold)*

[43] Other translations use different wording.

Perspectives on the Existing Christ in the Book of John[44]

The Existing Christ and the Scripture Texts

Critical study of Christian scriptures suggests the emergence and consolidation of the different texts of scripture is the outcome of 'communities' of authors writing for 'communities' of readers. It is also suggested that following the historical death of Christ, the texts of scripture and orthodox beliefs founded in scripture, evolved in both those 'communities' through a kind of 'survival of the fittest texts' selection process driven by the 'social ecological' factors and forces in Christian settings or ecologies. If we consider how social media develops and works today, such considerations are indeed tenable. There are parallels in the emergence of 'orthodox knowledge' in the social media, where we find communities of authors writing for communities of readers, and what emerges advances through a 'survival of the fittest' process as determined by the forces at play in social media ecologies.

Besides being shaped by spiritual reality, the scriptures have been shaped the carnal realities of the time. Scripture should be read and understood with critical discernment towards both realities.

[44] It would benefit the reader if they have read and have some familiarity with the Gospel according to John.

Three hundred years of critical-historical enlightenment has affected and is affecting our reading and understanding of scripture[45]. In turn, the place and role of scriptural texts in matters of faith and Christian religion is changed. *Christ does not stand or fall on the texts of scripture in themselves.* Christ is real in existence itself, not in only the meagre, abstract and fragmented texts of scripture alone. With or without the lens of historical-critical perceptions, scripture attests to the existence of Christ before the temporal birth of the historical Christ. Scripture also gives evidence of the existence of Christ after the temporal death of the historical Christ.

We experience Christ in us and in existence, pro-actively delineating and forming our spirit, mind and hearts. Knowing this spiritual reality through our existing, we encounter spiritual reality and engage it in our personal existence in existence itself. Through Christ activations in us and through Christ activations in existence external to our person, we are formed in the likeness of God manifesting the very essence and properties of the ultimate

[45] In the great debates concerning the reliability of scripture based on historical evidence, the debaters forget that we cannot compare scripture with any other ancient texts. Suggesting that because there were more Christian texts than other kinds of ancient texts somehow validates the meaning of the Christian texts is a pitiful red herring. Whether ancient Greek texts or any other texts of antiquity are reliable based on historical evidence, matters little in the grand scheme of things. When we are talking about the Word of God, we are discussing existence itself. This reality can help in sifting the carnal from the spiritual in the messages of the texts. The basis for the Gospel is the real existing Word of God; nothing less. Scripture affirms what we find really present to us here and now, scripture does create that reality which we presently access.

significance meaning and purpose of Existence or Existing. Spiritual existence is Christ active in existence and active in our personal existence affirming God and affirming God in us.

Scripture validates our individual and communal spiritual experiences; and, our personal and communal spiritual experiences validate scripture. In other words, we find support for our personal and communal spiritual experiences in scripture; just as we find support for scripture in ourselves, in one another and in spiritual community. Scriptures are mere documentations of spiritual experiences of the Word of God forming spiritual creatures. We look to scripture to support discernment of Christ in ourselves and in existence. While it may be beneficial if we could be certain on the authorship or the history of the texts of scripture, what really matters is to discern whether scriptural texts reveal God and God in human terms (i.e. Christ). Such discernment enables us to corroborate our actual personal and communal existential experiences. We can only read and understand scripture because of present existential experience of God indwelling forming the reader according to Christ after the spirit; and, in reading and rationally understanding scripture our spiritual experiences are affirmed.

Divine inspiration of reading and understanding scripture is personal. It is in what we personally see, hear and understand spiritually from what we make out of the temporal text from our temporal seeing, hearing and understanding. We may individually see, hear and understand the text differently. At different times with different knowledge and background, the Gospel message, being the Word of God forming us spiritually here and now, is constant. The Gospel in the Book of John is God's message in temporal text. As an instrument of communication of information, the text can be used in different way to provide its outcomes. One way is, when at some point, the text leaves its writer and stands on its own. Comprehension is triggered by the interplay between the text and the reader. The source of message is no longer the original writer. In a sense God becomes the source the message. The writer's original intent no longer stands and it becomes irrelevant whether the writer was inspired or not, or whether the writer was in some trance or not. The writer as intermediary is left out. If the reader discerns God's Word in the text, that is between God and the reader. The reading is affirmed by a reality whose existence is not dependent on either the text or the reader. God's Word derived out of the text of John is what we are actually discerning of the presently actually existing Word, given what was set down and what we see.

Honest and authentic efforts to find, engage and use Christ and Christ's ministry, were and are informed essentially by the spirit of Christ actively forming us in our actual present. The work of the spirit of God within us radiates out of the spirit, mind and heart of Christ actually in our person.

The Book of John

The reality of human need and human frailty asks where is God in the individual person's living. What is God and what does God do for the individual person's living?

In the book of John, there is an articulation of the role of the Spirit of God, variously identified as the spirit of Truth, the Holy Spirit and the Spirit of Christ all active as the Paraclete[46]. These provide a foundation within us, through which there is means of salvation and holiness, in formationally-following Christ.

Throughout the book of John, Christ articulates and establishes God's living Covenant inherent in God. God's living covenant is written in existence itself. In existence, God indwelling us forms us according to the living Covenant. This forming according to Christ after the spirit, is a *Christ Covenant* inhering God, which is written in our personal minds and on our personal hearts. The Christ Covenant is our actual and real union and communion with God indwelling according to Christ after the spirit. This Covenant is personal. It is between each person individually and at once with God, Christ and the Spirit.

[46] The Paraclete calls to us alongside us. We can hear and recognize the calling. We can see and recognize what we see. The Paraclete is the spirit of Christ shaped into specifics that reach out for us in terms we can relate to and recognize. The Paraclete is the connection between us and the reality of Christ. It is our response to the Paraclete that lets us sense and recognize the experience of our active formational-following Christ.

From a position of absolute worldly power, Pilate asked Christ in the book of John (John 18:35-38), "What is truth"? In Pilate, we have a pragmatic, rational and worldly perspective. Cosmopolitan Rome is not weighed down by Hebrew tradition, established religious or cultural customs. The best among them found their truths in the world after the flesh according to the world after the flesh. Pilate states in a question, what Rome had learned from several centuries of worldly experience: there is no truth. If you have the power of might, truth is what you want it to be. Christ stood to say otherwise. Truth is the Word of God. Our salvation is in knowing Truth and being of and from it. Pilate did not know spiritual Truth. Pilate had a sumptuous life, full of all that the world in his day could give, yet he was separated from God by the truths he adhered to. If Christ had tried to win Pilate to Truth by doing carnal miracles and presenting carnal wonders, then would Pilate have believed Christ and his Truth more? Perhaps he would … until Cesar found someone to perform greater carnal miracles and present greater carnal wonders. Christ presented only the Truth of Existence and Existing to Pilate. The texts indicate traces of the Spirit of Christ through the Paraclete in Pilate awoke a fear that convicted Pilate of the unrighteousness of Christ's arrest, trial and sentencing to crucifixion.

We are created with the Light or Word of God within us. We are creatures born into the Light of existence. We live, by nature of second birth, in and with faith, hope, charity and Godly love. In the Gospel of John, Jesus makes this "as clear as the noonday sun". In the few verses of John 3:1-21, Jesus teaches about being born again from above, begotten into a life of spiritual things. The Light in us actively shines over and in us. By nature, we are spiritually formed to be just, righteous, merciful and loving to others.

John 3:1-21, is a substantive and clear message: it is a watershed pronouncement. John 3:1-21, establishes a divide in regards to the scriptures' presentation of the spiritual things of God. This separation presented by Christ is without parallel in scripture presented before Christ. In John 3:1-21, Christ gives his message to a teacher and leader of Israel directly, without any supporting carnal analogies, metaphors, etc. This passage illuminates the rest of the book. Indeed, it sheds light on the whole of scripture, as no other teaching from Christ does. The encounter between Nicodemus and Jesus was significant and its recording provides an enduring testament in regards to knowledge and understanding of Spiritual life and wellbeing.

Christ spoke and taught Nicodemus about birth from above, that is about spiritual life. Christ does not go on to create a movement based on this teaching. The point of the lesson is to make clear that spiritual birth from above is separate from the life in, of and from the flesh. Following the lesson, Christ himself in his life manifested or expressed God through spiritual life born out of the things of God. Christ did in his life what we should do when we piously follow Christ and what we do when we actively follow in our existing and being.

The Word dwells in us and we do not receive it, because we are distracted by and choose this world and we engage in this world's temporal forces, neglecting the call from God within us. In Christ's temporal life and in temporal life before and after that, the Word dwelt among us, and we did not receive it. Those who respond to the calling of Christ's Covenant become spiritual children of God, embodying ultimate existential significance, purpose and meaning.

There is an ever-flowing ambiguity in John's Gospel from start to end. This suggests the Gospel was directed to at least two audiences. It addresses those who hear, see and understand things of the flesh. It addresses them in their terms; terms they can grasp and comprehend. They will undertake to follow Christ after the flesh as much as possible, as best they can. It presents miracles, signs and wonders, along with physical evidence as authority given by God. It represents people with worldly, physical needs seeking worldly solutions to their worldly needs. This is done with a view to getting their attention to turn them away from their bondage to worldly things, and turn towards freedom in the spiritual things from above.

Some people seek immortality in the merely bodily or carnal world. They are forlorn. Salvation is in the eternal moment that we are. Holiness is in what we presently are and what we presently do. In themselves, miracles are good, but they are only the start, not the end of Christ as described in the texts. The signs or miracles in John's Gospel are there to lead and to move us towards favouring and selecting for spiritual things. They are presented as scaffolding that allows us to learn that we should turn and direct our person to the spiritual.

The Gospel of John also addresses itself to a second audience who do hear, do see and do understand "Christ after the spirit". It addresses them in terms that they grasp and comprehend by their spiritual person so they actively follow Christ and further their discernment through Christ.

This ambiguity finds expression in a persistent lamentation from Christ concerning those who followed him after the flesh and believed only because of the physical miracles and their desire for carnal gain. At the end of the Gospel, Christ greets the disciples and provides them with physical evidence of his presence. These things are presented to the disciples long after the Spirit of Christ through the Paraclete had been promised to them. The Gospel records Christ's lamentation for those, who like Thomas, hear physically but cannot hear spiritually, see physically but do not see spiritually, and understand the world but do not understand the Kingdom of God. That John's Gospel presents the disciples as remaining captive to the snares of carnal life, even to its last pages, is not to be underestimated. If they, in their experience, were so bound, we must remain vigilant of such powerful forces in which we are submerged while we live in the flesh.

Throughout John's Gospel, there are two kinds of hearing, seeing, understanding and being. People hear, see, and understand carnally, that is physically or corporeally. The dynamic of primarily living and being carnally, is driven by carnal forces, for better or worse. People can also hear, see, understand and be spiritually. The dynamic of people's spiritual living and being is driven by spiritual forces at play in a spiritual reality cast in 'people terms'.

This Christ reality is the grounding and framing of our personal spiritual being. Through it we are spiritually born, come alive and live.

The early church established a ground and frame from which spiritual existence issues or comes to be, in existence itself and in individual people as well. It was necessary to spell out God's relationship to people as understood through Christ. How does the spiritual world relate to the bodily or carnal world and the dynamic forces at play there? What was needed was a ground and frame that could stand up to critical scrutiny and be actually grasped by people so they could follow Christ, as God incarnate. John 1:1-18 sets down the basic ground and frame of spiritual life. As was the case in John 3:1-21, it accomplishes its purpose in a short passage that plays itself out through the rest of the Gospel.

The Gospel of John opens by establishing the foundation on which personal created spiritual life exists. That foundation is that the Word was in the beginning. That in the Word was Life, and this was the Light. Later on we, find that the Light is in people, personally. This means that Life and the Word are also in people themselves, personally. These things come alive when the breath or spirit of God is breathing or spiriting us, forming birth and forming life of our spirit. We are personally bound in union to God through an existing reality: that reality is Christ.

The Gospel of John closes with teachings about the Spirit of Christ through the Paraclete and the nature of the Paraclete. God has created us with God within us, calling us to the Light that is within us. On our own, we can do nothing in regards to salvation or holiness. Nevertheless, we are not on our own. We are being formed with God in our innermost essence. We are formed to commune with God through our communion with Christ. The communion is proactively guided by the Spirit of Christ shaping our personal Christ-specific reality.

When we discern, act, and experience that reality, we hear differently, we see differently, and, we understand differently. In that reality, our spiritual being forms and participates in the infinite and eternal things of God. This spiritual forming utilizes our carnal lives. Our 'full' created existence and experience are not merely spiritual but includes our carnal temporal selves. While 'man does not live by bread alone', neither can people live without bread. We are born of flesh or water, and of Spirit. In this spiritual world, we can act and exist in Christ-specific ways while yet in the flesh. We can be just, righteous, merciful and loving in this carnal world.

These spiritual things are things we do for others, through God's grace in us, because of what we are. These are not objects external to our person. We seek for and find them, in order to get our share of our living them and doing them. Christ did not live to secure justice, righteousness, and mercy for himself or for God: neither needed them nor wanted them. Christ did not come to condemn and say people were not just, righteous or merciful to him during his sojourn in the world. Christ came and Christ himself was just, righteous, merciful and loving to the world … even to his dying act of divine justice, righteousness, mercy and love requesting that God forgive his people for not knowing what they were doing in executing him

Justice, righteousness, mercy and Godly love are things that through grace we do in an intimately personal way. These are not done to us or for us. These are things we ourselves do. Being Christian means being of and doing these spiritual things, as God would do them. Both God's relationship to us and our relationship to God, determined in how we are created, enables us to be just, righteous, merciful and loving. As merely bodily or carnal entities, we are not just or unjust; righteous or unrighteous; merciful or unmerciful; --- we simply are. We can live as more than bodily or carnal beings by being spiritually born into a spiritual life that arranges our carnal self to be atoned to God and the things of God. As far as God is actively in us, we can be Godly through being just, righteous, merciful and loving. This being born again from above, into an existence in which we participate in the things of the Spirit of God, is not a transformation of our bodily or carnal selves. It is a forming into our spiritual selves.

Born Again From Above – The Great Divide

In John 3, Nicodemus approached Christ. Why did Nicodemus come to Jesus? In his mind, given the signs and miracles that Jesus had been doing, Nicodemus according to his beliefs thought Jesus had come from God. Nicodemus want to know why God sent Christ. What was God's message? Nicodemus came to ask about the things of God. For Nicodemus proof or evidence of God's workings in our world was in the signs and miracles. The signs and miracles referenced by Nicodemus were things seen carnally, with which people interacted carnally.

While carnal signs and carnal miracles are reported in John's gospel, there is no proof or evidence of spiritual things in those carnal signs and carnal miracles. For his part, Jesus had come from unsatisfying encounters with people who experienced only the carnal aspects of his message and ministry. They followed because of the carnal signs and carnal miracles, and Jesus did not trust faith formed on that basis (John 2:24 – 25). For his part, Nicodemus also came because of the carnal signs and carnal miracles.

Jesus speaks plainly with the learned Nicodemus, in making the immediate point that that the spiritual world is apart from and different from the merely carnal world. Jesus anticipated that Nicodemus was ready to learn about spiritual life. As presented in John 3:1-21, Jesus did not give Nicodemus a chance to ask any questions. Instead,

Christ proclaimed. As an individual's carnal person is born into the merely carnal life, that individual's spiritual person is born from above into spiritual life, (but not without first being born into the merely carnal world). According to Jesus, flesh does not give birth to spirit. In pursuit of spiritual life and growth, we must carefully and studiously consider whether we are pursuing, dealing with and experiencing things of the flesh or things of the spirit. Speaking of earthly things and doing merely earthly things, is not of the same order as speaking of heavenly things and doing heavenly things. Jesus understood and accepted that many, who came to him and followed him, may have relied on the carnal signs and miracles to decide to come to him and then decided to follow him. From Nicodemus, Christ seemed to expect more direct and better understanding.

When we go to the scriptures in search of Christ and the reality of Christ, do we search for spiritual things and reality? Or, do we satisfy ourselves with merely carnal things recorded there that quieten our carnal fears and carnal anxieties? If predication, that is prophetic foretelling, tells us about earthly events, such knowledge is of this world and its doings. That does not help us in regards to our spiritual condition. It reveals nothing of Godliness that will help us to be more spiritual. In effect, the flood and the exodus from Egypt were carnal things of this world. Knowing the historic details of the flood would make us no more knowledgeable of the heavenly world or further us along in our spiritual journeying. In searching for Christ in the scriptures, it is distracting to become engaged in carnal signs, carnal miracles and prophesies concerning carnal, temporal events. In themselves, signs and miracles can be good and useful. It is when we idolize them and seek them, rather than Christ, that they become obstacles and barriers. Such distractions can obstruct our search for the Light as set in scriptures. Whatever place those carnal attractions have, they do not help us to know what we should be or what we should do. We must be wary the fowler's subtle snares, if we are to mount up with wings as eagles ascending into the things of God.

Jesus never lost faith in people. Indeed his death is a testament to his Gospel message. Christ wanted others to know and see that his life was greater than the bodily or carnal death so deeply feared by people. It is clear in this encounter with Nicodemus that Jesus' words failed. His gospel message was not heard by the carnal oriented Nicodemus. His gospel message was based on what he knew from above. What he presented he said, he had seen from above. The Gospel message from above, having been received or understood only in temporal and carnal terms, did not cause Nicodemus to believe or even start to understand heavenly things.

Nicodemus as a teacher and leader should have known and been focused on the mercy behind the signs and miracles and derived his understanding of Godliness not from the carnal signs themselves. Attention is to God and the things of God, not on the carnal signs and carnal wonders. As soon as Nicodemus indicated, he thought Jesus was a teacher from God because of the signs done by Jesus, Jesus immediately cut to the chase and directed Nicodemus to spiritual birth or being born again from above – over and above or separate from one's merely bodily or carnal birth and carnal life. Whether persons' with little learning believe because of carnal signs, carnal miracles and carnal wonders, or whether persons' with great learning believe because of carnal signs, carnal miracles, and carnal wonders; neither is secure given Jesus' response concerning the basis for spiritual life and the workings of spiritual living. The 'Nicodemus approach' does not address the fact that 'those who *do not* come from God' also come with carnal signs, carnal miracles, carnal wonders, and foretelling of carnal events. In themselves, those things are not indicative of being from God.

Indeed, many think that the basis of faith or 'fear of God' rests on God being physically or carnally powerful, without limits. But, spiritual life does not rest in any kind of physical or carnal power. This is the message of John 3:1-21 --- and the message of the Cross, which stood even to crucifixion and death. Those who base their faith and their salvation in carnal power could not and do not understand the Cross. To them it would be and it is senseless and foolish. It was senseless, foolish and an embarrassment 2,000 years ago, and to those whose faith rests in the wrong place it remains an inexplicable, senseless embarrassment today. These people struggled to explain the Cross 2,000 years ago; and they struggle to do so still. Their rationalizations and forced explanations fall short, coming to rest on superstition and magic.

Carnal reality is comfortable with and is readily persuaded by merely carnal life. The carnal world is a world full of carnal evidence. It affects us physically, bodily and carnally. To this day, many who call themselves

Christian continue to await a carnal messiah, who will come to deliver us from merely bodily or carnal needs and provide us with our merely bodily or carnal wants. That messiah is to come with carnal power and do carnal battle to win the carnal world and all its blessings for God's chosen and elect. This perspective misses the message of John 3:1-21.

Satan can perform and does perform carnal signs, carnal miracles, and carnal wonders, as well as foretelling of events, but is not of God and cannot enter the Kingdom of God. What sets Satan apart from God? Satan is not set apart by the carnal world. Satan is set apart because Satan is not spiritually in God, of and from God. Satan cannot by nature manifest the essence and properties of God. Satan is not born again from above. Satan does not have spiritual life. The mind of Satan is not the mind of Christ. Satan does not love God, and has not Godly love of anything.

We may find evidence of the existence of spiritual life in our merely carnal world --- comparable, for example, to when we see the merely carnal effects of a wind[47], while not knowing what causes such effects. We might find evidence of righteousness, justice, mercy and God's love in our carnal life, but we will not understand these things through carnal life. In regards to spiritual life, birth and being, evidence of spiritual life, cannot be explained by referencing the merely carnal world. Things of the spirit do not come from the flesh and they do not partake of those carnal, finite temporal things of flesh. What we know of our temporal lives does not inform us about our spiritual

[47] John 3:8

lives. What we know of our temporal lives is knowledge that comes from *outside* our person. What we know of our spiritual lives comes from *within* our person. There are two kinds of knowledge: one arising from the nature and properties of the world after the flesh; the other arising from the essence and properties of God. Our actions are driven by one or the other. Carnal actions stop in carnality. Spiritual actions harness carnal things to reflect the essence and properties of God. All the same, they remain separate from the carnal because the carnal cannot grasp the infinite and eternal: darkness cannot comprehend or overcome the Light.

The spirit is not causally connected to the merely carnal world. God created the merely carnal world, and while we may see evidence of God through the merely carnal things God created, we cannot understand God through merely carnal things. The merely carnal world will in itself, not reveal the heart and meaning of the spiritual world. Knowledge of the merely carnal world does not generate substantive knowledge or understanding of the spiritual world. The desires, expectations and assumptions that arise in us from merely carnal life, are not the desires, expectations and assumptions that arise in us from spiritual life. Merely carnal living can be described as living in, of and from the carnal world or the world of mere flesh. *It is a world that is neither good nor bad. It simply is.* The bodily or carnal and spiritual worlds are not by nature antithetical or adversarial. The carnal life, of those who believe in and pursue Spiritual living, must be reconciled or atoned to the Spirit of God.

In John 3:1-21, Christ reframes the very ground of the reality of our existing and existence. The real is not the merely carnal things; it is the spiritual things (and their place and role, relative to the carnal things). Carnal things are utilized to support salvation and holiness grounded in the precepts of God, which are given to us through spiritual reality. Christ in effect defined reality as the infinite and eternal Kingdom of God, which is our existential union with God, into which we enter through being born again from above and in which we participate through our spiritual lives. As is evident in scripture, and in our own sense of Christ, Christ taught and illustrated that people go through a birthing process to become new creatures destined to walk the way of holiness by formationally following in spiritual reality. Christ sets down a spiritual foundation or ground for that reality, and Christ sets out a spiritual framework, within which we live spiritually. This is the basis for the great divide present in Christ's teaching. Consider the teachings of the Sabbath by comparing for example Leviticus 23, with John 5, 7 and 9.

Consider the 'creation controversy' of the last 150 or so years reveals the significance and magnitude of this reframing in our time. That antagonistic controversy concerning whether creation follows the literal description in Exodus or whether it follows some other form, i.e. evolutionary theory, is a controversy about this carnal option or that carnal option. It is very much a 'Nicodemus approach" controversy. The animosity it has caused, and the resources that has been expended on it, are all very much in 'Nicodemus approach' territory.

Christ clearly and strongly lays down in John 3:1-21 what matters to him about creation. He selects neither carnal option; nor does he waste any precious resources or time discussing or debating such carnal sophistry or options. Christ puts forward a new reality, at least a different reality. This Christian reality reverberates throughout the Gospel of John and shows itself through the whole expanse of scripture. This shift in biblical pronouncements, made clear by Christ, represents a divide between the old creation of the world after the flesh and the 'new' creation of the world according to the spirit of Christ. Those who engage in this reality, have a new life, lived in a very different world, from those who continue to be snared and mired, by the unfettered forces at work in the things of the carnal world.

Access to spiritual creation is through the infinite and eternal Christ that is God, in human terms. It is in our hearing, seeing and understanding the things of God and in hearing, seeing, understanding, our intentionally and actually entering into and experiencing spiritual life. The 'proof' of this creation is Christ present, here and now. The proof of Christ and of this reality is in our actual spiritual experience. It is not in the bodily or carnal, temporal experience of the kind that Thomas seemed to require (John 20). Christ is the manifestation of the Light and Word of God in us. These things give us the capacity to experience existence spiritually.

Nicodemus twice indicates that he does not 'connect the dots' from his knowledge of and understanding of his merely carnal world, to an understanding of the spiritual world. He cannot fathom our spiritual birth or creation from above, or our spiritual life of God. He has eyes but does not see; ears and does not hear; he has understanding but does not know or understand about spiritual things from above. All the same, Nicodemus has an urge to reach for spiritual life that calls him, hence his visit to Jesus and his incredulous questions. The Light and Word in his heart, seeks knowledge and understanding beyond the carnal world --- for this reason he does not dismiss Christ outright when Jesus talks to him about being born again from above; he listens to Christ's message. Up to that point, he simply was not aware and did not understand.

There may seem to be some implication, that because Jesus immediately directed Nicodemus to birth from above, that Nicodemus was not born again, not godly, or just, righteous and merciful. This is nowhere explicitly put forward by Jesus himself. What is explicit is Jesus' immediate rejection of the merely carnal understanding of spiritual life, displayed initially by Nicodemus. Jesus was compassionate towards those who believed merely because of miraculous signs, but did not trust the steadfastness of the faith of such believers. When he addressed Nicodemus, Jesus put the external evidence of mere signs and miracles aside. Instead, he directed Nicodemus to the internal experience of personal birth from above. He directed Nicodemus to the Light and Word that is within the 'born again from above' person's life. Jesus pointed to the internal evidence of birth and life from or of the Word. Salvation and holiness is of God and from being born again from above, and then pursuing life spiritually in justice, righteousness, mercy and Godly love. Christ's presentation through the dialogue with Nicodemus towers above and illuminates the old scriptures' prevalent prophetic voices, telling of people who have ears and eyes, but do not hear or see, who do not understand or know; of people who listen and look, but do not hear or see; people who do not know, understand or possess the Kingdom before them.

Consider Isaiah 55. Water that is not water is offered to people labouring for spiritual salvation to satisfy spiritual thirst. Nourishment that cannot be purchased is offered to nourish the spiritual growth of seekers. Those who are not seeking are urged to seek and find, while they have time. The Word of God comes from God into people, just as water is sent from heaven to water the earth to stimulate seeds, in order to have as a result, bread for those who hunger to be spiritually satisfied. By nature and creation, we have Light and the Word of God, i.e. the Seed, in us. Grace comes to us from heaven above, to awaken us as the earth is awaken by rain, to stimulate the Seed within us (which is the mind, spirit and heart of Christ in us). We are being born again from above and are nourished by the Spirit into mature spiritual life and well-being.

According to the scripture, Nicodemus was a leader and teacher. We can surmise that he adhered to the tenets of his faith, followed its doctrines and rules. We can assume he sought salvation and holiness, this was the reason he approached Jesus. From his side of the discourse, we see Nicodemus' understanding is only of this world --- the carnal world. We can assume he was a "good" person. We can assume he studied and had knowledge of scripture, the law, and the teachings of the prophets. We can assume he diligently and faithfully adhered to and tried to follow the scriptures, the law, and the prophets as understood by him and his community. Yet, he did not consciously understand the world of the Spirit of God. He did not seem to consciously "see or hear" the Kingdom. He did not consciously know or understand the Kingdom. He did not seem to have conscious experience of spiritual life.

It may be that the Word of God in Nicodemus influenced him in his living, but not in such a way that he had a ponderous consciousness of that influence, its source or actualization in him. There was no conscious spiritual foundation by means of which he could intentionally direct himself to grow and develop his knowledge and understanding of spiritual things. He was caught in a world 'ruled' by understanding of the merely carnal: a foundation of sand and an understanding not grounded in the Spirit of God. We do not know after they completed their encounter, whether Nicodemus 'heard' the message, and if he did, whether it opened his eyes and understanding.

Just because he was not conscious of his spiritual life that does not, in itself, mean that he had no spiritual life. Being born again from above and growing spiritually is not dependent on our conscious knowledge or understanding. It is possible to be saved and holy and not know why one is so. Many have been saved and were holy, and did not fully know or understand that. Many will be saved and will be holy and may not fully know reflectively or understand reflectively. Yet it is clear in their presence that they are of God. As was said, the spirit listeth where it wills ... and we do not know where it comes from or where it goes. What Jesus was saying to Nicodemus was to take his eyes off the merely carnal and look at the spiritual to see the Kingdom, which is at hand. Seeing such a Kingdom, one can know, understand, and enter it manifesting the laws of Christ. In entering, comes conscious experience of the Kingdom --- here and now.

If what Nicodemus knew and understood satisfied him, Nicodemus would not have sought out Jesus. Nicodemus would have corrected what Jesus said to him. Instead, Nicodemus reflected in wonder. There was something in Nicodemus waiting to be born and waiting to live; perhaps what was happening was actually being born and coming alive.

The merely carnal world has its own laws: natural laws and man-made laws. It has its own ethics, its own beliefs, and its own values. Transient, carnal structures can arise and fall; none of them with any intrinsic good or bad, or intrinsic, spiritual value. People living merely carnal lives have carnal eyes that carnally see, and they have carnal ears that carnally hear the things of their carnal world. They have carnal understanding of their carnal selves and their carnal world. All that seeing, hearing and understanding fails when it comes to knowing and understanding spiritual life. Bodily or carnal life has no intrinsic spiritual significance. In this world, might is right --- but might comes and it goes. Nothing really matters one way or the other. It is pointless and directionless. It is a machine without spirit: empty and void of eternal significance or being. People limited within the terms of bodily or carnal existence, make do with their abilities within such terms. Some eat; some are eaten. All aspire to be as much as they can be within the terms of merely bodily or carnal existence. Some acquire carnal power and exert it. Others pursue illusions of power to the point of sad pathos. All the same, carnal life is never without some touch of grace. As such, carnal life can in some measure, point to the things of God that are above carnality.

Christ did not come to condemn carnal life, but to save the promise in the birth in spiritual life. Bodily or carnal life was also created by God, and it is good. It is crucially important not disparage bodily or carnal life. Many have confused this and have devalued bodily or carnal life. Bodily or carnal life is good and it accomplishes wondrous things --- but it is not spiritual life. Spiritual life can only come from being born again from above of the things of the spirit.

What makes John 3:1-21 such a powerful message is that as scripture it separates the mixture of bodily or carnal and spiritual things. These are not blended here; they are separate. Christ comes with Light to clarify the Word of God by un-mixing spiritual life from merely carnal life and demonstrating what leads and what follows in what 'God wants of us'. Some have focused their attention on the carnal signs and miracles, and other carnal things, and in so doing, have missed the Word of God before them. Others have lost sight of the reality of the bodily or carnal world and have as a result lost the meaning and purpose of spiritual life. We must be born of water and of spirit. We are not merely spirit. Our salvation and holiness is from our spiritual birth and life, but there would not be a spiritual life for us, if we were not first born bodily or carnally. Our bodily or carnal living, can point us to spiritual things; but it is not itself spiritual.

Consider the Neo-impressionist art, which uses many small points, which our eyes can transform into images that we see, but are not actually on the canvas. Consider the words we read, which are merely ink on paper, but we turn into words with meaning. Consider an act of kindness, mercy or justice we experience that turns our attention to the Word of God in us, and allows our inner Light to reveal God's justice and mercy written in our hearts and on our minds. Consider how scaffolding helps us climb, or consider moulds that allow for the shaping of bronze artwork. The bodily or carnal world is not be disparaged, but neither is it to be worshiped and so grab our attention, that our spiritual formation is arrested.

Light, ever present in John's thinking and writing, allows for the experience of sight. Sight generates understanding, which generates knowledge. Knowledge and understanding implies possession. The understanding is an understanding from spiritual experience and life, not merely bodily or carnal experience. Without being born again from above, we do not see the things 'of God', and consciously do those things, or experience and understand them. Despite seeing and understanding miraculous signs in merely carnal terms, without spiritual life and without spiritual experience there will not be authentic personal knowledge of God or Christ.

Light is present to us whether we are born again from above or not. Though Light is present in us, it is we ourselves who personally do not see or understand. Though Light is present in us, it is we who personally do not possess experience or knowledge of the Kingdom. Even if we were born again from above, and if we follow the Light given to us, we may not completely know. Even if we are saved and are holy, we still may not reflectively or fully "see". We might not fully possess awareness of the blessings we have. We would see then, as through a glass darkly. Clarity comes through our direct, personal encounter with God in our spiritual life. We understand spiritually through our encounter with the mind of Christ, which is distinctly or intelligibly written in our hearts and on our minds. The mind of Christ specifies or sets out spiritual actions for us to undertake. Engaging in spiritual actions generates experience and knowledge of the things of God from above. This knowledge and understanding convicts and persuades our judgment. It allows us to make decisions to believe, to have faith, and to follow.

Consider the other side of the great divide generated by Christ's ministry. Moses had spoken to God, who provided actual carnal tablets with external carnal laws tangibly inscribed on them. Moses created and carnally set down a lengthy set of laws and rules for people to follow. Moses established a priesthood to oversee the laws and rules, including rituals and observances, codes of conduct, etc. This priesthood oversaw the implementation of the laws and rules, to the letter, by the people. There is nothing personal in this except obedience to the external laws or rules.

Christ set nothing down. He came, ministered and left. Christ did not leave behind any carnal thing. Christ did teach about the Spirit of God and the things of God. Christ did leave the Spirit, and manifestly illustrated this (John 20:21-22). Christ's ministry as reported by John talked about those personally born in the image of God. Christ taught about being personally born again from above. He taught that spiritual things are different and distinct from carnal things. Christ made it abundantly clear that God is in us. Christ said that the Spirit of Truth has been provided to us. Christ made it clear that he was in us, as we are in him. The Gospel is clear that the Word of God is within us, that the Spirit and Mind of Christ are in us. The Word of God in us is released by Grace that nurtures us into spiritual maturity and life in God's Kingdom. Christ left us insight into God's Grace through the presence of the Spirit of Christ through the Paraclete's calling us. In the absence of the influence of Grace, we require just laws written into codes and rules; in the presence of Grace, we require the law within --- written on our hearts in our minds. Which is to say, on the one hand we have the written law; on the other hand we have Grace.

We can know carnal things from our carnal lives, and not by being born again from above. We can be born again from above and have spiritual knowledge and understanding, while not knowing a lot about things of this world. This is to say, we can be spiritual yet not understand to be able to explain to others in terms they comprehend, about our spiritual life. Indeed, we may not fully and reflectively understand our own spiritual life ourselves. As was said, the wind blows where it wills and the merely carnal world does not understand what causes the things 'of the wind', or what the things 'of the wind' cause --- this is state of ignorance evidenced by Nicodemus in the encounter described in John 3:1-21.

We find some people, in the absence of schooled learning, who have been born again from above and who in their walk with God are just, righteous, merciful and loving. Some have been able to put on Christ and had the Spirit support them directly. These spiritually knowledgeable, (but otherwise 'ignorant'), people have profound understanding of God: they see, enter and possess the Kingdom. Their understanding and knowledge arise from their experience of the Spirit and Light in them, and this triggers external experience of Godliness in what they then do. They walk along with the schooled, but for their part in their salvation or holiness, they do not require the merely carnal knowledge gleaned from carnal life in this world and its temporal history.

Faith itself does not grow from merely bodily or carnal experiences or merely bodily or carnal knowledge. Nicodemus believed (a view shared by many from diverse faiths), that God and the things of God could be comprehended and known by experiencing signs and miracles --- and other merely carnal things and events. A miracle may be of God --- but in itself, it reveals nothing spiritual of God or God's nature --- nothing of the things of God. It tells us nothing of God's comings or goings, for only what comes from above (i.e. spiritual things), will lead us to spiritual knowledge and understanding. Faith is the province of those born again from above of God's spirit.

Faith is the province of those born both of water and of spirit, who grow and develop spiritually by following God's laws, written in our hearts and on our minds. In these passages from John, we have the deepest and clearest teachings of Christ concerning the carnal and spiritual things relating to salvation and holiness.

In effect, Christ here separates the merely carnal messiah and the merely carnal signs and miracles of such a messiah (including healings, armies battling victoriously, carnal wealth and well-being, and limitless carnal rewards), from the spiritual messiah of God, arriving with salvation and holiness, with a call to follow in the way to salvation and holiness; to be born again from above and to pursue justice, righteousness, mercy and God's love.

No one has gone to heaven who did not come from heaven --- that is to say what originates from only water, flesh or carnal will not of itself be eternal or go to (i.e. enter) heaven. Spiritual life begins in heaven, it mixes with water or bodily or carnal life, and it may direct bodily or carnal life. Spiritual life itself is not directed by carnal life, for on its own carnal life is darkness without light. Bodily or carnal life may satisfy bodily or carnal urges, needs and wants; but it cannot satisfy spiritual urges, needs or wants. What the spirit can provide for carnal existence, carnal life cannot provide for spiritual existence. All life is created by God, both carnal life and spiritual life. We can live carnal lives, and ignore spiritual life. It was not the pursuit of salvation and spiritual life that generated the events that killed Christ; it was peoples' attachment to carnal life and its carnal demands, urges, needs and wants. When it is written that people loved darkness --- it means that people prefer and choose carnal life without the Light of the Spirit and Mind of Christ.

The one and only child of God is also that part of God that is people, and that part of people that is God. The Son of God is present to us in us today. Through Christ's begotten (i.e. not created) presence, God is in us and accessible to us. Through the presence of Christ in us, we can be existing expressions of God's grace in temporal human terms. It is this accessible presence of God through the mind and spirit of Christ that makes the essence of Isaiah chapters 58 and 61 a real possibility for us individually and collectively. This presence in us is not our personal salvation or Godliness, though the presence participates in our salvation and holiness. The presence does not come into play until we choose it by affirming it, lift it up and follow it.

Condemnation is a consequence of applying laws that forbid. It is the law that condemns, not the judge. The law does not reward right doing, it condemns wrongdoing. Because we have God in us we can follow God's ways. God is in us to lead us, not to condemn us. We are created with the Light in us not so we would have a means to judge, and in judging condemn our imperfections. Grace rewards right doing. For in doing right, in being just and in having mercy, we experience holiness through God's Grace. That part of God in us, the Light in us, is not there to reveal the dark in us. It is there to reveal the Light to us. It illuminates the Way. God in us does not measure guilt or sin, the Light measures or illuminates our salvation and holiness. We are convicted by what we know, not by the dark, which has no knowledge of God. We cannot 'pay for' any degree of sin. The old law was set up to bring worldly justice to worldly lives. Even if it was given to us by God, it was not God's law or Word, but a set of temporal laws for us. Condemnation and payments of restitution were based on those worldly laws suited to life in darkness. The law satisfied worldly needs and wants. God's laws written in our hearts and on our minds are different. This is Christ's Gospel: that we are saved by God's grace and nothing less. Our conviction leads us to choose God, and let go our meagre existence in darkness. God does not cover us in darkness. We live in darkness, God brings Light, which Light when lifted up allows us to live in and exist of the Light.

God did not send an avenging angel to condemn and destroy. God sends salvation, but people act in the darkness. It was human action in the dark that killed Christ. When carnal life is ruled by carnal forces, life is life in and of darkness, in other words is not life at all. When carnal life is ruled by the intelligence of the mind of Christ, carnal life aligns with spiritual life and we live lives in and of the Light. As written in the Gospel according to John and as taught by Jesus long ago, people continue to live and be in the dark, lured by the things of this world: preferring and adhering to them.

Nicodemus was a teacher of Israel and a leader of his 'church' council. Within his own faith, like the thousands before him, he may have been just and righteous and merciful. He may have been born from above and pursued spiritual living, as far as he was able. He may have been looking at the wrong things, the wrong ways and missed seeing, knowing and understanding spiritual life.

Knowledge, not even spiritual knowledge, is not a pre-requisite to salvation or holiness. The command was simple: "Follow me." The faithful and true of heart and mind will come to hear and see, to know and understand, then to have conscious reflective awareness of possessing the Kingdom, here and now.

After many prophets, and after Christ's gospel messages, still neither the people in the streets nor the teacher leaders in the temples, understood and accepted. Even when Christ espoused justice, righteousness, mercy and love in merely carnal terms, they did not believe in his teachings, but persisted in the shelter of their darkness. Indeed, in their turn, the disciples also failed to understand --- at least initially. Tragically, since then many 'people in the streets' and many teacher leaders in church roles, failed to understand. Many remained rooted in signs of carnal miracles and signs of carnal temporal prophesies coming true. Many remain rooted in mere carnal signs today. When Christ wept for Jerusalem, he did not weep for nothing. It is not surprising then that at the end of Jesus' earthly ministry, Thomas had not yet moved on from an understanding like Nicodemus' carnal view. Christ there lauds those who do not see carnally, but believe because they can see spiritually and understand spiritually. Christ was aware that his temporal life was very brief and that only very, very few people would see him physically in time and place. The writers of scripture for their part wrote with a hope for the quick physical return of Christ. In fact, they were aware of what Christ knew --- most all of humanity would not experience the incarnate temporal Christ in time and place. We can say that the witnesses to the incarnate Christ were so few and their experience so brief, in effect no one experienced Christ as a physical, temporal entity. When Christ refers to people who will not hear, see, touch or experience the physical incarnate Christ in time and place, he points to all of humanity. Christ's commendation to those who do not carnally see or touch, yet believe, at the end of John's Gospel, is immediately followed by the writer saying that Jesus had performed many signs. The writer says he has written these down so that people would believe because of the carnal signs or miracles. Perhaps then Christ wept again…

In creation, only one comes down from heaven --- God in human terms: Christ in spirit and mind. At the time of our creation, heaven was already with us and was within us like a Seed being germinated in the activation of the Word. Our spiritual life is in being born from above and living spiritually while we "yet in the flesh". We are called to salvation and holiness by the Word in us and we are shown the way of holiness by the Light in us. Before we are born, the essence and properties of God is written in our hearts and on our minds, for us to understand with our acquisition of the mind of Christ. So it is with everyone born of the Spirit. Their spiritual lives come from above, not from the carnal world. The carnal world will not make sense of where spiritual life originates or where it goes to. There is evidence of Spiritual life in the fruits of the Spirit appearing in carnal life: in the exercise of Godly justice, righteousness, mercy and love.

Without the born again from above birth, there will be no entering into heaven. Lifting the Son of God or the Son of Man refers to lifting God in us. We do not lift God. We lift God in us, that is, we lift the infinite and eternal Son of God --- the Word or Light in us. This part of us comes from above. It is a seed within our nature. Grace, like water, comes from above; it quickens the seed and gives us birth from above. When we lift the 'Person' in us (i.e. Christ), we choose salvation. In lifting the Light within, we see a different reality. When the Word within shapes and leads us, we follow into the reality of spiritual life and holiness. As the Israelites had faith in Moses' snake lifted high, so Christ in us lifts up spiritual life for us. As a result, people can and should have faith and belief to be born again from above and into a spiritual life of justice, righteousness, mercy and Godly love. One must see, believe and follow spiritual things to find eternal life.

If one is looking for a messiah who will condemn evil doers and reward a chosen few, then they are mistaken in their merely carnal understanding of the things of God. Salvation and holiness add to the merely carnal. It infuses, lifts and transforms the merely carnal, through the emergence of the spiritual to form and shape the merely carnal. God is not going to undermine the merely carnal world --- it is what it is – that is how it was created. Those who are lifted beyond the merely bodily or carnal through being born again from on high, are lifted into the Kingdom of God. There is no alternative to the merely carnal world, in the merely carnal world. God adds he does not destroy. God adds the spiritual to the merely carnal: he will add justice, righteousness, mercy and love. This God achieves through Christ, through the mind of Christ written in our hearts and on our minds. Satan destroys, and adds nothing.

We make terrible, terrible mistakes when we confuse our carnal sense of justice with God's Justice. We must see merely carnal things for what they are. It is difficult to do so, if one has invested all of oneself in the merely carnal. It was very difficult for Nicodemus to give up his cherished merely carnal beliefs concerning salvation, holiness and carnal redemption. It was difficult for the people populating John's Gospel. Many of those people required carnal, tangible miracles in order to believe and to follow. Given their needs, carnal miracles were done and they then believed and followed. Perhaps in the believing and following, their spirits came alive and infused their lives. Perhaps in the following, the Word in them spoke softly, then loudly. Perhaps, the obstructions to the Light in them, lifted and they began to see. Perhaps the way was prepared by their carnally based beliefs, and their carnally induced following, prepared the way, and levelled the road. Perhaps these things, allowed the lame to walk and not be disabled but instead healed. When we are born again from above into spiritual life, we will plainly see the eternal and ultimately significant things of God, and we will abide in them. Perhaps Nicodemus did just that in his time.

Given this watershed pronouncement in John 3:1-21, we can revisit John 1 with this understanding in hand. The Word of God is the One who connects people and God.

It comes from above, and through it, we rise up. The common spirit or essence affords us atonement with God. It is the mind of Christ. The beginning of course is our beginning. What came to us was with God and it was God -- that aspect of God that reached to us in human terms. Life derives from God. Things exist to us, because we have experience of those things. We experience carnal things in merely carnal ways. We can experience spiritual things in spiritual ways. What is more our experience of and understanding of spiritual life can change our carnal life and our carnal existence. Our spiritual life can infuse our carnal lives, and align or atone our carnal being with the mind of God. This is the work of the Word of God.

Life for God's children is more than merely bodily or carnal life. The more is what comes from the eternal and infinite essence and properties God, and it is given to us through the Word of God. We have no other means of seeing or knowing God or the things of God, except that such sight is given to us by the Word of God in our being created by the Life that is in the Word in us, and in our being receptive to the Light created by God in us. We see by means of this Light given to us by God. In addition, what we see and experience spiritually, we understand and know spiritually.

It seems we have the Word of God within us. We are created with the Light in us, but all the same we can live bodily or carnally without reference to that light or Word. In our bodily or carnal world we can carnally see, and carnally hear and carnally understand carnal things; yet live in spiritual darkness, blind, deaf and without spiritual life. Nor is this an either or situation. We can live our lives using more or less Light. Less means living with less infusion of the spiritual into our carnal living.

The depravity of bodily or carnal life is that in itself carnal life cannot understand or comprehend spiritual things or spiritual life. Carnal experience can point to God, but we reach God only by being born again from above, and by spiritual living. By nature, merely carnal life does not understand or comprehend spiritual reality, spiritual birth or spiritual life.

All persons are given Light. The purpose of the Messiah was to awaken spiritual life past, present and future. He has not been recognized as the Word of God present to people to enlighten people. Yet all persons have Light, and all persons could recognize the Word in them. Still, people prefer the dark of satisfying bodily or carnal existence that quenches bodily or carnal thirst and provides bodily or carnal comfort. People seek bodily or carnal well-being derived from transient bodily or carnal life dominated by carnal might serve directionless carnal ends. Christ provides a way to spiritual salvation and holiness. People did not understand. Nicodemus did not understand. The people amongst whom Christ stood did not understand fully. However, they were given a road map: "Follow me." Be born of God. Find God, then be born of God and in doing Godly things grow in God.

Moses provided carnal laws for people to use in their carnal world. Even so, those same people were created with the Word and with Light in them. People experienced the mix of carnal life and spiritual life. We see this mixture in the writing of the prophets, so full of spiritual insight and wisdom, while at the same time addressing the lure of carnal rewards and comforts. Caught up in the moment, in history, politics, and temporal predications; much of the old scriptures addresses spiritual life ambiguously, through darkly carnal glasses. Moses used a 'legal' covenant – a carnal contract backed up by carnal signs. Christ did not use carnal signs to affirm the spiritual ting of God. Christ used the laws of God actually written in our hearts and on our minds: he used grace and truth.

Christ is the Covenant. Being born again from above is not a carnal covenant bound by carnal or biological parameters. The Gospel of Christ is different from the messages of Moses and the Prophets. John records the unique message of God's Messiah concerning salvation and holiness.

John 20:21-22 reports one of Christ's last calls to his disciples, for them to follow him. Christ says that they are to do as he did. As God sent Christ to them, Christ sends them to others. As Christ did in his ministry, they should do in theirs. Christ breathed on his disciples, and told them to receive the Spirit. (This was long before the Pentecost event, as reported in Acts.) However, in actuality they already had the Spirit. Though having the Spirit, they had yet to hear, yet to see and yet to understand. Carnally or carnally breathing on them was intended to redirect them to spiritually catch the breath of God and to live spiritually. Those who actively grasped what Christ said they should receive, take on spiritual lives. They who 'receive' the Spirit are able to forgive sins --- they can exercise mercy because they are not bound or restrained in carnal snares and bindings of the forces of the world after the flesh.

Given the choice, what is the value of choosing a spiritual life? If it does not provide carnal, carnal benefit then what use is it? Why is being personally just, righteous, and merciful the right choice for people? The choice for spiritual live is a choice for peace with God and reconciliation with the very meaning of existence. It is the difference between salvation and death, between holiness and deprivation. The choice for spiritual life is a choice for a greater and more intimate participation in God.

According to Christ those who do evil deeds, prefer life in darkness. People who do good deeds love the Light. They lift the light up and are formed by following the Word. In following Christ, we do good deeds. In doing good, we love the Light. We must be clear; following Christ is not merely a matter of joining a church, attending that church, and keeping the doctrines of that church. Nowhere in the Gospels will we find such instruction in Christ's teachings or messages. We follow Christ by having the mind of Christ in us, as our mind; in having the mind of Christ in us filled with the spirit of Christ in us; and, in so being we 'intent', we act and then we spiritually experience good deeds. There is wisdom in congregating in church to help one another to achieve these things. Doing these things feeds our love of the Light and Word. When we live by the truth, we do the truth and we are set free by the truth to enter into truth   --- the Kingdom of God.

The Paraclete

During the incarnate life of the historical Christ, people had access to the temporal Christ, but they also had access to Christ within them and the eternal Christ in existence itself. They had the Word of God active in them. They had the Inner Light. They had access to God's Truth through Christ. Despite all that, many could not see, hear or understand: being fixed on things external to their person, they could not recognize God indwelling through Christ. In scripture, the disciples, (and subsequently many of the apostles), seemed always to be looking for God's salvation in the world outside themselves. They did not concern themselves with personal spiritual forming till after Christ's *external, carnal death* and *external, objective carnal or bodily absence*.

The Christ Covenant is inherent in reality. God calls us to that Covenant through the essence of Christ indwelling our person. To us, God is sensibly and intelligibly present in the distinctions and specifics that are the Christ reality. In reality, Christ is the sensible and intelligible definition of the existential relationship of our union with God, the terms of the union (the 'Christ Covenant' inherent in reality) is being inscribed in our hearts and minds in God indwelling our person. God's indwelling forms our spiritual persona according to Christ after the spirit.

It is evident in the book of John that the explicating of Truth in the flesh, which Christ undertook to do in carnal terms, failed. People continued to look outside themselves to the world of flesh. They could not and cannot sense, see, hear, know or understand spiritual things from a flesh and blood perspective. That failure demonstrates that salvation and holiness are not carnal outcomes. The Truth is not explicated from one person to another. Truth is not an abstraction or a process of reason. Truth is experienced by our spirit because we are spiritually in it of and from it.

Christ tried to teach the disciples that *when he becomes carnally absent*, then they will hear the Paraclete alongside them calling to them the spirit of Truth and they will respond spiritually because Christ prepares this in eternity.

John 14:5, 16, 17, 26 and 15:26, as well as 16:7, 12 and 15 speaks to the "Paraclete, the Spirit of truth". In John's text, the Paraclete shows up 5 times and the Spirit of Truth shows up 5 times. The two are identified as the same, therefore referenced 10 times. That along with the surrounding texts gives the Paraclete a significant place in the book of John. To this, as will be shown, these passages relate to Christ's discussion with Nicodemus in John 3; as well as the Prologue in John 1. The Prologue reads as though it is a summary of these passages involving the Paraclete or the Spirit of truth.

The Paraclete has been considered by some to be Christ's ghost (i.e. Holy Ghost). The word ghost is the translation for the Greek 'fantasma'. Ghosts are connected to persons of flesh and are limit by the actual flesh. A ghost is a kind of person after the flesh, continuing a carnal existence in some kind of tangible flesh and blood sensible form. This is its attraction. The Paraclete is the Spirit of truth calling us alongside us, but it should not be confused with 'ghosts' that serve to meet our biological needs to endure in the flesh.

Some translators[48] have used ghost instead of spirit in their translations. This kind of 'corruption' or disfiguration, for good or ill, feeds things of the flesh, for better or worse. The confusion over ghosts 'of flesh and from the flesh' and things of the spirit was not acceptable to Christ in his time --- it caused him to weep over Jerusalem. It is not acceptable today. It reduces people's grasp of God indwelling according to Christ after the spirit to carnal superstition and phantasy.

The Paraclete as one alongside us calling us illustrates that *by nature God or Existence purposes our spiritual person.* In the calling is the purpose. The purpose is to exist and be existentially ultimately significant and ultimately meaningful.

Paraclete is an unusual word in scripture. The notion and word is introduced by Christ and only discussed by Christ in the book of John. The word and its meaning are difficult to decipher and understand. Para means to the side of, or being alongside of. Clete (Kletos) means calling,

[48] It merits pondering whether the notion of *Christ's ghost* was put forward by church leaders to control the gullible and superstitious, or whether it was put forward as an effort to reach the superstitious and gullible for their own benefit. In any case, it was not done lightly or slightly. And, it would have had untold unproductive impact on many, many people over hundreds of years.

that is, 'to invoke'. This spiritual invoking from alongside us calling is *a calling from God that we respond because we recognize it.*

Setting aside grammatical considerations, Paraclete is the spirit of Truth 'alongside us' *actively* 'calling us'. What distinguishes the Paraclete from the spirit of Truth is personification. The Paraclete is the spirit of Truth when that spirit is active alongside us actually calling our existing person. The Paraclete counsels and comforts according to the specific distinctions that make up the 'face' of Christ after the spirit, advocating the spiritual truths of Christ. This is done within us in Christ-specific terms that we recognize and sense intelligibly.

The very meaning of the word 'Paraclete' puts the Paraclete *alongside but outside our spiritual person*, as opposed to the indwelling Word of God or the Spirit of Christ or the Light all of which are inherently manifest within our spiritual person. The Paraclete may invoke or call to us, but the Paraclete does not form or generate our spiritual person. The 'actively calling us' or the invoking our spirit originates in the essence of God or Existence within us, flowing through our minds and completing itself in us. As Job in his time experienced, we can *hear* the Paraclete calling, advocating and invoking, but we see the actual Word of God or the actual spirit of Christ because we in, of and from them in our being or existing. The Light that allows us to recognize our spiritual birth and forming emanates from God. We can respond to the calling and guidance of the Paraclete by making and implementing a plan of living aligning our cognitive, emotional and social life in response. We hear the spirit of Truth calling, as sheep do the shepherd; we recognize the voice and know its meaning. As a child recognizes and knows its parent's voice, even though at the time it may not comprehend or understand fully. We are supported by the Spirit of Christ through the Paraclete, in recognizing and assenting to God's incessant calling.

Our spiritual person though is not a response to or a reflection of the calling. Our spiritual person is a distinct and specific act of God indwelling presently forming our essential spiritual person in God of and from God by way of real Christ-specific distinctions.

In regards to the spirit of Truth and the spirit of Christ, these have always been present in existence and in existing and there would be no need to send them to us as they are already within the person. Christ was putting in relief and drawing people's attention and focus away from external things and to things within our person, in order that the deaf could hear and the blind see.

John 3 is a watershed pronouncement, which sets the foundation that situates the Paraclete, the spirit of Truth relative to God indwelling forming our spiritual person according to Christ after the flesh. The passages concerning the Paraclete follow Christ's washing his disciples' feet at the last supper. The work of the Paraclete is servant work, liking washing guests feet. The Paraclete uses Truth to support and comfort. The Paraclete reveals the things of God to provide clarity for judgement and separating or washing away the unclean.

John 17 provides a glimpse of existing on the spiritual side of the watershed pronounced in John 3. We read that the saved and holy bring glory to Christ (John 17:10), rather than Christ bringing glory to them. We are Christ's purpose: that we be saved and be holy, which can only be through Christ. We also learn what eternal life is. It is not ghostly endurance of the flesh. Our personal eternal life is: "to know God" (John 17:3), which knowledge is according to Christ after the spirit forming our person spiritually. The Paraclete is our grasping of Christ's purpose.

The Light shone for Christian communities when they turned their eyes away from the familiar appeals of the carnal and carnal, and turned their eyes to the reality of Christ in their existence. This lifting of Christ in them illuminated and enlightened their spiritual forming. When Christ was active in them and when they engaged the reality of Christ in their existence, then there was formational impact that changed their existence. This was the case then and has been the case since.

The Johannine teachings and tradition stand as though to direct the disciples and apostles towards God indwelling through the spirit of Christ. The book of John differs in this regard from the synoptic Gospels. In Christ's historical life, the disciples followed "Christ after the flesh" and Christ was aware of this. After the death of Christ, it was the disciples who required a bodily resurrection of flesh because the flesh is all they had grasped and come to know. They needed to touch the resurrected body's flesh and blood wounds. The external knowledge they acquired from Christ and their external experience of the Christ they had followed had little impact on them knowing "Christ after the spirit". Searching to carnally grasp Christ, they had failed to understand the eternal existing Gospel of Christ at the core of spiritual existing and being. Because he saw this, Christ taught them about the Paraclete and indicated that the Paraclete would come to guide them in his temporal absence.

The Paraclete intelligibly presents the truths of the actual infinite and eternal mind of Christ (i.e. the spirit of Truth). Such presentations serve as 'guidance systems' in our cognitive processes, such as learning, experiential learning, discerning, decision-making, problem-solving, judgment and adaptive process. These presentations also allow us to organize information for quick reference, as well as help us to construct thought laboratories where we can trial things or conduct thought experiments in the abstract before practicing in real life.

These things that come together within us to guide us are merely reasoned presentations of general truths of spiritual things, which act to support discernment during our spiritual formation. These are not the hand of God forming us spiritually. They are not Christ after the spirit.

In the flesh and blood absence of Christ, in developing a plan to live piously the disciples would have to understand things on their own. They would have to represent within themselves what Christ had presented to them. They would have to be able to think about and know Christ from Christ's working within their persons. They would need to have what they grasp to be as close to the actual reality of Christ as possible. They would trial and test, then refine their grasp of Christ. In their reflecting and thinking, they would have to rely on the general truths of the actual indwelling God through the spirit of Christ, as well as their recollections of the historical Christ (which recollections were subsequently shared with others through stories, then committed to various texts).

We can acquire *sensory experience of the workings of Christ and of Christ within our person.* In the absence of the actual bodily presence of Christ, we can cognitively construct in the abstract a passive exemplar or model of Christ. We can also acquire sensory experience of Christ external to our person through historical reports, and reports from other people's experience of God's indwelling according to the spirit of Christ in them. These experiences can be weighed against the reality of the mind of Christ and the truths of that mind through the use of trials, experiments and reasoned demonstrations.

The Paraclete coaches us to see and hear, so that when we look and attend to the Kingdom, we can see and we can hear the Shepherd whose voice we come to know. *Out of the Paraclete comes a framework for critical thinking based on Christ: that is, Christ-specific critical thinking or discernment.*

We have sensory experience of external things of the flesh, as well as internal things of the spirit. We have sensory experience of the external Christ, but that experience and knowledge is through our bodies or flesh. It is not prima facie or immediate. We also immediately and prima facie experience things of the spirit that is: God indwelling; God indwelling in human terms; and, our spiritual union with God. It is as if the Paraclete and the spirit of Truth's urging is binding us to Christ. These experiences and knowledge are our spiritual experiences and spiritual life. We are aware of them because we 'exist' them.

We learn about Christ after the spirit because what is presented to us directly by God from our spiritual forming according to the spirit of Christ within our person is re-presented in our cognitive functioning as a model of Christ. Our source of this information and knowledge, not limited by our finite bodies, is clear and is complete. *When we seek Christ after the spirit through the Paraclete's intelligible urgings, we to recognize then grasp or catch within our person the spirit of Christ and Christ existing. As Paul put it, "...then shall I know even as also I am known ... face to face..."* Our experiences point us to the direction in which we focus, but it is our actual spiritual experience being sensed that is the basis of our knowledge of God indwelling through Christ.

Our experience of our forming in God of and from God is internally sensed by us. This is different than our sensing the intelligible urgings of the Paraclete. The Paraclete is a Christ-specific guidance system and laboratory of learning. The Paraclete is not is not the spirit of Christ. While the Paraclete is a guide and counselor to our individual person, the spirit of Christ actually forms our individual person spiritually. These are two different things and processes. *Our personal manifestation and usage of the*

Truths of spiritual things instructs us and trains our 'spiritual ears' to recognize the Shepherd, the Shepherd's work and the fruits of that work. We are connected to God indwelling in specific ways, by means of which we are fruitful branches of the existing Vine that is Christ. We actually apprehend or grasp the spirit of Christ indwelling through intuitions of existing and being and we experience that apprehension or intuitive grasping. These are real spiritual things. In our grasping we are spiritually alive or real.

We also temporally learn about Christ and God from the knowledge we gather from our external sensing, from reading texts, hearing stories, seeing activities or hearing evidence of God's presence in the world. Our source of information and knowledge external to us is limited, incoherent and incomplete. We learn about Christ after the flesh because of what is presented to us from outside our person, through history, reading, hearing witnesses, experiencing external events, etc. All these are re-presented in our cognitive functioning as a model of Christ. When we see Christ after the flesh through such a model, we only catch a possible resemblance to the spirit of Christ and to Christ, because, as Paul put it[49], "For now we see through a glass, darkly.... now I know in part..."

The disciples could passively follow an accessible but external to their person "Christ after the flesh" cognitive model and in doing so be obedient to Christ and God's commands. We need to be careful to discern and distinguish, when we are discussing the real spirit of God

[49] 1Cor13:12

or spirit of Christ and when we are discussing abstract re-presentations of Christ. Unlike indwelling the spirit of Christ or the indwelling spirit of God, the Paraclete is external to our person, though within our minds guiding and lending intelligibility to what we experience from within. Our obedience to God and Christ is honoured when we follow Christ after the flesh, in our daily living. On the other hand, through spiritual discernment and judgment coached by the Paraclete, they could and would then recognize their inner spiritual birth and forming. Christ becomes accessible in the spirit through their being in God of and from God. In recognizing and affirming the indwelling God through the spirit of Christ they actively follow Christ, from within their person. These inner spiritual experiences are sensed by us and the experience can inform the exemplar: the Paraclete or spirit of Truth within our thoughts.

We need to be careful to discern and distinguish, when we are discussing the real spirit of God or spirit of Christ and when we are discussing abstract re-presentations of Christ. Unlike indwelling the spirit of Christ or the indwelling spirit of God, the Paraclete is external to our person, though within our minds guiding and lending intelligibility to what we experience from within. Our obedience to God and Christ is honoured when we follow Christ after the flesh, in our daily living.

The Paraclete in John's Gospel

John 16 is a very interesting chapter in the book of John. It seems to pick up where Christ's discussion with Nicodemus in chapter 3 left off. After a brief reference to that kind of discussion, Christ illustrates the notion of 'letting go things of the flesh and becoming of the spirit', by considering the emotional change experienced by a woman giving birth (John 16:21-22). It is physically painful and difficult to let go the flesh, just as it is painful and difficult to give birth. One mourns and grieves living according to the world after the flesh with all its binding attachments. But with the birth comes joy for the created life and the emotions of loss become nothing. Living to the spirit spawns the creating of our spiritual person. The disciples would need to let the world, including their attachment to Christ after the flesh; and, they would grieve and mourn their loss. But with spiritual birth and life comes joy for their new life according to Christ after the spirit.

What is interesting is that Christ told them that this would not happen if he remained with them in the flesh. But, that in his absence he would send the Paraclete and the Paraclete would call them to spiritual birth and life. Significantly, the whole chapter is about the Paraclete and the Paraclete's work. It is clear throughout the whole of the book of John that the Spirit is shared by God and Christ and each of us personally. It is not the spirit that Christ will send; the spirit is already present to us therefore there is no need send it. We know that the spirit of Christ is infinite and eternal; therefore he is not sending the spirit of Christ, nor for the same reason the spirit of God. He is not sending the mind or heart of God. Christ is sending something that had not been and perhaps could not be part of his temporal ministry. Christ was sending a 'calling' or rather a caller calling alongside us in us, but not from within our spiritual person.

According to John 14:16-17, as the meal of the last supper was concluding, Christ said he would ask the father to send his followers the Paraclete, *another* advocate alongside calling the spirit (*not calling the carnal by carnal means)*. The Paraclete is the "Spirit of truth" that advocates for spiritual birth and life, by calling people alongside them. The Paraclete's calling illuminates alongside us, until the Light or spirit of Truth emanates from within us. This would include the Paraclete's 'calling', which calling is not heard by people after the flesh. The world according to the flesh, we are told cannot see hear or know and therefore cannot accept the Paraclete's urging. That world is a carnal world that senses carnal things. People after the spirit would hear, see and know this calling. They would experience the spirit's calling and the concurrent spiritual birthing and living; they would sense it spiritually and know it intelligibly. Verse 14:17 says that people know Christ because he lives "with" them, as the Paraclete, and lives "in" them as the spirit of Truth. In fact, the disciples did not know; they could not see, hear or know the Paraclete or the spirit of Truth. But, the text says, because the Paraclete or spirit of Truth "will be in" them, they will know him.

John 14:19 says that soon *the world* (i.e. the carnal world) will not see Christ any longer[50]. But then the disciples, when they have the Paraclete in them and the spirit of Truth does its work in support of spiritual birth, they will see him --- not after the flesh, but after the spirit. On that day (verse 20), they will see, hear, sense and know personal union with God indwelling forming their spiritual person according to Christ after the spirit. Christ's lesson concludes saying that because Christ lives (not after the flesh, but after the spirit), so the disciples will live after the spirit.

Verse 26 tells us that the Paraclete is also the Holy Spirit[51] and that Paraclete will be sent by the father to "teach" all things --- the things of God. When the father teaches, the teaching is sensibly and intelligibly written in our hearts and on our minds and is etched in the forming of our spirit distinctly and specifically according to Christ after the spirit. Moreover, what Christ tried to teach (and failed to teach in the flesh), the Paraclete would urge in spirit. In chapter 15:26, we find that the father sent the Paraclete through Christ. Christ is providing the Christ-specifics, which are taught to us when God indwelling etches in our person's individual heart and individual mind in our forming or generating according to the specifics Christ after the spirit. The Paraclete ignites our personal motive to prefer the spiritual things of God. The Paraclete

[50] Ironically, since then there has been an uninterrupted and failed pursuit of Christ after the flesh to assuage the needs and wants of the flesh.

[51] I.E., That is, the part that makes the Holy Spirit intelligible, calls urging our person to union with God indwelling.

illuminates and in so doing guides, reveals and leads. We are drawn to the Light that gives life and motivates us to assent to union with God.

Christ's teachings at end of the last supper described in John 14:15-20, and 26, as well as John 15:26, sets the stage for *life without Christ in the flesh.* The Paraclete, the spirit of Truth is an advocate preaching the Gospel of Christ from within. In so doing, this Advocate proves that those who are in the flesh of and from the flesh are "wrong about sin and righteousness". This had been demonstrated in both the establishment's response to Christ and the inability of the disciples to grasp Christ's message. Christ leaves this world and goes to the Father to be seen only in a person's actual spiritual forming according to Christ after the spirit. The Paraclete's urging and the Spirit's Truth are not in words or messages. They are in an urge to be formed in Truth of and from Truth, which Truth is Christ distinct and specific. Chapter 16 is directed to our actual becoming and being, not to abstract discussion, rules or laws. The urging is for us to form spiritually in the distinct and specific fashion that is Christ.

According to the text, if Christ is before us in the flesh we do not see, hear or know him in the spirit. In verse 16:8, it clearly says that unless Christ is gone in the flesh and is no longer externally present to our body; the Paraclete will not come to people. If people are looking for Christ in the flesh external to their individual person, they will not see Christ in the spirit internal to their person. People had been and were waiting for a carnal Messiah to carnally deliver them from carnal tribulations. But when the Messiah came and proclaimed the Word of God --- the message was rejected outright or not understood. If the external, temporal Christ of flesh goes, then the Paraclete will come calling with a voice that we can spiritually sense, spiritually recognize and hear, then spiritually know and understand; and so, spiritually respond in heart and mind. The calling is a true calling to Truth itself. The calling is not only a call but also an explication of the Word indwelling forming our spiritual person according to Christ after the spirit.

The Spirit of Christ's nature through the Paraclete spirits (sparks or invokes) us to recognize, hear, see, and understand the laws of God written in our hearts and on our minds. These laws, in human terms, are the accessible reality of the mind of Christ, present in us here and now. There is one true Paraclete, who is common to all and serves each person individually. The Spirit of Christ through the Paraclete, like an athletic coach incites us to optimal spiritual action. By invoking and calling us, while alongside us, the Spirit of Christ through the Paraclete is our supporter, our vested counsellor, a comforter to us, indeed a proactive advocate in our seeking and finding true salvation and holiness. The invocations of the Spirit of Christ through the Paraclete, alongside us call for us to recognize the present spirit and mind of Christ within us. The Spirit of Christ through the Paraclete supports what comes into us when we follow Christ, but also what forms in us as the Word within shapes our minds and hearts. The critical pathways of the Paraclete are Christ-specific ways.

In the Gospels of scripture, it is clear that Christ was temporally "alongside" the disciples and the people in the flesh. While temporally alongside them, Christ was "actively calling them". The recorded outcomes were not encouraging. Christ recognized that the carnal world's carnal forces were moving to destroy him. It was time to prepare for his 'replacement' and to teach the disciples how his spiritual ministry would continue in his carnal flesh and blood temporal absence. God provides in creation an immaterial, temporally accessible presence in the spirit of Truth.

The Spirit of Christ through the Paraclete actively calling alongside us is not the Spirit of Truth or the mind of Christ as these are in themselves. Through the Paraclete, the spirit of Truth coalesces within as the sensible and intelligible presence of Christ, so configured that we hear its calling alongside us, as well as know and understand its active working within us. As Christ had been alongside the disciples and the people calling, in his bodily absence the Spirit of Christ through the Paraclete would be alongside calling them and us. The Paraclete does not respond to this call, we do. We respond through God's grace utilizing the Light and Word within. We utilize the reality which is infinite and eternal spirit of Christ, which when lifted up: lifts us. When Christ teaches the disciples about the Paraclete, he does not explicitly say or suggest that the Paraclete is new. He does say that he is sending the Paraclete to them. The Paraclete it would have been 'new' to them.

Christ was providing his disciples with a change of direction for their 'attending faculties'. If we persist in darkness and avoid the Light, we do so even though the Paraclete calls us to hear, to see and experience spiritual Truth. We are created with the Spirit of Christ, and with the Paraclete alongside us calling us. Even if we ignore that calling, the calling remains present in our existence.

In coming to an understanding of the Paraclete and

the Spirit of Truth, we find that both these are eternal and infinite things or truths. In Christ's impending temporal absence, the disciples would make use of the Paraclete to guide, advocate for, and comfort them as they interacted with the world about them and as they interacted with the spirit of Christ within them.

The disciples had not yet received the message of Christ; they would need the Spirit of Truth once Christ was gone. The failure to receive the message of Christ's ministry in the flesh, called for the revealing of an enduring influence from God. It called for Christ to speak about and teach about the Paraclete (John 15:26-27, 16:12-15). In John 14:17 the Spirit of Truth is spoken of as present. John 15:26-27and 16:12-15, speaks of the Paraclete as, yet to come. It was *yet to come to them at that time*, because up to that time they had Christ bodily before them in the flesh, but were frequently spiritually deaf, blind and ignorant despite Christ's ministry to them. While Christ was carnally present and they carnally followed him, they would not look within to find their experience of own salvation. They remained attached to the world after the flesh. The coming support of the Paraclete was for the sake of disciples, who being carnally oriented were not able to bear more at the time. Through the existential urging of the Paraclete's calling to ultimate significance, meaning and purpose, they disciples would find their way in due course and respond to God indwelling according to Christ after the spirit. In the absence of the incarnate temporal Christ, the spirit of Truth in us evidences the reality of Christ, here and now. Presenting that incendiary evidence, calls us and we respond. We look and find an existing activating presence not bound by time or space.

The Paraclete does not act in our salvation and holiness. The disciples' failure to receive the Gospel of

Christ at the time, along with the temporal death of Christ, required the Paraclete come to be at the fore of their persons. The Paraclete as the explicating, discernible spirit of God in us calls us. It guides us and supports us alongside our person as we proceed to discern the reality that is Christ. This reality was present before the temporal birth of Christ, and remains present after the temporal death of Christ. We tune into it by discerning Christ and following Christ, here and now. The spirit of Truth reveals to us the true spirit, mind, and heart of Christ. It shows us the specifics of God incarnate. Through the spirit, mind, and heart of Christ, we act, we become, and we are. Our spirit, mind, and hearts form Christ-like. We become and are Christ-like, that is to say just, righteous, merciful and loving.

If we look at the life of Christ as told in the Gospels, we find that Christ used the Spirit of Truth. As a person in the flesh but not of and from the flesh, he called up and made use of the spirit of Truth and gave voice to the Paraclete. Christ was no stranger to these two influences of God. The Spirit of Christ through the Paraclete has supported, advocated for and comforted the Godly. The Spirit of Christ through the Paraclete helps us as we reach for, find, grasp and hold the mind of Christ before us. It guides us as we follow Christ in spirit and in deed. We have as strong and spiritually powerful an influence to comfort and guide us as for example, Isaiah and Jeremiah did. All the support given to Christ, God gives to us. The Spirit of Christ through the Paraclete helps us navigate uncharted waters. It is not that we can simply reach out and catch God. Neither God nor the Spirit of God is comprehensible to us. We can only grasp God through human terms; we only grasp God through Christ.

We cannot follow what we do not know or

understand. To love God, a person must experience and must intelligibly know God in one way or another. To love others, a person must experience and must intelligibly know God in others in one way or another. In Christ are the specifics that we can within our own limitations, reach for, grasp, and take on for ourselves. We have the spirit of God and the Word of God welling up within us --- "spiriting us" as it were. Our spiritual understanding is in our spiritual forming according to Christ after the spirit. Our experience and intelligible knowledge of God and of God in other people, is given to us in our spiritual forming which enables us to love God and love others.

We have the spirit of God in us. At the same time, we are separated from God by the infinite and eternal nature of God being 'housed' in our temporal and finite body. The housing is either a binding snare flesh or it is the conveyance of the personal spiritual seed within us. To be Truth to our essential person, the spirit of Truth must be personally intelligible to us one way or another. The spirit of Truth is intelligible to us because God's Truth is made distinct and specific to our person's knowledge and understanding in human terms. The encounter is not mystical, it is sensible and intelligible: we know our union with God indwelling according to Christ-specific distinctions that *by God's grace we recognize and respond to according to our person.*

We have the Spirit of Truth in us and with us by way of the Paraclete, and this light allows us to understand God to an extent. The spirit of Truth is not carnal. It is not an object of our senses nor is it, itself, an imaginative or cognitive construct. It is not a creature of our personal experience.

The spirit of Truth and the Paraclete are two

powerful influences that guide, comfort, and enlighten us. They are alongside us calling us. They help us. We cannot be Paraclete-like. We cannot be spirit of Truth-like. We can be Christ-like. It is in our spiritual nature to be Christ-like and through Christ be 'in God of and from God', no longer separated, but atoned. Christ is specific. Christ exists in human terms. We can take on the specifics of Christ.

Recognizing and responding to the Paraclete, and affirming the Truth, we can passively put on Christ after the flesh. In so doing, it remains that what we are doing is only an echo. It is an echo that can point us to the Word by means of which we actively put on the whole of Christ in spirit. In doing so, we spiritually become what God calls us to be – God's image in life. Unlike the Spirit of Truth and the Paraclete inside us and alongside us, the spirit and mind of Christ is not alongside us but is *in us and within us* --- the heart of what we are. While the Paraclete with truth and power is alongside us, Christ is in us and we are in Christ. Individually and personally, we are in Christ; and Christ is in us individually and personally. We do not and we cannot follow the Paraclete or the Spirit of Truth, though these influence us as we formationally-follow Christ. As a reality, Christ is not limited to me. Christ is present to each individual personally, but also common to all individual persons, who reach for, find, grasp, and possess the reality of Christ.

Christ is not in our carnal bodies or in our carnal minds as an object apart from our essential person. Christ will not be discerned in brain waves or neuroscientific measures. Those are 'sounds' of the 'wind', they are not the wind. The cause and effect of investing cognitive functioning does not and will not speak to the existential 'cause' of the spiritual cognition or intuition. The science of objects of the flesh, external to our person is not the science of 'objects' of the spirit internal to our person. Confusing the flesh and the spirit, people do turn to such objects of the flesh. For example, in pursuit of Christ after the flesh people *were given to believe* and did believe that they were physically ingesting the substance of God, based on the now discarded notion of transubstantiation. People often talk as though the indwelling God or Christ is in our bodies or minds but *apart* from our person. We cannot 'talk' to the indwelling God or Christ in us. Christ is in our person, and our person is in Christ. This we can sensibly and intelligibly experience and from our experience intuit, but talking to the indwelling God or Christ would be tantamount to talking to ourselves. All the same such discussion can be beneficial in several ways. But, 'talking' to the indwelling Christ implies Christ is not truly 'in' us but is actually outside our person as an object we can talk to. Unlike the indwelling God or Christ, the Paraclete is only alongside us and can 'talk' or call to us. Our communion with God is in our spiritual union with God: in God of and from God according to Christ. *Our union with God is in communion (i.e. what we existentially have and hold in common) with Christ.*

Christ came with a message. The world did not hear it. It did not see him. Christ was not received and was not understood. Spiritual forming is caused by God indwelling. Spiritual forming does not follow from and is not caused by Christ's temporal incarnation in the flesh in history 2,000 years ago, as person existing outside our persons. Nevertheless, the message became flesh and dwelt among us as an object external to us. It further becomes flesh and dwells among us in abstract texts and stories. In his time, Christ articulated what the image of God in human terms was meant to be. The message was not heard or seen or understood in carnal terms.

That was then. Now, we find the message not in history but existing within our person. In Christ, we can recognize what we should be spiritually. In the mind of Christ, we have the parameters and distinctions of our spiritual minds. In the heart of Christ, we have what our hearts aspire to be spiritually.

In John's Gospel, people kept themselves focussed on the carnal miracles and signs. They did not see past those things. They stayed focussed on a carnal Messiah, they did not see past their worldly needs and carnal aspirations. Christ knew his temporal presence was a temporary presence. Christ also knew his temporal presence had little effect or people's spiritual birth or living. Like any human, Christ wanted live in the flesh. Christ never chose carnal death. When the choice was spiritual life or carnal death, Christ chose life. The cost of bodily or carnal life is spiritual death; Christ chose spiritual life and bodily or carnal death. Christ saw people focussed on external things. He saw them focused on carnal signs, wonders, and miracles. He saw them focussed on his temporal person, wanting temporal triumph over their temporal enemies and over bodily or carnal death.

Like the Paraclete before him and the Paraclete after him, the temporal historical Christ called people from alongside them. He was also calling from within them; most failed to hear. Many were called, few followed. Those who followed struggled in bondage of carnal, bodily or carnal snares. Fear and anxiety of bodily or carnal, physical death continues to have dominion over many individuals who do not let go the carnal things of this world to embrace the spiritual things of God in order to find and embrace salvation and holiness.

In his last temporal hours, Christ taught the

disciples, that in his absence, with his message in hand and with them holding him high, the Paraclete, who would spiritually guide them 'alongside' them, would supportively help them ambulate the way of salvation and holiness. People would use the Paraclete to follow him when Christ in his absence, was no longer present in the flesh. They would turn their eyes away from the temporal Christ and focus on the eternal Christ. The Spirit of Christ through the Paraclete would support them and urge them to discern the ever-present reality, which is Christ: to choose that reality, to be in it and of it. Christ told his disciples that he would not stay in this temporal world. In his absence, they would be given access to the Spirit of Christ through the Paraclete, to approach in Christ's name or ask in Christ's name. They would be heard on their own, without Christ asking on their behalf. They would use the Spirit of Christ through the Paraclete to learn what they had not yet grasped about Christ. Having put on the spirit of Christ and acquiring greater understanding of Christ, they would hear, see, and understand the spiritual things of God.

Christ was not satisfied that his disciples had 'overcome the world'. The concern expressed was that the followers would go astray and be scattered by the forces of this world. In John's Gospel Christ says he would ask the Father to send the Paraclete to support the disciples in his temporal absence. The Father would make them aware of the Paraclete and its role for them. The Paraclete would be with them and would be alongside them calling them to the Truth of the Word in them.

Over hundreds and hundreds of years, the Church infused itself with worldliness. This was not acceptable. For example, the Protestant dissenters of the 16th and 17th centuries looked past the Church of their day to directly approach God to find justice and righteousness. Luther retreated to scripture that had stood secure over time. In denying the worldliness of the Church by anchoring himself to scripture, it was not Luther's intention to deny us the Spirit of Christ through the Paraclete in our time, and to deny the Spirit of Christ through the Paraclete as given in John's Gospel. In our time, the pursuit of knowledge of scripture in itself is loosening the textual anchor that scripture was thought to be in the 16th and 17th centuries. Those who would study the meaning of scripture in terms of the texts, stories and histories of scripture alone, leave us explanations that confuse more than clarify.

We have not been given the Paraclete so we could perform carnal wonders, do carnal wonders, or speak of carnal things wondrously. All manner of people do these things across the entire planet and over the centuries. The Paraclete is given to us so we can be in God's ultimate existential significance Truth, and so that Truth can be in our being and existing. If there are carnal signs and wonders and if there are carnal miracles, these are good in themselves. However, we should not mistake the carnal for the spiritual. The spirit of Truth has always been with people, but alone it does not suffice. The presence of Christ activates the spirit of Truth for us so we can utilize its guidance, its leading, and its support. In the absence of the temple instruments, we use the spirit of Truth to engage and relate to God in our daily lives.

The Paraclete and the Work of God

The Paraclete points to the Light within and to our spiritual forming. The Paraclete helps to put us into a place of experiencing, sensing and intuiting our spiritual generation. When we sense and know that we are saved, then what? What is the purpose, meaning or significance of Christ forming us in God of and from God? We are not saved to be idle worshipers or remain in constant prayer. Union with God does not call for perpetual bliss and celebration of union. Union with the God of Christ calls for service to others. Like Christ before us, we are saved, to do the work of God. This was the lesson of Christ washing the disciples' feet during the third Passover festival. This was also the reason for Christ laying out the role of the Paraclete in John 21. The Paraclete's invocation calls for each individual to personally become Christ-like and in doing so, assume Christ's mantle to do the work of God.

The Paraclete leads us towards Christ. In our spiritual forming we are spiritually atoned or reconciled; we affirm God and our self in God. The world we live in remains at odds with our personal existential atonement and reconciliation. The Paraclete, the spirit of Truth continues calling, advocating, invoking and comforting, while we, possessing a spirit forming according to Christ, turn to the world in which we live, aspiring to reconcile it as far as possible. In being born from above, it is we who through Paraclete learn how to arrange the world so that it is atoned or reconciled to Christ after the spirit. Our temporal actions are framed by justice, righteousness and mercy, as well as forgiveness and love. We are counselled, guided and comforted by the Paraclete, still alongside us calling us to do God's work.

We are saved to serve. It is that simple. But, history demonstrates how people undertake to serve is not necessarily how Christ served. God moves within us, so that we do the work of God outside us. The very last thing Christ did (in some form or other) according to the book of John was to feed his disciples. He *served* them. Christ provided an example --- the disciples merely ate and where satisfied to be fed. After feeding them, Christ asked Peter whether Peter loved Christ more than other people loved Christ. Peter said yes. Peter's yes indicates he had not grasped Christ's Gospel. Christ provided guidance by instructing Peter to do God's work by feeding Christ's sheep. When asked whether Peter loved Christ, the answer should have involved a love that involves "feeding the sheep" and washing the feet of others. Two more times, Christ posed the question. Two more times, Peter said yes, but not 'Yes. *I will feed your sheep*'. Both times, Christ advocated for Peter to feed Christ's sheep.

Peter's responses (including his question about what will happen to the 'disciple Jesus loved') did not indicate that Peter understood what it means for him to 'love Christ'. It is not at clear that even after having be invoked by Christ 3 times to affirm what it means to love Christ, that Peter had at all grasped what Godly love is. Indeed, Christ goes on to say that while Peter had served Peter, Peter's life would change and he would no longer follow his self-service. Peter followed Christ to meet Peter's self-serving carnal goals and aspirations. The Christ Covenant is to work to "feed the sheep" that belong to Christ. Peter would go where he did not want to go: Peter would be led by service to others who belong to Christ. In future, Peter would be bound to Christ and he would go where Christ leads him, not where 'Peter after the flesh' might wish to go. This serves Christ's purpose. The notion that this teaching is a temporal foretelling of the kind of carnal death

Peter would have, does not serve Christ's purpose or mission.

Christ says the Paraclete will prove the world wrong. The Paraclete, the spirit of Truth parses the things of the flesh and the things of the spirit. The Paraclete will parse and separate the things of the flesh and the things of the spirit within us. The Paraclete will make the spirit of Christ *known* to the disciples. According to Christ the Paraclete only *re-present* what belongs to Christ and will guide into all truth. The Paraclete is of and from the Truth but is not the Truth. The Spirit of Christ utilizes the Paraclete to help us discern the things of heaven including our being spiritually formed into the Kingdom of God and then our using our birth right in the Kingdom of God to live according to the spirit of Christ in this world. The report concerning the Paraclete in John 16:7-16 concerns having counsel and guidance in dealing with sin, righteousness and judgement which are cognitive acts. The Paraclete takes the place of the temporal, flesh and blood Christ. Though acting as a *temporal and accessible* counsellor and guide, the Paraclete's call is actually eternal. This is not about being saved, but it concerns the way to salvation and the way back from salvation to living in this world

The Prophets and the Paraclete

In John 3, we find Christ saying the Spirit 'listeth were it wills'. The infinite and eternal 'comings and goings' of God are beyond our finite comprehensions limited by temporality. All the same, we are in God and God is in us. We share an actual existing. From our shared existing, we have prima facie, an ineffable and inarticulate but deep existential experience of union with God as well as an *unintelligible* awareness of God and knowledge of God.

Our awareness of our union with God is the Light within illuminating our spiritual existing and being. This experience becomes *intelligible*, when through the Word we put on the mind of Christ so that the distinctions and specifics that make up the mind of Christ also make our mind. In putting on the mind of Christ, God's Truth is common to our person and to other persons who are born from above according to the specifics of Christ.

In created human existence, the *Spirit of Christ* through the Paraclete has always been alongside us calling us, urging us to discern the distinctions and specifics of the things of God. Some people did tune in to the Spirit of Christ through the Paraclete and others did not tune in and did not respond. Those who found and grasped the truth of God and Christ reached to the depths of the spirit and discerned a measure of truth. We can find these glimmers in the prophets, for example Isaiah and Jeremiah, which allowed them to articulate Truth in some measure. In the texts of scriptures, the infinite and eternal get mixed in with the mundane and worldly. While addressing the worldly needs and wants of the human condition as they found it, prophets also let out rays of light whose truths have stood the tests of time. The voice of God steadfastly powerful, was heard and was spoken by those who heard the Paraclete's calling, in the midst of the clamour and noise of the trappings and doings of the temporal world that they tried to make sense of.

While holding onto the desires and wants of their times, the prophets aspired for attainable hope of spiritual salvation however unclear. With the support of the Spirit of Christ through the Paraclete, they journeyed towards God. Perhaps unbeknownst, they found the reality that is Christ, and made the journey in just, righteous and merciful ways that were Christ-specific. Their knowledge and understanding was enlightened, as far as possible for them. We look and see that their yearning was given some satisfaction, caught up in the twists and turnings of their temporal world, coloured and surrounded by confusion and errant pathways.

Like the ancient prophets, we too embrace and use the Spirit of Christ through the Paraclete, the spirit of Truth to respond to and understand spiritual things. In the terms of the Christ Covenant inherent in Existence and in Existing the spirit of Truth goes from calling alongside us to being within us, no longer calling but manifesting; from guiding and counselling to spiriting us; and from advocating on our behalf to presenting us as a Truth offering.

The Spirit of Christ, the Christ and the Paraclete

From personal experience we learn that there is Truth; and, that Truth grounds our spiritual existing in temporal tabernacles in eternity. It separates what is transitory about us from what is not transitory. Truth is then an important instrument for people who aspire to personally exist as much as possible in eternity with ultimate existential significance, meaning and purpose. How do we access this tool and how do we learn to use it? We acquire knowledge of Truth and the positive or affirming application of Truth from personal experience, personal sensing and personal knowing. Our personal experience of Truth can be passive or active; it can be random or ordered. The truth of God through Christ is active and ordered according to Christ after the spirit or God indwelling in human terms. Immediate and direct experience, sense and knowledge of God and Christ are in our existing or being in God of and from God indwelling through the spirit of Christ. Our experience of God is made intelligible through the spirit of Christ. There is order in things according to the spirit of Christ. While Christ atones or reconciles our spirit, we reconcile our temporal carnal living to Christ after the spirit. In our temporal reconciled existing or being is our response to our experience of Truth according to Christ after the spirit.

It is Christ who allows us to relate to God in human terms. In precipitating and putting on the mind and spirit of Christ, we incarnate Christ by having Christ in us forming us. We do not do the same with the Paraclete or the truth represented in the Paraclete. Our end and purpose is not just to passively see, hear, sense or understand Christ, passively follow and do remotely do as Christ would do; our spiritual end and purpose is to actively become and be

Christian in the spirit of Christ forming us spiritually and to fully be so while in the flesh.

Christ was not twice born. He did not have to form his person according to the spirit of Christ; it was already in that form. Christ did not require counsel, guidance or comfort from the Paraclete. Christ would not have used it as the disciples or we would need to use it. The image of Christ 'receiving the spirit', for example like the dove descending on Christ in John 1:32 is to provide people with a bodily or carnal example in temporal time and space terms, illustrating in an easily relatable fashion that there are two aspects to living a physical bodily or carnal aspect, and a spiritual aspect. In reality, Christ was never without the spirit of God or the Spirit of Christ.

The mind of Christ is the truth of God in sensible, intelligible human terms. This is the only means by which we can make any sense of and have any understanding of God. The properties of the mind of Christ is shared or held in common by those whose mind is manifest according to Christ after the spirit. These properties are common to all minds that are manifest according to Christ after the spirit. The properties are real in the individual person; the commonalities are abstractions or cognitive constructs. In this life we do not live alone and in isolation.

The properties of Christ are manifest in our personal properties and our existential knowledge of these properties is in our actually being. In actively, actually being or existing according to Christ after the spirit, *the Spirit Christ precipitates distinctly and specifically in our person, our mind, our spirit and heart*. While this happens to us personally, Christ actually lives through other people existing or being according to Christ after the spirit or existing or being in God of and from God.

Towards the very end of John's Gospel, the resurrected Christ *carnally* breathed on his disciples telling them to receive the Holy Spirit. Why did Christ do this? Why 'carnally' appear a week after his carnal death, then breathe on them and then tell them to receive the Spirit? They were fearful and hiding behind locked doors. Many times Christ had told them that the spirit of Truth was in them. He had often said that God was in him and he was in God and in them as well. They had the Spirit in them but they remained grounded in the inadequate passive understanding from carnal things. They continued to be drawn by the carnal. In John 20:19-29, Christ did two things: first, he carnally breathed on them and then taught them the meaning of that illustration.

When Christ was to leave them carnally and would no longer appear as a carnal, temporal person. He told the disciples that in his absence God would provide the Paraclete to guide them. In his carnal absence, they would 'receive' what they already had, but had not to that point discerned. Yet, a week had passed since Christ's death and they had not yet received the Paraclete and had no strength or comfort alongside them calling them. It seems they kept waiting for some external carnal sign or miracle of the flesh. Because Christ carnally breathed on them, they appeared to 'receive' the Paraclete. The enactment points them inwards to help move them to look for and find a cognitively constructed mental exemplar of Christ then utilize it in judgement, decision making, and comprehending. If not the disciples, then *the audience of the book of John* required a more tangible or mundane way of grasping birth from above. The author of this Gospel understood his audience of that time. By breathing on the disciples and telling them to receive the Spirit, the audience had a means of understanding, even if 'through a glass darkly' that they had something within that could help them. Immediately following that scene, Christ carnally proves to Thomas that he was present in order for Thomas to believe. Christ teaches them that those who have faith without carnal evidence are blessed and the way to the Paraclete is not obstructed by external things.

Christ could have left us laws, as Moses did. Christ could have left us scriptures[52], as the prophets and the Gospel and Epistle writers did. Christ did not. Christ could have left us rites, rituals, ceremonies, acts of religiosity, or written and signed covenants, as many others have. Christ left us none of these things. What Christ did leave ***for me***, is the Spirit of Christ through the Paraclete 'alongside me calling me' today so that I hear, see and understand God's Truth, recognizing and finding God face to face. Christ provides the Paraclete to all people. Just as the disciples had tremendous difficulty letting go the things of the flesh that they valued of the world after the flesh, everyone is challenged to let go what they have come to value of and from the flesh, with all their seductive illusions.

---

[52] On reflection, Scriptures seemed to play a modest role in Christ's ministry, which is demonstrated by the meagre references to scriptures in the Gospels. Altogether, there are 22 references to scriptures in the entire Gospels combined, a number are duplications. There are 3 references in Mathew, 3 in Mark, 4 in Luke and 12 in John. When we review the references, it is clear Christ and the writers of the gospels knew and referred to the scriptures. The priests and people at hand also knew the scriptures referenced by Christ and the writers. Significantly Christ never says that any of his words come from scripture, he says his words are not his own, they are from God and his experience of God. Christ left us the Paraclete to help us discern the spirit of Truth. Others left us the scriptures. Christ did not leave us carnal words on material paper; Christ did not leaves us 'dead' things; Christ left us access to the living Word, that is Christ left us Light and spiritual life. We have the Paraclete, the Truth and the Word in us. It is for us to present the mind and spirit of Christ to ourselves and to one another. Truth does not diminish the importance of the scriptures; it highlights the importance of the Spirit.

Revealing the Christ Covenant Over Three Passovers

Introduction

We are spiritually made up of the stuff of God's essence. In Being and Existing, God affirms existence as we spiritually experience and know it. There is inherent in each of us, (and in God), an 'affirming' or an affirmation of existence forming us according to Christ after the spirit. This is the nature or essence of existence. We know it because we exist. We are spiritual bound to God in a kind of existential covenant rooted in our essential existing in Existence and Existing. The distinctions and specifics that make up Christ are the 'terms' of this existential covenant. The existential covenant is a Christ-covenant involving God and our individual spiritual person. The covenant in our person's heart, spirit and mind is a living Covenant in God, of and from God. It is rooted in our being, and is realized in our becoming. It is real. While we exist, this reality is within our grasp. While we live, we can grasp it, hold it, and possess it. God's covenant with us is fulfilled when we, in following Christ, do God's work.

This covenant relationship is the heart of Christ's messages throughout the Gospel according to John. It is how we embrace God forming us through the indwelling spirit of Christ and it is our means of holiness. Christ's work is to engage us and form us; our work is to actively follow Christ so that Christ forms us. For our part, being formed spiritually we are doing the work of God through our living.

The teachings of Christ in John's Gospel imply a personal covenant between God, Christ, and each individual person. The Covenant unites people, binding their person into union with God through Christ. The Passover Feasts are events that remember God passing by the Hebrews' homes, when God destroyed the first born of Egypt. In the Exodus storey, the Hebrew homes were sheltered and protected from death. Among the numerous important descriptions of events, teachings and instructions in the book of John, the writers tell about three Passover feasts attended by Christ in Jerusalem. The writers themselves were not present; they did not see, hear or witness what was said or what happened. How did they know about or understand those things they did not experience? Did they add notions and nuances to the texts to further their personal understanding or to help their readers better understand the three messages from the three events? We do not know and we will not ever know. In our reading of their accounts we should ask what should their accounts demonstrate or illustrate given our actual experience of Christ after the spirit, here and now. First and foremost the written texts ought to affirm the rest of the book of John, and the rest of the book of John should affirm the accounts in the texts. Overall, we know what the message of the book of John is: it is written in our minds and on our hearts; it is given to us when we put on Christ and when we take on the mind of Christ. This standard is what illuminates our reading of the texts. What those carnal writers intended to carnally share with our carnal eyes and ears, is relevant but not critical. What is critical is the Light within revealing the indwelling Word of God to enable us to comprehend the scriptures.

John tells of three Passover Feast times in his Gospel[53]. The Christ Covenant is explicated during these Passover Feast time passages. Surrounding these three touchstones in the Gospel, Christ teaches how as he is lifted up in us, God passes over our bodies of flesh and into our own spirit, forming us according to the spirit of Christ. Incorporating Christ, we are dwellings for God. Christ's actions and teachings around three different Passover Feast times sets down

1) the means of 'exodus' from carnal bondage and carnal captivity to the world according to the flesh --- the world external to our spiritual person,
2) personally incorporating Christ spiritually as the means of accessing and acquiring spiritual life, and,
3) models of God's work and doing God's work in our existing or actually being, which point us towards recognition of the things of God and our spiritual forming within our essential person.

People engage God through incorporating Christ or having Christ embedded in their existence forming them. We need

[53] See John 2:13, 6:4 and 13:1. It is noteworthy that in substance it is the second Passover Feast time in John that parallels the single Passover Feast time in the other Gospels' Passover Feast time. John further utilizes a third Passover time that differs in form and substance, but aligns in timing with the synoptic gospels.

to existentially ingest or incorporate Christ, as both the bread of life from heaven that nourishes the spirit (6:35) so that our personal spirit does not hunger or thirst; and, as the living water (7:37 and 4:10-13) that wells up within, to nourish our spiritual being.

The first Passover time[54] in John's Gospel is associated with Christ clearing the temple of the means of carrying on the carnal rites, rituals, ceremonies and sacrifices associated with communing or relating to God. These were carnal tools mimicking atonement, reconciliation and holiness. The rituals and ceremonies of sacrificing of animals, the burning of incense and offerings, were in place so people could engage God in relationship through those carnal offerings. Christ was really clearing out traditional carnal ways of relating to God. He goes further and suggests the stone temple, in all its majesty, could be torn down with no consequence. In effect, Christ implies that God does not dwell locally in the temple. Indeed, tear down the temple, as Christ had 'torn down' the sellers of the means of carnal offerings and carnal sacrifices. In not so many words, the lesson is not to let the rituals, rites or ceremonies obstruct our relating to God; not to let the temple priests stand between ourselves and God. God is not contained within the temple walls, outside our selves. Clear out the temple. Then, tear it down. Christ sets aside the carnal church of his day. He sets aside its rituals, rites and ceremonies. He set aside the worldly, carnal means of communing with God. Isaiah wrote of God's repugnance for empty burnt offerings and sacrifices. Christ went past words to action and cleared the temple, so we could undertake true offerings of personal justice, righteousness, mercy and love to directly commune with God.

[54] All four Gospels describe the clearing of the temple event.

The clearing of the temple and the tearing down of the temple metaphors are entirely analogous to personal cleansing of a body or destroying by tearing down a body. The cleansing metaphor holds. As the temple was cleared of the sellers and money changers of carnal things, so our person is cleared and cleansed of the trafficking of carnal things. In regards to tearing down the temple, what is it that is being torn down? Is it the stones or the building, as some scoffers assumed? If so, then it would be a person's body that would be torn down and destroyed. Some writers of scripture assumed that and for example suggested that the tearing down of the temple was analogous to Christ's body being torn and destroyed by crucifixion. They presumed or framed that Christ saying he would raise it in three days, was analogous to his bodily resurrection three days after the crucifixion. This view is very much a carnal view, focussed on the body as a temple. But, in fact there is no need for Christ to have a body that is torn down and destroyed. The analogy is of temple to us as persons, not to Christ as a person. The temple is like our carnal person, not like our carnal body. It is our carnal person that needs to be torn down and destroyed and it is our spiritual person who will be lifted and raised. It was the character or persona of the temple that Christ would tear down, because the temple, like many church structures, had become an idol. The part of our person that is in bondage and captive to the world after the flesh is not our body, but *the carnal person tabernacled* in that body. It is our carnal person who is trafficking in carnal things, who needs cleansing. The begetting of our spiritual person is also the tearing down and destruction of our carnal person. The body, while it lives, tabernacles or houses a carnal person or a spiritual person --- these do not co-exist.

God was in the temple that Christ said he could tear down; God was outside that temple as well. Also, God would be in the temple that would be raised up. What then was so objectionable about the temple that Christ would want to tear it down? It was not the stones or the building per se. The temple, as 'church' structures sometimes do, had become an idol serving its keepers. It was this idol and idolizing that was offensive and subversive to Christ's Gospel message. Christ would tear down the idol and raise up or lift up the Truth. The analogy fits. The spirit of Christ tears down our carnal person when Christ is being lifting up in the emergence of our spiritual person and our essential selves lift Christ within our person.

God lives through Christ in us and amongst us, not in the temple. We can find God in us directly: no ceremonies, no rituals, and no intermediary priests. Indeed, if the temple were to be torn down (as it had been and as it was going to be), its absence would not be significant or of real spiritual consequence. How long does it take to raise the true temple of God? Three days. In mere days, we seek God and finding God we pursue Godliness. The Spirit of God wells up within, while the Spirit of Christ shapes our spirit and forms our mind, not in decades of years, but in mere days, indeed in minutes.

The first Passover Feast event talks about tearing down the stone temple constructed by carnal people and living instead in a temple constructed by God, which we can enter and become part of. Death cannot enter into this house of God, in which we are sheltered and protected.

Ours is not an exodus from the tyranny of a pharaoh or another people. We are captive to a carnal world. We are held in our carnal snares. As long as we are held captive, we are bound in a situation in which we are separated from God. At our 'Passover time', we are not passed over. God finds us and passes into our innermost selves. We move from looking for God outside ourselves in temples of stone, to seeking and finding God within ourselves. There is a place for the carnal temple or church. There are places for carnal ceremonies, rites and rituals. However, these places do not house God. These things are outside us, designed for us to use for our purposes. We may use churches and priests today. We may still use carnal, flesh and blood ceremonies and rites as aids. We no longer confuse real personal communing with God incarnate, through the reality of Christ, with any carnal substitute.

The second Passover time event in John's Gospel is associated with the bread of life and with living waters, with nourishment of the spirit. It is associated with 'eating the flesh' of Christ and 'living water' (i.e. the blood) of Christ. While those around Christ concerned themselves with carnal things, Christ was speaking of spiritual things. Our spirit is formed and nourished through Christ, here and now, by our actual existential ingesting or incorporating Christ into our existing. Incorporating Christ in our actual forming removes the separation between God and us.

This actual temporal presence of the Eternal dwelling in us is God working through our flesh and blood, to form and mature our emergent spirit into eternity. Our spirit encounters God and while incorporating the spirit and mind of Christ as our essential self, God gives our spirit life. Our eternal spirit is fed while we live in this temporal world, in this life. The spirit is not transformed magically. The bread of life does not feed the carnal body, as everyday bread does. The bread of life, while we exist carnally, forms and feeds the spirit in our lifetime. Salvation is secured in our present living and holiness is accomplished in our present life. Our spirit is nourished by the spirit of God in us as the mind of Christ is precipitating or incarnating within ourselves.

The third Passover time event in John's Gospel is associated with serving others. Christ washed the disciples' soiled feet, as a very ordinary everyday offering. God's purpose is to serve people. Christ doing God's work, served people. Christ accomplishing God's work, served people. Christ serves the disciples by washing their soiled feet, to illustrate what 'eating the flesh' of Christ and 'drinking the blood' of Christ means in action. (In Luke's Gospel, Christ says he is among us as one who serves. He is not among us to be served.) Those who follow Christ; those who believe Christ into their being; those who do as Christ would do; do and accomplish God's work, in serving others. Those who love God love others and serve others. (This point was make above while commenting on Christ's last lesson to Peter (John 21:15-22). In the absence of doing God's work, we are neither saved nor holy. We do the work of God first for our love of God and also for our love of others.

Christ clears the obstacles we cling to, that keep us from personally relating to God directly. Christ calls for the emergence of 'people' temples in which God is manifest. He establishes himself as the reality required to connect be in union with God. By incorporating Christ our personal spirit matures into spiritual life. We feed on the eternal and present Christ, here and now. God feeds our spirit here and now and gives us life from above. Christ demonstrates what it means to feed on God within, by doing and accomplishing the distinct and specific work of God. The Christ Covenant is a promise of spiritual forming between

God and us, as God's spiritual creations. We repent from our carnal selves and turn to our spiritual selves. We do not transform from carnal to spiritual. We let go the carnal and embrace the spiritual, to forming Christ-like maturity.

Strewn amongst their obscure grappling with temporal needs, desires, and wants, we find in the prophets' ancient calls to God's covenants intimations of the Christ Covenant. They seemed to sense a covenant with an intimacy that did not leave any separation between God and people. How this would be, does not seem clear to them. In that obscurity, they also sensed a solution that would bridge God and people. God is at hand, not outside of and separate from people. They sensed spiritual atonement. They sensed the atonement or covenant, as in a glass darkly through the mists of this world. They had intimations that the terms or laws of the living Covenant are not be set down on stones, housed in a wooden ark in a temple. They sensed a special covenant between God and us. The terms of the living Covenant were within, and the Prophets felt such terms within themselves. The terms of the living Covenant were written then in their hearts and on their minds, as they are now written in our hearts and on our minds. They sensed the terms and the presence of that Covenant; we too sense the same. In the fulfillment of the living Christ Covenant, we see God face to face; we portray the lineaments of Christ after the spirit. We hear the intelligible voice of God and discern Christ in the hearing. In Christ, we have the reality of that Covenant before us as the Christ Covenant made specific and clear to us by Christ.

The First Passover Time - Finding and Engaging God

In the midst of the first Passover Feast time in John's gospel, Christ heroically cleared the temple of the carnal trappings of offerings, sacrifices and worldly means of trying to interact with God. When asked 'by what authority' he cleared the temple, Christ did not appeal to higher worldly authority, to Moses or any prophets or rules of priests. Instead, he suggested that the temple and its authority could be torn down --- in effect without spiritual consequence. According to Christ, the entire stone temple of 1600 square feet could be torn down and replaced with a 'temple' in a matter of days. People assumed he was talking about stone blocks built into a temple. But, Christ would have no interest in tearing down or building up stone temples. Christ was talking about tearing down the idol that the temple was and clearing out the idolatrous pretenses of carnal offerings and sacrifice. Here was a call for an exodus from bondage to the temple of the priests and bondage to the things of the flesh, to the freedom in personally housing God within our spiritual person, while spiritually housed in God.

The clearing of the temple described in the 2nd chapter of the book John, foreshadows the discussion between Christ and Nicodemus in John 3. There Christ clearly separates the things of the flesh from the things of the spirit. Christ may have cleared the Jerusalem temple of its worldly trappings and called for a house for God that did not have such trappings in John 2. But, in John 3, Christ teaches that we should also clear our person of its worldly trappings so that our spiritual person could rise up to house the very essence of God indwelling, actively forming our spirit according to Christ after the spirit and to be housed in that essence.

If the temple is cleared because there is no essential need for the temple itself, (or the Ark of the Covenant, the Tablets of Stone with their inscribed laws, or any other carnal prop of the temple); and, if the temple is further simply torn down, then how shall we relate to God? In the absence of the overwhelming presence of the Temple and its lofty priests, and in the absence of powerful carnal blood sacrifices to assuage guilt and make symbolic atonement with God, then what shall we do? Where shall we find God? How shall we engage and commune with God? Likewise, if we undertake to tear down or bind the person of flesh and destroy its seminal role in our existing, then how shall we find and relate to God?

It only takes minutes or hours to find God within and worship the Word, directly and personally. It takes only hours to undertake repentance, reconciliation and atonement, as well as salvation and holiness. In three days, Christ said he could raise a new temple created by God. In a matter of days, Christ could raise a temple that actually houses God and is filled with activities that are of God. As God houses or tabernacles us, so we are created to house God. We house God in a matter of days, not years. We are designed to house God; that is our purpose and end. God's laws written through the mind of Christ; are written in our hearts and on our minds. We are spirited dwellings, not vacant carnal vessels moved by winds external to our person.

Christ articulated in action what the Prophets before him proclaimed in fragmented words: God does not require burnt carnal offerings or carnal sacrifices. God does not dwell in temples, (See for example Isaiah 66:1). God dwells in us when we dwell in God. What God requires is that we do the work of God. In the end, the physical temple and its impediments, established to support and help become obstacles to direct and immediate, personal communion with God.

We engage God through the reality of Christ. We commune with God and participate in the things of God by fulfilling Christ in us. What God wants of us is written on our hearts. What God expects us to do to find salvation and holiness, is written in our minds. Our directions are already in hand. God's Word actively dwells within us. We are created with the Light as our innermost essence. When we engage the Word in us, and we see through the Light we have from God, the spirit and mind of Christ emerges within and we become shaped into Christ-likeness. God is in us through Christ, and through Christ, we are in God. We are spirited by God through the reality of Christ, here and now. Christ is God with us: Immanuel. God became flesh and the Word made his dwelling among us, as well as within us.

When Jesus, as a boy, was presented at the temple for purification and consecration to God, two doves were sacrificed to 'seal' that covenant with carnal blood. The dove sacrifice was not to secure forgiveness. It was not a payment for sin, though it was a blood sacrifice. The doves' blood was shed to seal the consecration. As the Christ, Christ drove the dove sellers from the temple. The valued carnal life blood was not needed. Carnal death serves no further purpose than the ending of carnal life. Sacrifice was not required for consecration, or for forgiveness of sin or guilt.

Neglecting the primal attraction and true carnal influence of the temple and its carnal bloodletting sacrifices and offerings, leads to misunderstandings of early Christian experiences and misunderstandings of the challenges faced by leaders at the time. These were and would be carnally captivating events that seize the participants in the core of their carnality. Carnal and physical needs easily mislead us. They did then. They force compromise. John's Gospel reluctantly includes the magic and lure of carnal miracles and wonders in order that people would listen on account of their carnal experience if not Christ's ministry, if not for the sake of Christ.

Today, the deep primal attraction of participating in symbolic ritual sacrifice and performing pacifying rites is still with us, appealing to those whose physical and carnal needs, desires and wants overwhelm them. For his part, in John's Gospel, Christ does not replace one carnal temple for some other different but still carnal temple; he does not replace one set of sacrifices and offerings, with a different set. Idolatry is rooted in the carnality and is separate and apart from spiritual things, whether the idol is a temple or a ritual. Christ intends to free us of the bonds of earthly temples, and worldly modes of relating to God (i.e. various kinds of sacrifices and offerings). Free of such worldly bonds and with direct personal relationship to the reality of Christ, people can put on Christ and acquire the mind of Christ. Being spiritually formed of Christ, people can, along with Christ, assumes the work of God: to love and serve people.

Christ, in his Covenant, does not require the sacrificial spilling of bodily or carnal blood. There is no need for a theology to prop up such ill-conceived notions. Christ requires justice, righteousness, mercy and Godly love in personal terms.

During our temporal flesh and blood life, that is our carnal life here and now, we must incorporate Christ into our spiritual person and spiritual being. Our bodies are mere housing and are not the subject of our existing and existence. As we will see when considering the second Passover Feast time in John's Gospel, we must 'eat the flesh' and 'drink the blood' of Christ while we actually live in this world. Christ incarnate must pass through our temporal existence so that *we are* in Christ, of and from Christ. We are spiritually formed here and now in being born and living into the world of spiritual things of God, while we live in the temporal world. We become Christ-like while we actually live. In doing so, we do the work of God in this life: we serve God by serving others in this life.

The Second Passover Time – Incorporating Christ

Before the celebration of the second Passover Feast time in John's Gospel, Christ encounters the Samaritan woman at the well (John 4:7-14). We are told that Jacob had provided a well for his descendants that supplied water for generations and quenched their thirst. Carnal living requires water. The well was a source of carnal life, whenever they were thirsty; they had only to drink the water. Thirst came regularly. The water from the well quenched a carnal thirst that would come again. The thirsting of the spirit is not quenched by carnal satisfaction, regardless of ritual, ceremony or rite. Carnal satisfaction may distract us away from spiritual thirst, but spiritual thirst requires spiritual water. Christ introduces the woman to a different kind of water --- 'living water' for those thirsting for spiritual life. This water is not ingested from outside us. It arises from within us, from within our spiritual nature which involves God's nature. The spiritual water flows endlessly through our spiritual selves; it is what we are, when we are in God, of and from God. It is poured out for us, from within us. Those who drink the living water will not thirst spiritually again.

Right after his encounter with the Samaritan woman, Christ's disciples offered him food to eat. Christ directed them to consider his food, or to consider the spiritual food on which he, Christ fed (4:34). His food is to do the will of God and accomplish God's work. His food is to serve people. God harvests those who serve others, into eternal life.

After feeding the 5,000 with the five loaves and two fish, Jesus counsels the people to direct their attention not to their filled stomachs and the kind of food that perishes, but to food that, like the living water, satisfies forever (6:26-40). Christ counsels them to work for food that endures into eternal life. The discussion goes on to compare the manna from heaven, which had to come each day to feed that day's carnal hunger, with the bread of God. The bread or sustenance of God gives life eternal, not life not for a day.

The food that Christ had, which the disciples did not know about, is the same food that we presently have through Christ. It is God's essence in the form of spiritually nourishing bread of Existence and Existing. Christ provides both spiritual bread and spiritual water from on high, to feed and quench hungry thirsting spirits. Christ is that bread and water, and we have that bread and water within us, feeding and watering our spirits eternally. If people eat that bread and drink that water, they will not spiritually die, but will spiritually live forever. That bread according to Christ is his 'flesh'. That water likewise is his 'blood'. When we follow Christ we are encountering Christ in our temporal existing. We are existentially incorporating or ingesting Christ spiritually, which extend in our flesh and blood actions.

As Nicodemus had done in John chapter 3, the people at the feeding of the 5,000, took Christ's references to bread and water, and to flesh and blood, to be merely carnal bread and water, and merely carnal flesh and blood. They asked for a carnal miracle, for carnal bread that would satisfy their carnal hunger forever. What he said to them made no sense to them. Christ said the people must eat his flesh and drink his blood or they will not have any life in them. On the other hand, those who eat his flesh and drink his blood would have eternal life. His flesh is food; that is, bread for the spirit. His blood is drink; that is, water for the spirit.

In a sense by doing what Christ would as Christ would do it, we ingest[55] and incorporate Christ into our daily living. This pious and serious taking in Christ after the flesh, sensitizes us and allows us to recognize the workings of the spirit and the Cross within us. In 'eating' and 'drinking' Christ after the flesh externally by what we do, we lift Christ. From within us, God indwelling according to Christ after the spirit internally forms our spiritual person to become and be as Christ is. Christ is in us and from within pour person he provides living water and living bread.

Those who existentially eat Christ will live because of Christ. What the people did not understand is that Christ was counselling them to incorporate him spiritually, as they incorporate bread and water carnally. *Externally* they could ingest the flesh and blood of Christ by following Christ after the flesh. Internally they have Christ housed in their flesh and blood to receive what comes into a person as they assent and affirm their spiritual formational-following Christ. The Word manifest in *Christ within* and in *Christ without* responds with Life emanating from one's personal spiritual life. Incorporating Christ allows us to participate in the infinite and eternal. Spiritual hunger and thirst are done away with. They are replaced with eternal spiritual fulfillment. By grasping Christ and spiritually ingesting Christ; we existentially incorporate spiritual food and drink in our own individual spirits that in maturity will no longer

[55] When we talk about ingesting Christ or incorporating Christ through 'eating' the body or 'drinking' the blood, let us keep the following in mind. There is no 'five and dime' Christianity. You cannot acquire Christ on a Wal-Mart shelf; there is no fast food 'McChrist'. There is no 'Christ for Dummies' book to follow. When it comes to following Christ, the 'pabulum and milk' must give way to existentially ingesting the real living body and real living blood residing in the reality that is Christ.

hunger and thirst spiritually.

The second Passover Feast event reported in John's Gospel falls between Christ's talk with the woman at the well and his talk with those he had fed with the loaves and fishes. In these passages, we discern that as temples of God, we 'incarnate' Christ by incorporating him into our essential selves. We eat Christ and drink Christ, and in so doing we become Christ-like. When we eat carnal food and drink carnal water, we have carnal energy. When we eat and drink Christ, we have spiritual energy. As bread and water feed us and we grow, and grow strong, so we are fed by Christ and our spirits grow, and grow strong.

The bread of life comes from heaven, and is present to you and me, here and now. Here and now, you and I can eat it and feast on it. When we eat that bread and incorporate it, we will not hunger spiritually any more. Living water comes from heaven as well, and is present here and now. Here and now, you and I can drink it till we are spiritually quenched. When we drink that living water and incorporate it, we will not thirst spiritually any more. However, we must eat and drink the reality Christ, here now, and while we are in the flesh.

This living water and living bread will not become a part of us without going through our temporal life and temporal selves. Our actual living must grasp the reality of Christ and in grasping take on the work of Christ --- to serve others. As temples that house God, we are animated by formationally-following Christ and being as Christ would be, and doing what Christ would do, as he would do it. When we existentially ingest and incorporate Christ, the Word of God within comes alive and acts. The spirit of God in us moves and we are led by the spirit and mind of Christ. We become born from above and we live the spiritual things of God. The bread of life, unlike carnal bread is not static. It lives and gives life. God's grace is that this bread passes into us and spirits us with the mind of Christ lifted up, for us to follow carrying 'a light yoke'.

Spiritual living involves actively incorporating Christ, here and now. This incorporating, i.e. this 'eating the flesh' and 'drinking the blood' of Christ is our real world existence. Spiritual repentance is repentance from merely bodily or carnal living, with the purpose of turning to spiritual living. Spiritual repentance is not merely a matter of turning away from sin, not merely a matter of not existentially ingesting or incorporating sin. We can repent from sin, without turning to God in which case, we acquire neither salvation nor holiness. Spiritual repentance is not merely turning away from attempting to feed our spiritual hunger with merely carnal food and activities. Spiritual repentance and salvation is not just turning from the carnal then turning to the spiritual. It requires activating ourselves spiritually. Spiritual repentance and salvation, is using the Light we have to stop actively attempting to use the things of the carnal world to be saved; and to actively use or incorporate in us the spiritual things of God to be saved spiritually and being saved, to be holy.

We live as flesh and blood, and such carnal living can be much and can do much. However, it remains merely carnal. We cannot live spiritually, by simply reworking the things of this world, even if reworking them demonstrates awesome power and miraculous wonders. No merely carnal thing or merely carnal action can cause the merely carnal world to nourish us spiritually. We are only nourished spiritually by God incarnate here and now, by our actively incorporating the reality of Christ or God dwelling with us, within the terms of our being.

How can we actively incorporate the reality of Christ into our existential becoming and being? We need a traversable road or way. We need a gate that we can actually go through. We need someone who we can actually follow, once we actively turn to God. What we need must be incarnate and accessible to us. What we need to do, must be doable here and now. To incarnate God into our becoming and being and to become and be spiritual, we must actually formationally-follow Christ, here and now. The call to follow God in human terms has always been present. It is present now. It always will be present. As alluded to in John 6:45, it is God within us who calls us and leads us. During his ministry, Christ's call to follow was pervasive in his teaching and messages.

Christ incarnate is God in our world; Christ incarnate is God really dwelling among us in an accessible way. Christ is here and now dwelling with us and as accessible to us as our food and drink. Rather than food and drink that perishes, Christ incarnate is food and drink that is imperishable and that gives eternal life to those who in their flesh and blood existence ingest and incorporate the present Christ in mind and spirit. We incorporate Christ personally, directly and in an immediate way. We make the heart of Christ our heart. There are no by-ways, mediating steps or persons between us and God, for the Word is immediately present to us, as is both the spirit and mind of Christ. We incorporate Christ, when like Christ before us; we do the work of God. God's purpose for us is that we serve others with justice, righteousness, mercy and Godly love. Setting up a rite of eating Christ's flesh and the drinking his blood, as a means of grace in itself, is to mistake the work of God that Christ did and does. Christ served people: service is his flesh and is his blood. That is the Christ we existentially incorporate and ingest.

There is a difference between earthly hearing, and, hearing as Christ would hear; between earthly seeing, and, seeing as Christ would see; between earthly understanding, and understanding as Christ would understand. Grasping Christ with our essential being here and now, so that we actively hear, actively see and actively understand as Christ does, is what is meant by 'eating the flesh' and 'drinking the blood' of Christ. The eating and drinking is in the reaching, the grasping and the holding high of Christ. This is grace that generates new spiritual creation.

The new spiritual creation is not simply a vessel that houses or 'tabernacles' God. We existentially ingest and incorporate God in our present actual existing or being. The spiritual creature is being created by God and exists in the creating. Earthly life and its activities are not all evil and repugnant. Earthly life has powerful meanings and purposes. The temptation to put those special and significant experiences in the place of our relation to God is always before us. For those who yet have to find and participate in the reality of Christ, the temptation makes sense. It is an imperative to lift up these earthly things to have some sense of meaning in this life. Such meaning falls short. It is Christ who must be lifted and not earthly substitutes. We are to use our daily life and everyday activities to incorporate Christ. We must be careful not to try to turn 'a sow's ear into a silk purse'. This is especially true given the profound advances we make in knowledge and understanding of earthly things. We should not try to transform mundane earthly life and things, into heavenly things just because we wish it so and it is convenient. Given recent advances in science and technology, now or very soon, we probably can or will be able to turn a sow's ear into a silk purse. Whether it is a sow's ear or a silk purse, the thing remains a merely carnal thing. As Christ reminded so often, the things of the spirit are of God, the things of this world are not things of the spirit.

The Third Passover Time – The Work of God

After the clearing of the temple and making clear that God's dwelling on earth is people, and after establishing that God dwells in us as far as we incorporate Christ into ourselves (in our becoming and being), John's Gospel describes another important teaching in the third Passover Feast time event. The teaching is about serving others. This teaching at a meal before the third Passover Feast time was in the shadow of Christ's impending arrest, condemnation, and temporal death. It is an important teaching.

The content of Christ's teachings surrounding the single Passover Feast time referenced in the Gospels of Mathew, Mark and Luke, seems to better align with the content of Christ's teaching in the second Passover Feast time mentioned in the Gospel of John, rather than with the third Passover Feast time mentioned in John's Gospel. On the other hand, the timing of the Passover Festival time referenced in the Gospels of Mathew, Mark and Luke seems to better align with third Passover Festival mentioned in John, rather than the second one. This is not accidental or a mistaken difference. The event of the Third Passover Festival time in John's Gospel makes a purposeful and important point in the teaching message of the last supper, as reported in John. The message is different from that in the other Gospels. Christ washed the disciples' feet during supper. Foot washing usually occurred when people entered indoors, not during the meal. The whole episode is an intended and purposeful disruptive innovation… to use a modern change concept.

Christ demonstrates by example, the work of God, which he came to do. He washed his followers' feet at the last supper meal. In this action, Christ models the significance, meaning and purpose of Christ. (In Luke, there is reference to Christ actually serving the meal itself.) Washing of the feet was not in itself a deep lesson. It was not an earth-shattering event, not an awesome miracle, not an overwhelming display of power. It was not an act of extraordinary help to the poor, the oppressed, or the despised. It was not a sign that might have impressed and won over people. It was simply Christ doing an ordinary day thing: washing feet in a very ordinary fashion.

The work of God that Christ does is not an awesome, overwhelming carnal miracle. The work of God is to spiritually serve people. This was the work of Christ and this is the work Christ gives us to do. In these spiritually driven but common everyday actions, we manifest God's justice, righteousness, mercy and love. In this we find God's love. Christ incarnate came to demonstrate that God serves people in everyday living. (A powerful testament to this is 1 Corinthians 13.) Like Peter during the last supper in John's Gospel, we do not naturally think that God serves us in our everyday living. The reporting of this ordinary but significant event is in a critical place in the Gospel of John. It carries import. Here is demonstrated Christ's most important command: Love God and love one another. As God serves people, people should serve one another. To do the work of God, Christ serves people; to do the work of God those who follow Christ should serve others. In so doing, they accomplish the work of God.

Christ broke bread and shared this with his disciples, instructing them to break bread in remembrance of him[56]. He was asking them to remember him whenever

[56] While only this "last supper" is recorded in scripture as a teaching, one would assume that Christ took the occasion of sharing mealtimes

they ate *the bread given to them by God* and in remembering him, serve others. Christ poured wine into a glass, indicating that the wine was his life, which was poured out for many. He instructed the disciples that they should remember him, when they drank *the wine given to them by God.* In remembering him and his life, they too should pour out their lives with love, in service to one another. As he served them, they should serve others. Christ is speaking about his disciples constantly ingesting him existentially; that is constantly incorporating Christ by eating the bread of service and drinking the wine of mercy in relation to other people. In addition, while embodying Christ in heart, mind and being, Christ as the Word in them generates their spiritual life.

Christ is serving. But here Christ is not 'the suffering servant'. Here, Christ is the servant turned friend. The service is as a friend to friends. The disciples are not servants. They are treated as friends. No longer master and servants, friends serve one another (John 15:15-16). Christ's pre-eminent service was, and is unconditional acceptance and love of others and service to them as friends. He put others as friends, before himself. This was not suffering, but joyful.

Christ's service to others, strewn throughout the Gospels, seemed often to offend the priests and 'church regulations', as well as the 'hardened hearts' of the established religions' enthusiasts of the day. Christ came in flesh and blood, preaching and teaching the way of

---

as opportunities to instruct his disciples on this very same as well as in other lessons. This would hold for both concepts expressed in the synoptic gospels as well as in John's Gospel. What this means is that in telling their Gospel's the writers wanted to emphasize what they wanted to impart to their audience or readers. Both the lessons are in fact repeated in different parts of the Gospels. Christ serves us and serves us with his life and being.

salvation from crippling and obstructive carnal illusions and delusions. These block our spiritual eyes, ears, and understanding; and they keep us from reaching for, grasping, and holding God personally and directly. Christ set out examples and teachings for us to use in our efforts to follow Christ actively in spirit, in mind and in our actions in the world. We follow Christ when we serve one another as friends, in very ordinary ways. Throughout the Gospels Christ put others before himself. We also can put others before ourselves. In his time, Christ did not ask that anyone should serve him as a slave. He asked that we serve God and serve one another as friends. God requires mercy, justice, righteousness and Godly love. Christ called for his disciples and followers to hold fast to the things of God, and to love and serve one another.

In this third Passover Feast time, Christ teaches and instructs his disciples about the Paraclete coming to each individual person. Within the terms of our person, we can access God through the present reality that is Christ. Those who assent, consent and affirm choose salvation guided by the Word of God within. They are activated and actualized in spirit, mind, and actions in the reality that is Christ, present to us, here and now. They can grasp God. In personally reaching for, grasping and holding God in our inner most being, we become and are creatures of heaven.

The spirit of Truth in the role of Paraclete had already been present to people as long past as people had been alive. Christ pointed the disciples to the Paraclete, which had always been present but unseen, unheard and un-understood by them. The disciples could utilize Christ in reality by listening for and taking direction from the Paraclete. The disciples were able to take on the work of Christ, and with the Paraclete's support and guidance, they could actually find their way.

During the last supper, Christ stopped and interrupted the meal to wash his disciples' feet. Chris was making a clear point about what his role in the world was, and what their role in the world should be. Christ then told them about the Paraclete. Following that, Christ prayed for himself, then for his disciples, then for all believers. In his prayers, he did not ask anything for himself. He does ask to be in his infinite eternal state of Glory in God's presence. His temporal work was done. He was returning to the Father. He was leaving this world.

Christ did ask for something for his disciples. Christ asks that they have the spirit of Truth and that they be protected from evil, while they are in the world. For all believers, Christ asked that they too should have what he asked for the disciples to have; and, what he had. What was it that Christ had? Christ had glorification because he loved God and did God's work of loving others. He had the washing of other's feet. He had service to other people. Christ had the spirit of Truth during his temporal incarnation, now he prays that those who follow him, should also have, like he had, the Truth with them and in them, so that the Word in them would emerge triumphant in their being and eternal spiritual life. To guide them and support the disciples in their acquisition of Truth, Christ redirected them from his temporal carnal self, and pointed them towards the things of God working within each of them. Christ drew attention to the Paraclete so that the disciples might better recognize its calling them.

God requires mercy not sacrifice. What sense then is to be made of the idea of Christ pouring out his life as an atoning sacrifice? Christ put people before himself --- he sacrificed himself to them by serving them. His life was not his own, it was given to others. Christ forgave. Christ, in turn, leads us to forgive and to love one another. When we serve, we forgive. That is why Christ washed Peter's feet, and told Peter to do as he had done. That is why Christ told Peter that, he (Christ) had to serve Peter in order for Peter to be of or partake of Christ. When we forgive, we serve. When we forgive, we love. We see the reason Christ asked Peter three times whether Peter loved; and, we see that each time Peter demonstrates that he tried but that he did not understand Christ's question or the correct answer to the question. Christ's life was an atoning sacrifice: his life given 'among us' to serving us, or to love us above himself. Christ picked up his Cross and dwelt among us doing the work of God. In loving others, Christ loved and served God. He completed the work of God by serving God not by being a substitute carnal blood sacrifice ritual that serves idolatrous 'religious' leaders but does nothing for God.

The prayer passages at Gethsemane were different. Christ did not pray for others. His prayers were for himself. His prayers were intense. In Luke's Gospel, his sweat was compared to drops of blood. Christ was facing the greatest trail of his life --- his death. Here is a human person experiencing the ultimate existential anxiety: non-existence. Christ loved life. His life's end was at hand. Were the 'tears of blood' and the prayers of supplication coming from a fear of pain or a fear of death? Which confronts people as the more fearful and unbearable: death or pain? I may be able to endure pain; for it passes then life goes on. Can I endure death, which does not pass? Did he endure pain for others? The primary consideration is that Christ, as a living person, confronted his death. He had the kind of response that a normal carnal person has. It was fearful. It was anxious. It was to be avoided if possible. Christ did not embrace death. Indeed, he prayed to avoid death. Death was imminent: Christ found consolation in fervent prayer. He did not diminish his fear by claiming an afterlife in, of and from the flesh in heaven. Christ overcame death in Gethsemane, while he lived here on earth as a temporal carnal person. At Gethsemane, Christ prayed for himself and at Gethsemane, Christ claimed victory over death. Christ left this legacy for us who enter into Covenant with Christ.

Following the last supper in John's Gospel, Christ prays for others. These prayers in John seem to have some similarities with the Lord's Prayer. There is quite a difference from the prayers that followed the last supper in the other Gospels. We must carefully read that difference in regards to its meaning and significance, especially in light of the last supper also being so different in John compared to the other Gospels. In John's Gospel, he had washed their feet to teach them about serving one another. His work as a person living among us was completed. Christ then prayed that his followers would complete the work of God in their personal existing. God's will is that Christ's followers would love God and love one another. Evil emerges when love is misplaced and, temporal life loves its carnal self more than it loves God and loves others. His prayers are for them that they might complete their work, which is the work of God.

The birth a child is the birth of hope to a family. This is true of kings and paupers. For kings to ensure there is someone to succeed them in 'kingship'. To paupers to ensure there is someone to care for and serve them in their infirmary or in their old age. Both these hopes are hopes of temporal times. The child is born to serve, but is first served. A child, who is served well, serves well. A child, who is neglected or abused, neglects or abuses in turn; although that suffering child may overcome the evil in this world and may serve well. The book of John does not report on the birth of Christ. The other Gospels do. But it is clear in John's Gospel that Christ is Mary's son. He was born, was a child and youth. Why was this important in the Christ story? Why not have the Messiah come as a fully created fully adult person? Christ came to serve as a child who serves his family and parents. Those who follow Christ are obligated with the responsibilities of child-ship or son-ship. Those who do God's work serve their parents, their brothers and sisters.

Woman, here is your son… When being crucified, before dying, he passed on his child-ship to 'the beloved disciple'. Here is the last temporal act initiated by Christ in John's Gospel. He asked his loved disciple to assume his responsibilities and burden as a son; that is, he asked his beloved disciple to 'follow him' by assuming his responsibilities as a child to provide his mother with hope for her future: to serve her as a her first born child would, that is to say, to serve her present needs and coming infirmaries of age. In passing on the torch of his temporal carnal life's familial purpose, Christ called on John to assume his role as a child of humanity. In passing that torch to John, it is passed to every child born with the promise of hope within them --- the hope of doing God's work to serve. As Christ commended his mother to John, so Christ commended his sheep to Peter, and commends the care of others to each person in communion with Christ.

It is no surprise that after the temporal death, the risen Christ remains true to his calling. First, we find he prepares breakfast for his disciples and feeds them. Then he teaches Peter what it means to follow Christ. The prophets had taught the message years ago, but many had not heard the message, which Christ then tried to teach Peter. God does not want carnal sacrifices or burnt offerings, God want justice righteousness, mercy and love. God does not want people to love him in carnal terms. God wants people to love God by doing the work of God which is to manifest justice, righteousness, mercy and Godly love in our actual existing and being. He asks Peter three times whether Peter truly loves him. Three times Peter says yes, each time more emphatically and not comprehending what Jesus meant by love or true love. Three times Christ instructs Peter to feed 'his sheep'. He reminds Peter to stay focussed on Christ by following him and not get distracted by others.

Those who love Jesus do not have to say so loudly and repeatedly. Proclaiming one's love for Jesus is not an end in itself. Those who love Jesus will simply say so in what they are and do. When we compare these passages, with the comparable passages in the other three Gospels, that is, with the prayers at Gethsemane, the power of these passages from the upper room in John's Gospel comes clearer.

How is Peter to feed Christ's people? The answer is to feed them the flesh and blood of the real and existing Christ; to have the people existentially ingest or incorporate Christ after the flesh and Christ after the spirit, in mind, heart and spirit. Peter should follow Christ by feeding Christ's people, so that people would, like Christ before them, do the work of God, by serving one another in justice, righteousness, mercy and love.

The Existential Christ Covenant

All four Gospels describe the arrest, condemnation, and crucifixion of Christ during a Passover Festival event. John reports two previous Passover Feast times, making three referred to in all. John also reports that Jesus attended the Festival of Tabernacles and the Feast of Dedication (Lights), between the second and third Passover Feast times. In the book of John, there is a preponderant use of the Passover Feast times as a backdrop to critical teachings in John's Gospel about our relationship to God. Christ participated in all the religious feasts and gatherings, including the Day of Atonement, the Festival of Dedication (Lights), the Festival of Tabernacles, and Pentecost. John's Gospel highlights the Passovers. The uses of Passover Feast times in John's Gospel are striking and special. Why were these particular times used to provide these related teachings?

Tabernacles or the ingathering celebrated the community coming together after securing the richness of the harvest. From the events surrounding Christ at the festival of Tabernacles (John 7:37), we have important teachings from Christ about the living water and the living bread, but we also learn of the *increasing separation and divide* between Christ and the priests of his community. We learn of the failure of people to receive Christ's teachings and message. Christ used these large religious gatherings to present his message and make his points. The Feast of Dedication (Lights) is mentioned in John 10:22, the failure to receive Christ's message progresses on to efforts by his own community, to stone him. Unlike these disconcerting references, Christ presents a restructured relationship between people and God during the three the Passover Feast times, in John's Gospel.

Why were Passover Feast times especially selected to present these core Gospel teachings? For example:

> Why not use the gathering of the Day of Atonement as a backdrop before the crucifixion? The Day of Atonement spoke to sin and guilt. It made use of carnal blood sacrifice of flesh and blood bulls and goats to rid people of their sins and guilt, and to secure atonement with God. It would be a good framework in which to establish Christ as a sin offering, whose blood was shed to atone for peoples' sins. The Passover itself recalls a time when God protected people from death.

or,

> Why not utilize Pentecost to speak to the Word of God coming to dwell with us. Moses was given the law and he in turn gave it to the people. Christ came as the Word incarnate to give that Word to his people. The celebration of Pentecost could easily be associated with giving to Word of God to people. These were not used that way in John's Gospel.

In all four Gospel's it is clear that Christ desired to celebrate the Passover Feast with his disciples. John identifies three Passover Feast times, during which Christ tries to teach the fundamental meaning of the Gospel. During these three times in John, Christ discloses a real and existential Covenant or inherent relationship between God and people, in which the essence and properties of Christ are the living terms of the Existent Covenant. The Christ Covenant between God and people through Christ, not only promised but actually gave people life – spiritual life. That part of existence, which is our personal union with God, is

Christ. As such, Christ is the Word specifying the distinctions of reality that makes that union possible; and, Christ, as the essence of God, generates those specific distinctions in our actual real spiritual person. The Christ Covenant is the nature of Existence, Existing and Being: the "I AM." Our personal; spiritual formation or generation within the terms of that Covenant manifests the essence of God indwelling according to Christ after the spirit.

God or Existence irrevocably destroys carnal lives that were not spiritually born in second birth, which precludes their existing with or existence of ultimate existential significance, meaning or purpose. They do not essentially participate in the infinite and eternal essence and existence of God.

The Christ Covenant is a revelation that God incarnate exists and in that existent reality, we have a relation or covenant with God. There are distinct and specific 'laws, rules or terms of agreement' in this covenant between us and God. These are the infinite and eternal distinctions and specifics of the mind of Christ, which mind manifests its self when these laws of Christ are invoked into our hearts and onto our minds, as our innermost essence. We are created and called to fulfill our spiritual selves through our fulfillment of that covenant. We know God when we know that God through Christ serves us. God serves us, and we serve others. We are holy when we accomplish God's work --- serving others by putting them before ourselves. The way between God and ourselves is the reality of Christ, which reality directs us to do the work of God.

When God in us emerges, we emerge spiritually. Christ deploys the Passover Feast times as a backdrop to freedom from captivity: from spiritual bondage to spiritual freedom. The three Passover Feast time accounts in John's Gospel, anchor a formational approach to the salvation and holiness covenant between God and people. The three aspects are:

1. In our spiritual forming from above being in God of and from God; and, relating to God personally through the reality of Christ, here and now, and so raising up the true temple of God in our existing and being.

2. Incorporating Christ by using the reality of Christ, here and now, in order to engage the Word of God within, and raising up Christ to draw all of oneself to him; in so doing become formed here and now into spiritual life of the things of God.

3. In doing God's work, Christ came and served people: we exist for God to serve us or to form us. We passively and actively follow Christ in serving others. In serving others, we passively and actively do the work of God. As we accomplish God's work, God's purpose is that we are become fruits of the true Vine. God's work is manifestly evident in our person.

It remained in John's Gospel for Christ to show the temporal support (i.e. the Paraclete) that we have from Christ and God in finding our way into and through the Christ Covenant, in his carnal absence, following his carnal death.

The laws of the Christ Covenant are written on our hearts and in our minds, and are played out in our becoming and being Christ-like. The activating spirit of God within us calls us to put on the spirit, mind and existence of Christ. We put on Christ and in so doing we covenant with God through Christ for spiritual life. The Covenant of Christ is a covenant of life. Without our spiritual birth from above and without spiritual living, there is no personal relation or bond between God and each person. In applying the laws of the Christ Covenant (i.e. the specific spirit and mind of Christ) our spirit activates. Salvation and holiness are not merely the absence of sin. The forgiveness of sin, whether unconditional or by blood sacrifice, may provide salvation from sin. Getting rid of the negative simply means we are free from sin. Such forgiveness does not necessarily provide salvation to a life of the things of God. Salvation to a life of the things of God is an act of generation not an act of forgiveness. The Christ Covenant promises life to those who follow Christ in spirit, mind, heart and in existing and doing.

The Christ Covenant is sealed with a 'sprinkling' of the Spirit, for example as when Christ breathed on the disciples and told them to receive the Spirit (John 20:22). This Christ Covenant is not sealed with a sprinkling of blood (e.g. of a sacrificed dove or goat), as might be the case with other covenants. The Christ Covenant generates atonement with God, through the generation of the spirit through birth from above. This atonement lifts people to God's purpose for them. Power is given --- the power to forgive sin. With the forgiveness of sin comes the power to break the snares and trappings that hold us captive. The spirited person, born from above of the spirit of Christ, can free the captive and proclaim promised Salvation. It is then for the freed captive to turn to the spiritual things of God to find, grasp and possess in essence, God through Christ. The shedding of blood for a guilt offering may make up for a shortfall or an offense. The blood indicates the cost, in flesh and blood terms, being offered up to undo the sin or the offense. The blood is spilt, the sin paid for in full, yet spiritual life has yet to be formed and be born. Spilling blood is not a means to salvation. God comes with mercy not sacrifice. Sacrifice is not salvation, it is only a try at undoing of a wrong, an offense or a shortfall, by providing a payment in kind for sin incurred. The forgiveness of sin does not itself engender spiritual life. If correcting wrong does not positively influence spiritual life, what does? Our covenant with Christ is that we will follow him. His Covenant with us is that if we choose to follow Christ, then we will find and possess spiritual life.

Our personal spirit emerges along with and in communion with the emergence of the spirit of God in us. The spirit of God is not 'passing over', but emerges in and stays with us. Within the frame of the spirit and mind of Christ, the spirit of God (the Paraclete), actively guides those who follow, giving us spiritual life personally. Altogether, these ignite our hearts and generate our actions and ourselves, so that we in essence become and are Christ-like. A new relationship emerges. A new Covenant is established requiring positive personal action in spirit, mind and heart. It is driven by the promise that the spirit of God in us, will guide us in Truth and set us free spiritually, to put on Christ in spirit, mind, heart and action. In this, the Spirit of Christ through the Paraclete supports us, by being alongside us calling us.

Christ's ministry spoke of God's relation to people and their relation to God, and the role of Christ in that relation. Christ is the Covenant between God and people. As Christ revealed himself, so he revealed the Covenant. God put his Covenant with people, in Christ. As we reach for, grasp and hold Christ in our innermost self, so we grasp and hold our Covenant with God. Without the reality of Christ, there is no Covenant with God. Without Christ, we have no relation to God. Together the three Passover

Feast times in John's Gospel, articulate Christ disclosing himself as the Covenant between God and each person. The Christ Covenant is the Word of God written in our hearts and on our minds --- come to life.

When Christ exerts authority, he says he is speaking the words given to him by God and about things that he knows because he experienced them first hand. He does not claim authority through a priesthood or church. He does claim authority from tradition or by scripture. Christ references living water and living bread. He speaks about 'eating and drinking'. He says, "it is written". This speaks to the people he addressed at the time. Christ references experiences he has from being of God. Christ shares what he experiences and knows from experience. He shares these things so others through him will know of his direct experience. In following Christ, we are not called to abstract knowledge or transcendent belief. We are called to experience what emerges within us with the support of the Paraclete. The Spirit of Christ through the Paraclete guides us into true experience of the living God within us from which we are born from above and into a life of the spiritual things.

Christ calls us to follow him into a living Covenant with God. The actual calling by the infinite and eternal Christ in the present is the Paraclete. The living Christ Covenant is sealed with a sprinkling of the spirit from above. It gives and feeds spiritual life. Because Christ lives, the living Covenant with God lives. Christ opens the gate; we follow. The Spirit calls within us; we hear and follow. We follow and we know what Christ knows, that God is in us and that we can have the mind and spirit of Christ. In such knowledge, we hear, see and understand the laws of God written in our hearts and on our minds. In such hearing, seeing and understanding we put on Christ in mind and spirit. Being so spirited, we undertake with Christ to do God's work. In return, we become part of God and participate in God's eternal being. The Christ Covenant is in human terms a living Covenant between God and us. The fulfillment of the Christ Covenant is the fulfilment of God's promise to us of existence of ultimate existential meaning.

Introductory and In-Depth Workshops

Workshops are available at reasonable costs, including overviews, working knowledge, in-depth knowledge, and consultations.

Aldo Di Giovanni
1-905-626-2536
aldo12@sympatico.ca

About the Author

The knowledge I have of my experience of Existence and Existing is a poor shadow of the reality of the experience. The words I craft to describe what of I have been given to know of the experience of Existence and Existing, fall short several times over. These meditations are deep, they are also plain; they are not 'lettered' or academic[57], and while the writing may not be cogent or clear, it is substantive and has some import. The living Gospel, New Testament Gospels and the works of several 'lights', support them.

Mine is an early 17th Century radical protestant or rather *radical Christian approach*[58] that combines with a mid-twentieth century Salvationist's understanding of the 'Living' and written Gospels. Into the mix is added a Methodist appreciation for experience and Light within, likely derived from that 17th century radical protestant legacy. My understanding is of a down to earth theology[59].

---

[57] This is not to say that I have not studied and learned, because I have. I have studied philosophy and scripture, in different places and at different times. And, this has also allowed me to see. But, my sure ground, to which I always return is God before me, God in me here and now.

[58] Mostly in line with Quaker and Spinozist thought.

[59] This combination may seem contrary on the surface. But, going past the appearances to the theology and grasp of the Gospels, these two movements have much in common. This was intuitively recognized by George Scott Railton, an early Salvationist 'preacher of Holiness', who prepared and published an intriguing and insightful article he titled: George Fox and His Salvation Army 200 Years Ago.

My approach to the Gospel is direct and plain. In my experience, Salvation Army soldiers I have met[60], as well as many other simple souls illuminating God's light before me, had a direct and plain grasp of the Gospel of Christ, its theology and doctrine. They lived their justice, righteousness, mercy and love and in doing so illuminated my way. I found in them, what God reveals to me in my heart and in my mind. No doubt my development within the Catholic Church in childhood has also influenced me. Places of worship and gathering, such as they were, illustrated the yearning people have for spiritual life. Needless to say, there has been much study and learning given over to the 'grist in the mill' of my understanding. In the end, I am a child of my age, within its traditions, speaking to the present and perhaps the future. The Gospel plain and deep has guided me in the past, it guides me now and it will guide me in the future.

For many years, many Salvationists came forward with sincere hearts: unconditionally caring ---- loving others and acting on that love, as Christ had done so long ago. (I speak of those Salvationists who I personally have encountered. And, it may be that with the passing of the years that such plain and direct actions, and, such plain embrace of Holiness, have passed on with their passing.)

That Salvationist foundation was practical and derived over many years and on many helping fronts from Christian 'doing in being' which came to be in individual

[60] I refer here on my experience of the many Salvationists I have personally known over the years. My source is those *living inspired Salvation Army soldiers* I personally encountered in my day.

and collective charity, apart from the establishment and propagation of the institution by 'leaders'. What caught my eyes was the 'living' in the people; their few frills and inessentials appealed to me. It was aligned to the dictates of the written Gospels but also of the living dictates of the living Gospel and was manifest in personal encounters with the mind and heart of Christ. I heard and took these notions into my heart, blending them with the old Quakers' and Methodists' purpose to do God's work by serving others.

In discussing the Gospel with people, I find that the abstract discussions themselves are confusing. We need to act and be to experience commonality; and in becoming by acting, know and understand. This illuminates. We need to grasp and know God in us. This illuminates. When we have deeply embraced God within and when we have acted Godly and have experienced God acting through others, then we can discuss the gospel with some focus and some clarity. That also holds as much or more in our effort to be holy. It begins with God in us; it flows through Christ; and, then becomes us.

My spiritual starting point is always simply God. When I get swept away in my personal struggles to exist and make sense of existence and humankind, I return to that simple Presence … that still small voice[61]. I turn to the Gospel within me. I look for the Gospel in others. I reach for the Gospel in scripture. I listen for and hear Whispers of God, here and now.

---

[61] 1 Kings , 19:11-13 (KJV)

References

Barrett, William, Irrational Man – A Study in Existential Philosophy, Doubleday 1962.

Brown, Raymond, The Gospel According to John (I-XII), Doubleday 2006.

The Gospel According to John (XIII-XXI), Doubleday 2008.

An Introduction to the Gospel of John, Doubleday 2003

Fox, George, The Journal of George Fox, Friends United Press 1976.

Maritain, Jacques, Existence and the Existent – An Essay on Christian Existentialism, Image Books 1957.

Spinoza, Baruch, Spinoza Selections, Ed. J. Wild, Chas, Scribner's Sons, N.Y., 1958, (This edition does not include the Footnotes in the TdIE.)

Spinoza, Benedictus de, 1632-1677, A Theologico-Political Treatise and A Political Treatise, 1951. Dover.

Spinoza Benedictus, Short Treatise on God, Man and His Well Being in The Collected Works of Spinoza, ed. and tr. by Edwin Curley, Princeton University Press, 1985.

The Correspondence of Spinoza, tr. and ed. with intro. and ann. by A. Wolf, N.Y., L. Macveagh, 1928.

Spinoza Complete Works, Tr. Samuel Shirley, Hackett Publishing Company, 2002

Tillich, Paul, Systematic Theology Volume I, University of Chicago Press 1975.

Systematic Theology Volume II, University of Chicago Press 1975.

Systematic Theology Volume III, University of Chicago Press 1975.

Other Publications

(Available at Amazon Books and Amazon Kindle Publications)

Christ-Specific Lifeskill Experiences and Experiments Coaching & Counselling.

Christ-specific Lifeskills Toolkit: *an Approach to Christian Life Coaching*

Spinoza's Christian Project: *Chemistry, Christ and Salvation.*

The Mind of Christ … the making of personal holiness… John, Paul and Spinoza

Unravelling Paul's Authenticated Epistles I-IV: Collected Commentaries on 1 Thessalonians, Galatians, Philippians, 1 Corinthians, 2 Corinthians, Romans.

God, the Satan and Job's Calling:
The Book of Job: a Radical Christian Study and Commentary.

Radical Christian Reflections on the Theology of John Milton's Paradise Lost and Paradise Regained.

Situational Mastery for Managers, Supervisors and Workers.

Emergent Seniors' Age-ability Framework: *An Ecological Framework for Positively Supporting Preferential Age-able Behaviours of Daily Living in Long Term Care.*

David Suchet
carnal

Printed in Great Britain
by Amazon

40162585R00175